PAINT PEOPLE in ACRYLIC *with Lee Hammond*

NORTH LIGHT BOOKS
CINCINNATI, OHIO
www.artistsnetwork.com

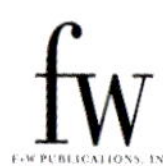

Published by North Light Books, an imprint of F+W Publications, Inc., 4700 East Galbraith Road, Cincinnati, Ohio, 45236. (800) 289-0963. First Edition.

Other fine North Light Books are available from your local bookstore, art supply store or direct from the publisher.

11 10 09 08 07 5 4 3 2 1

DISTRIBUTED IN CANADA BY FRASER DIRECT
100 Armstrong Avenue
Georgetown, ON, Canada L7G 5S4
Tel: (905) 877-4411

DISTRIBUTED IN THE U.K. AND EUROPE BY DAVID & CHARLES
Brunel House, Newton Abbot, Devon, TQ12 4PU, England
Tel: (+44) 1626 323200, Fax: (+44) 1626 323319
Email: mail@davidandcharles.co.uk

DISTRIBUTED IN AUSTRALIA BY CAPRICORN LINK
P.O. Box 704, S. Windsor NSW, 2756 Australia
Tel: (02) 4577-3555

Library of Congress Cataloging in Publication Data
Hammond, Lee
Paint people in acrylic with Lee Hammond / Lee Hammond.
p. cm.
Includes index.
ISBN-13: 978-1-58180-798-1 (pbk. : alk. paper)
ISBN-10: 1-58180-798-8
1. Human figure in art. 2. Acrylic painting--Technique. 3. Painting--Technique. I. Title.

ND1290.H36 2006 751.4'26--dc22

Edited by Mona Michael
Designed by Wendy Dunning
Production art by Kathy Bergstrom
Production coordinated by Jennifer Wagner

Metric Conversion Chart

To convert	to	multiply by
Inches	Centimeters	2.54
Centimeters	Inches	0.4
Feet	Centimeters	30.5
Centimeters	Feet	0.03

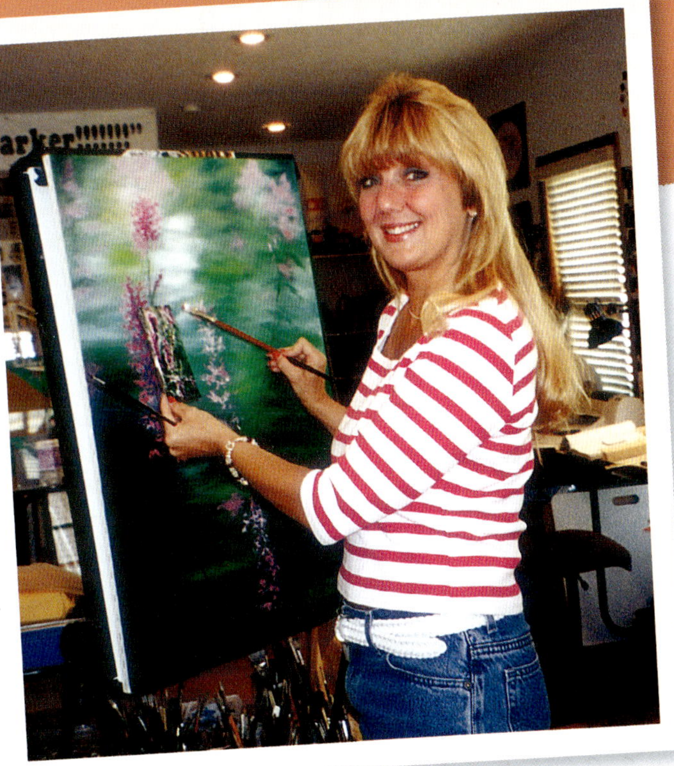

ABOUT THE AUTHOR

Polly "Lee" Hammond is an illustrator and art instructor from the Kansas City area. She owns and operates a private art studio called Take It To Art™, where she teaches realistic drawing and painting.

Lee was raised and educated in Lincoln, Nebraska, and she established her career in illustration and teaching in Kansas City. Although she has lived all over the country, she will always consider Kansas City home. Lee has been an author with North Light Books since 1994. She also writes and illustrates articles for other publications such as *The Artist's Magazine*.

Lee is continuing to develop new art instruction books for North Light and has begun illustrating children's books. Fine art and limited-edition prints of her work will also be offered soon. Lee lives in Overland Park, Kansas, with her family. You may contact Lee via email at Pollylee@aol.com or visit her website at www.leehammond.com.

ACKNOWLEDGMENTS

This is my second book on acrylic painting and I have thoroughly enjoyed working on it. Capturing people in portraiture has always been a passion of mine, and sharing my painting techniques with you is exciting. I am so happy to have the chance to combine the two.

The wonderful people at North Light Books have been my family for more than a decade now. They continue to support my ideas, and allow me to grow and expand as an artist and author.

Without their unwavering support, an art career would be hard to maintain. I appreciate their help and guidance more than I can express in words!

DEDICATION

This book is dedicated to all of the wonderful friends I have made because of my career as an artist. My trademark, Take It To Art, is a perfect description of my life. My art has taken me all over the world, helped me see and do things I never thought possible, and has been the vehicle for meeting the most outstanding people on the planet. It is a joy I will never take for granted. For those of you who have entered my life because of art, I hope you feel as lucky as I do! All of my books are dedicated, in heart, to you!

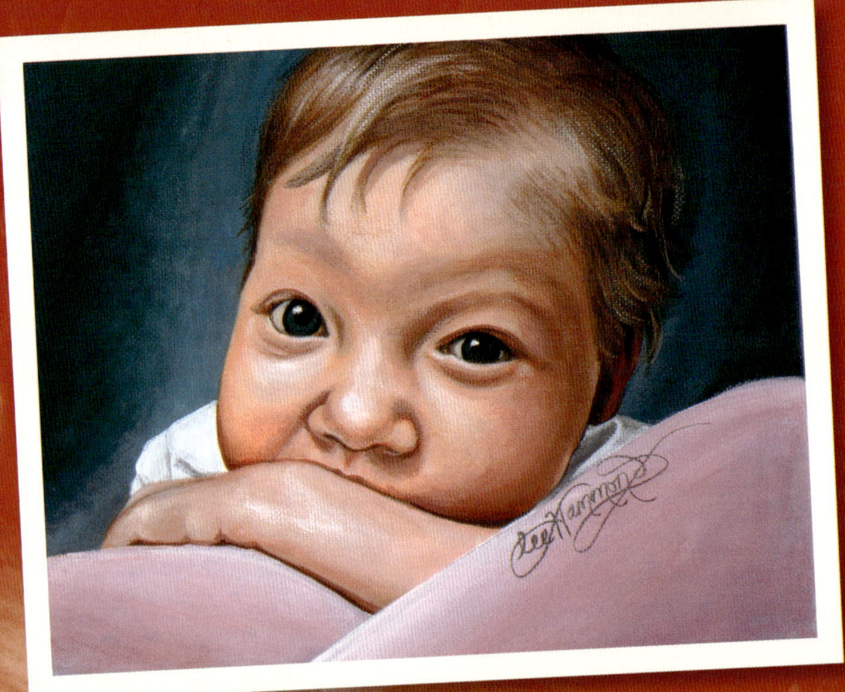

TABLE OF CONTENTS

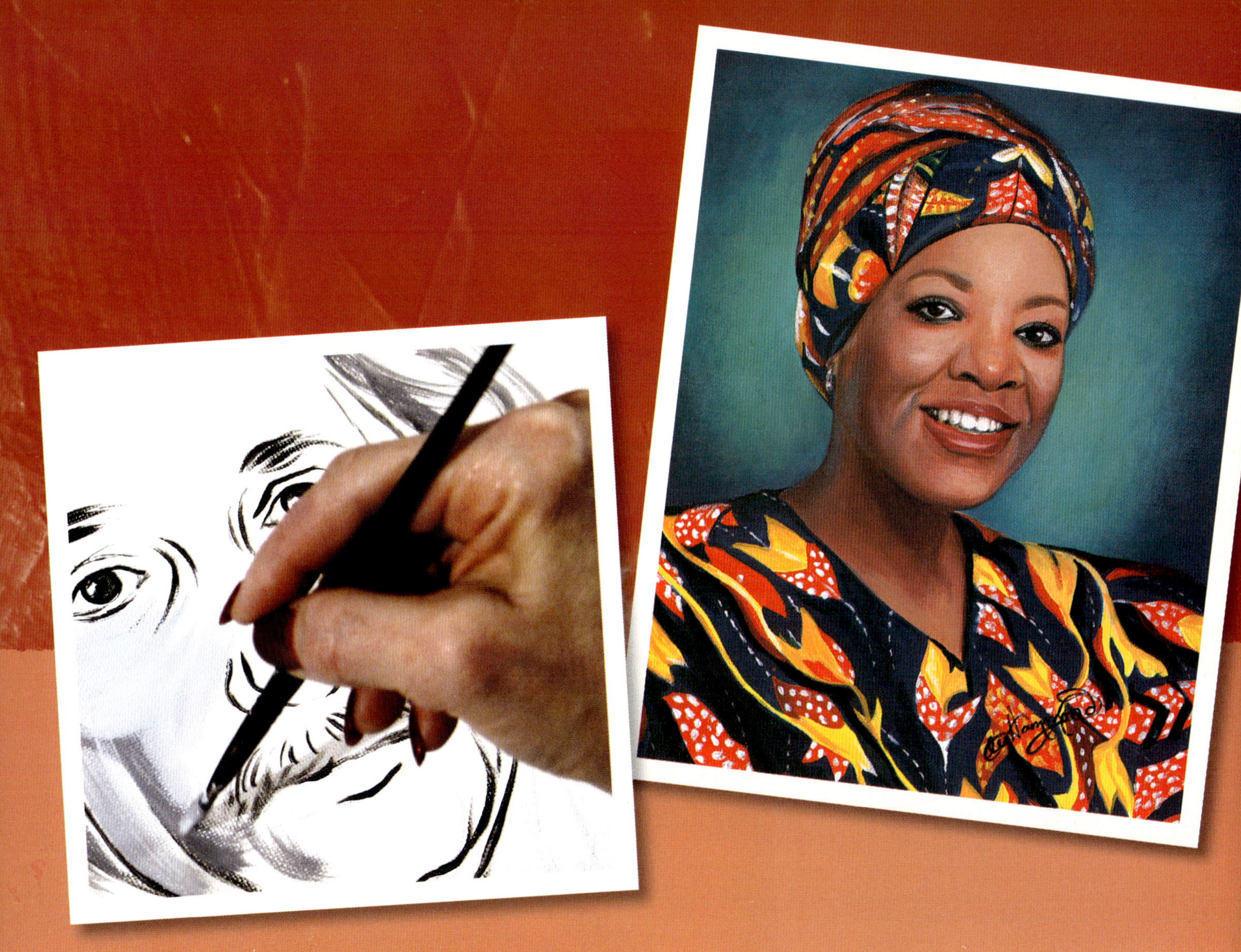

The Awkward Stage

Acrylic paintings are done in layers. The awkward first layers of the painting are an essential foundation to the art. The first layers involve thinned paint with a consistency more like watercolor, applied loosely. Think of the Awkward Stage as a color map. You're just laying the foundation of the colors you will build on later.

I have found that many students using acrylics for the first time become frustrated and give up too soon. Because the painting looks so sloppy at first, it is understandable to be unconvinced of a good outcome. It is hard to accept the fact that all paintings go through the Awkward Stage! However, if you hang in there for the rest of the process, you'll be amazed at the transformation.

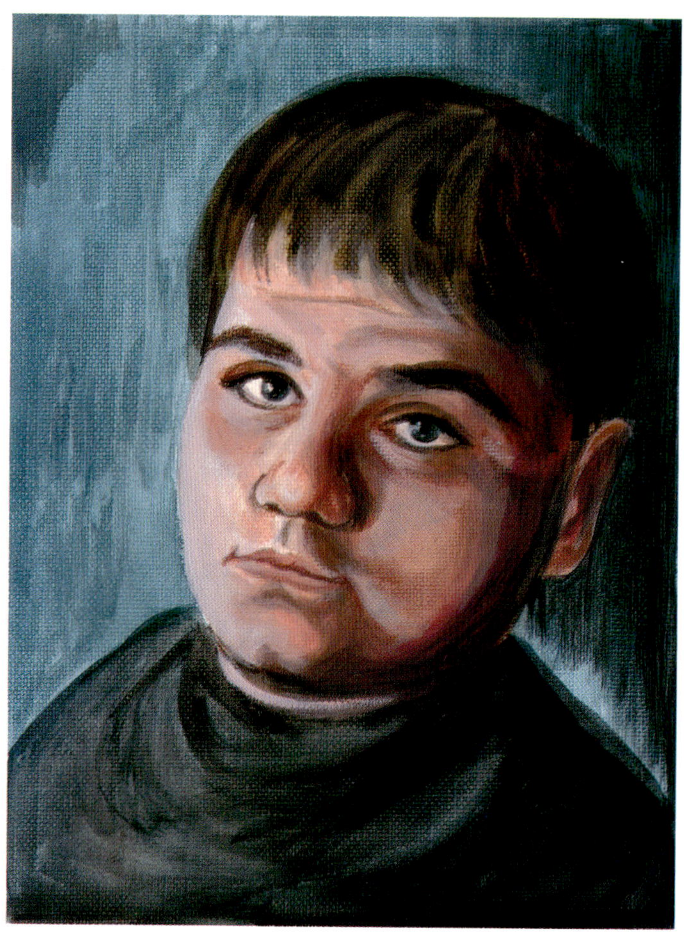

The Awkward Stage Creates Your Color Map
This awkward stage provides you with a color map or road map to follow. The paint is more like watercolor and the canvas shows through. The colors look weak and a bit muddy. This is where many beginners mistakenly quit.

The Final Layers Finish the Painting
When more layers of paint are applied, the artwork improves. Once you've reached the awkward stage and have your color map, you can then follow the map as you apply layers of thickened paint and add details. The canvas now is totally covered and the colors are much more vibrant. It is in the final stages of the painting that everything pulls together and gives the work realism. The effort is definitely worth it! The moral of this story is: Be patient and don't give up too early.

CHRISTOPHER DALE
Acrylic on canvas paper
14" x 11" (36cm x 28cm)

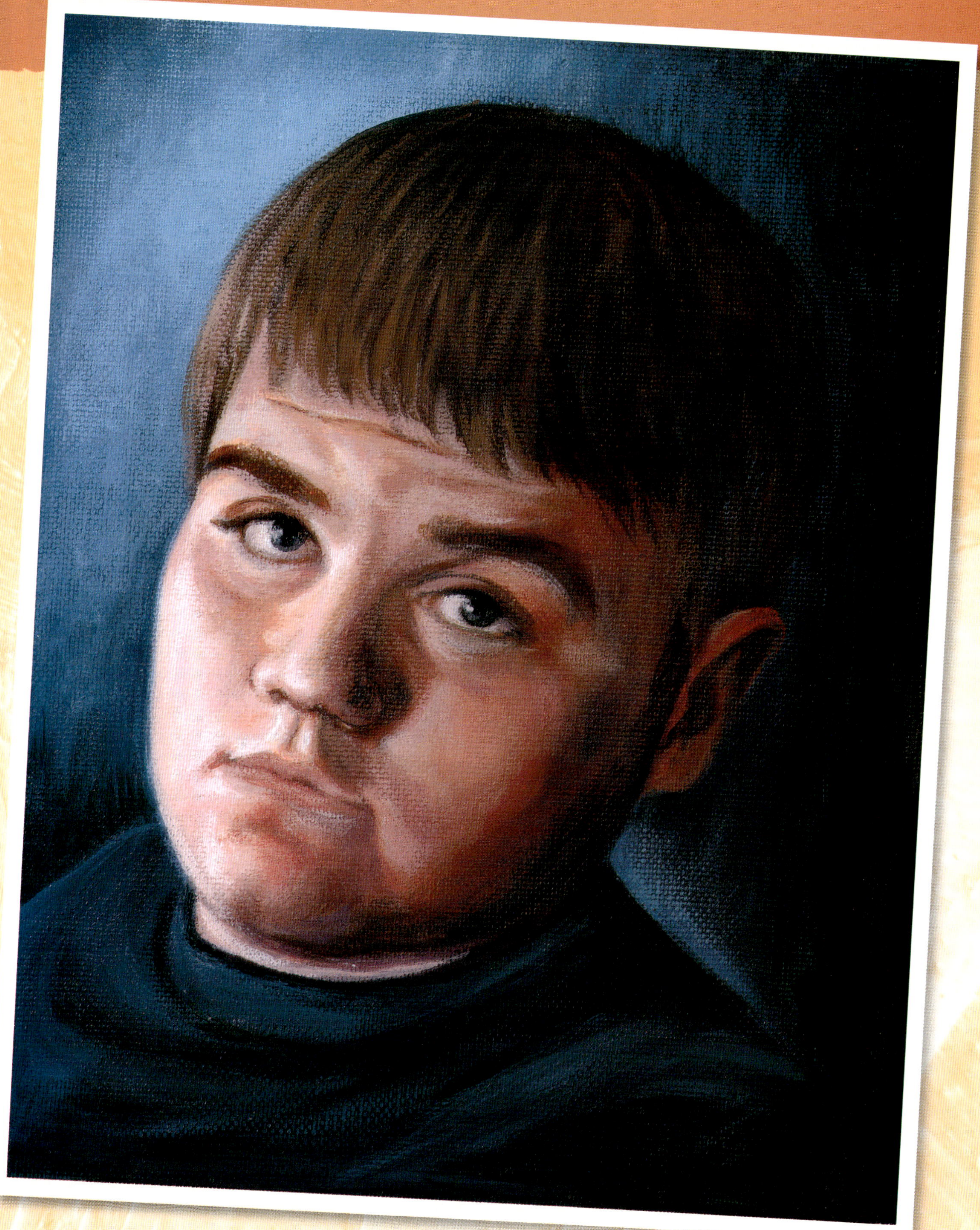

Paint Properties

As we just discussed, each form of paint—jar, tube or squeeze bottle—has different characteristics. Once you've selected the paint you prefer, you will find that individual colors have their own properties as well.

Opacity: Some colors cover surfaces better than others, appearing more opaque, while some will be more transparent. Some colors completely cover the canvas, while others are more transparent and seem streaky. With time and practice, you'll get to know your paints. Play and experiment first by creating some color swatches like the ones on this page. This will give you a better understanding of how each color on your palette behaves.

Permanence: Certain colors are more prone to fading over time than others. Most brands will have a permanency rating on the package to let you know what to expect. A color with an "Excellent" rating is a durable color that will hold its original color for a long time. A color rated as "Good" or "Moderate" will have some fading, but not a huge difference over time. A color rated as "Fugitive" will fade significantly. You can see this most often with yellows and certain reds. Try to avoid fugitive colors, but regardless of a color's permanence rating, never hang a painting in direct sunlight. Ultraviolet rays in sunlight are the primary cause of fading.

Toxicity: Good-quality paint brands will include some toxic colors. Some of the natural pigments that produce vivid colors are toxic, such as the Cadmium pigments and some blues. Never swallow or inhale these colors. Certain colors should never be spray applied; check the label. If you're working with children, always find a brand that substitutes synthetic, manufactured pigments for the toxic ones.

Cadmium Red Medium
This red is opaque and completely covers the canvas. Can you see the difference between this and the Alizarin Crimson?

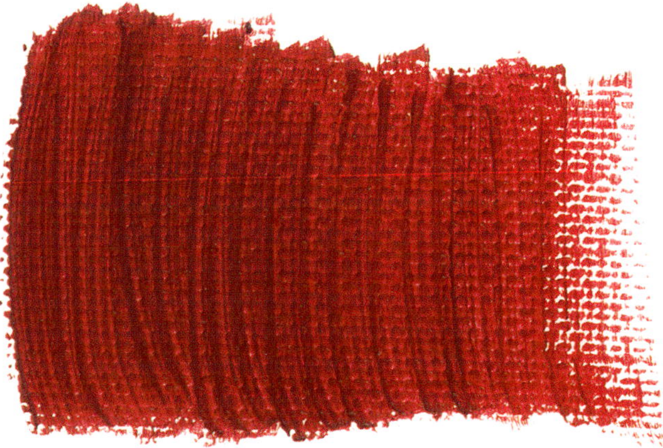

Alizarin Crimson
This red is dark but transparent in nature. It has a streaky appearance, letting some of the canvas show through.

Prussian Blue
This blue is dark but transparent.

Prussian Blue + Titanium White
Just by adding a touch of Titanium White to Prussian Blue, you can create an opaque version of it.

Thinning Acrylics With Water

Mixing acrylic paint with water makes it more transparent. This is useful for the beginning stages of a painting, when you are creating the basic pattern of colors.

Thinned acrylics are often used to create a look very similar to that of watercolor paints. The difference is that acrylic paint is waterproof when it dries. You can add more color without pulling up previous layers. Regular watercolor will rehydrate when wet paint is applied on top of it, usually muddying the colors.

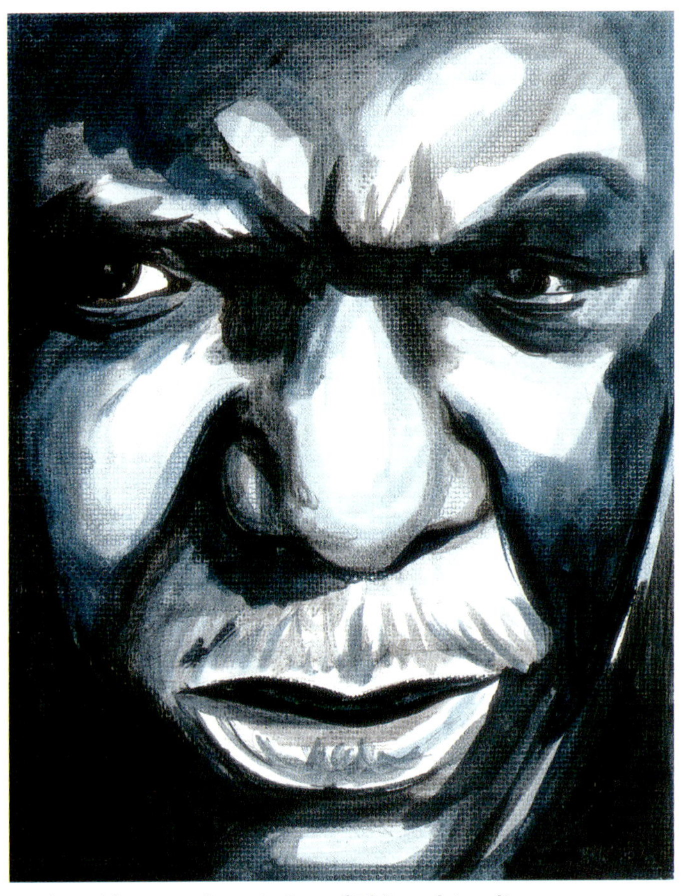

Begin With an Underpainting of Thinned Acrylics
Transparency can be created with acrylics by diluting the paint with water. It looks similar to regular watercolor paint and is a good underpainting for your acrylic work. First, establish the colors of the entire painting, including the background. Then, add more color for the details.

This example shows how I begin a painting. It looks very underdeveloped, but it gives me a good foundation to work on.

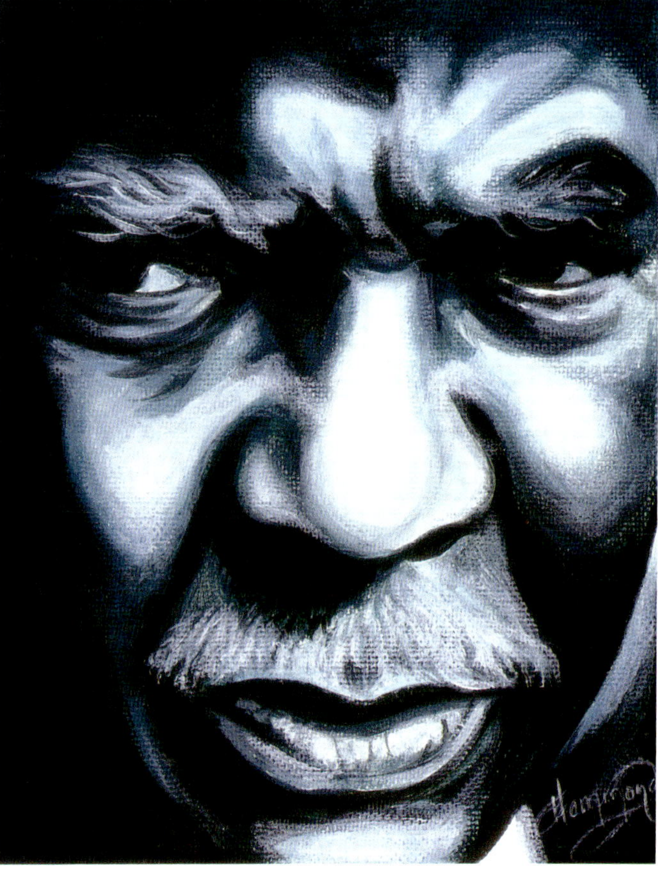

Finish With Purer Pigment
When you begin adding details to finish a painting, reduce the amount of water you add or use the paint full strength. This causes the pigment to become much more opaque. The thicker paint covers up the existing layer. You can see how the look of the paint changes.

Choosing Brushes

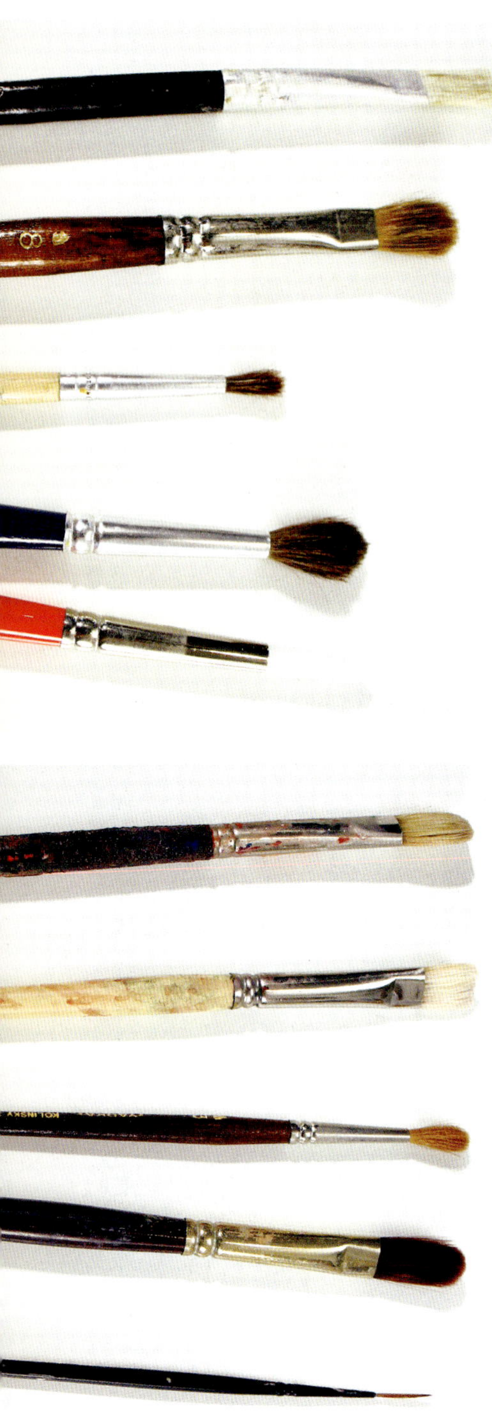

TOP: From top to bottom: stiff bristle, sable, squirrel hair, camel hair and synthetic bristle types.

BOTTOM: From top to bottom: flat, bright, round, filbert and liner brush shapes.

While there are endless varieties of brushes to choose from, I have included only the ones I use the most. Read all about brush basics here, and see the list on page 10 for the basic set of brushes needed for the projects in this book.

Bristle Type

The way paint looks when applied to canvas largely depends on the type of brush you use. Brushes come in a variety of bristle types.

Stiff bristle: These brushes are made from boar bristle, ox hair, horsehair or other coarse animal hairs.

Sable: These brushes are made from the tail hair of the male kolinsky sable, which is found in Russia. This very soft hair creates smooth blends. The scarcity of the kolinsky makes these brushes expensive, but they are worth it!

Squirrel hair: These soft brushes are a bit fuller than sable brushes, and are often used for watercolor because they hold a lot of moisture.

Camel hair: This is another soft hair that is used frequently for both acrylic and watercolor brushes.

Synthetic: Most synthetic bristles are nylon. They can be a more affordable substitute for natural-hair brushes, but paint is very hard on them. They tend to lose their shape and point faster than natural-hair brushes. Good brush cleaning and care (see page 15) are essential to make synthetic brushes last. Natural-hair brushes can be quite pricey. However, if cleaned properly, they will last longer than synthetic ones.

Long or Short Brushes?

You will see brushes with both short handles and long. Long handles are designed for standing at an easel, so you can paint at arm's length and step back and see what you are doing. Short handles are more for sitting and painting, and working on small details.

Brush Shape

Brushes come in different shapes, and some shapes are better for certain paint applications. Below is a list of the different brush shapes and the best uses for each.

Flat: A flat brush is used for broad applications of paint. Its wide shape will cover a large area. The coarse boar-bristle type is a stiff brush that can be used to literally "scrub" the paint into the canvas. A softer sable or synthetic bristle is good for smooth blending with less noticeable brush marks.

Bright: Brights are very similar to flats; however, the bristles are a bit longer, which gives the brush more spring.

Round: Use round brushes for details and smaller areas. The tip of a stiff bristle round is good for dabbing in paint or filling in small areas. A small soft round can be used in place of a liner brush for creating long straight or curved lines.

Filbert: This brush shape is my personal favorite. Also known as a "cat's tongue," the filbert is useful for filling in areas, due to its rounded tip.

Liner: The liner's small, pointy shape makes it essential for detail work. You can create tiny lines and crisp edges with a liner.

Hake: A hake (pronounced hahkay), a wide flat oriental brush made from natural hair, is excellent for soft blending.

Brush Maintenance

Acrylic paint is hard on brushes. Remember, once acrylic paint dries, it is waterproof and almost impossible to remove. Paint often gets into the brush's *ferrule* (the metal band that holds the bristles in place). If paint dries there, it can make the bristles break off or force them in unnatural directions. A brush left to dry with acrylic paint in it is as good as thrown away.

Follow these pointers to keep your brushes like new for as long as possible:

- Stick to a strict and thorough brush-cleaning routine. See the sidebar for my favorite cleaning procedure. (Note: Some paint colors stain synthetic bristles. This staining is permanent, but normal and harmless.)
- Never leave a brush resting in a jar of water. This can bend the bristles permanently. It can also loosen the ferrule, causing the bristles to fall out. (Sometimes a brush with five hairs is good for small details, but not if the poor brush started out with a hundred!)
- Always store your brushes handle-down in a jar, can or brush holder to protect the bristles.

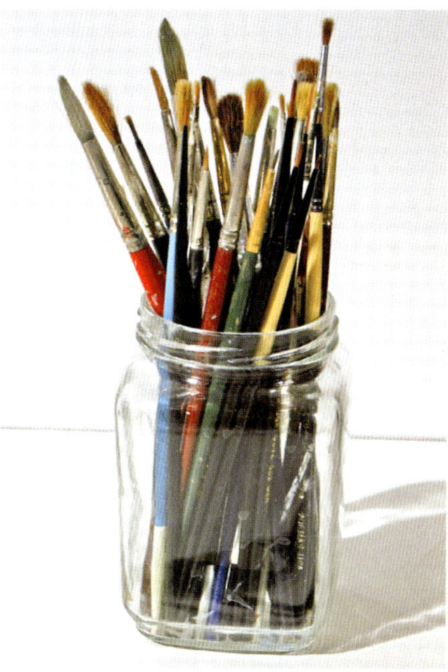

Proper Brush Storage
Always store your bristles in the "up" position!

How to Clean Your Brushes

1. Swish the brush in a clean jar of water to loosen any remaining paint.
2. Take the brush to the sink and run lukewarm water over it.
3. Work the brush into a cake of "The Masters" Brush Cleaner and Preserver until it forms a thick lather. At this point, you will notice some paint color leaving the brush.
4. Gently massage the bristles between your thumb and fingers to continue loosening the paint.
5. Rinse under the warm water.
6. Repeat steps 3 to 5 until no more color comes out.
7. When you are sure the brush is clean, apply some of the brush cleaner paste to the bristles and press them into their original shape. Allow the paste to dry on the brush. This keeps the bristles going the way they are intended and prevents them from drying out and fraying. It's like hair conditioner for your brushes! When you are ready to use the brush again, simply rinse the soap off with water.

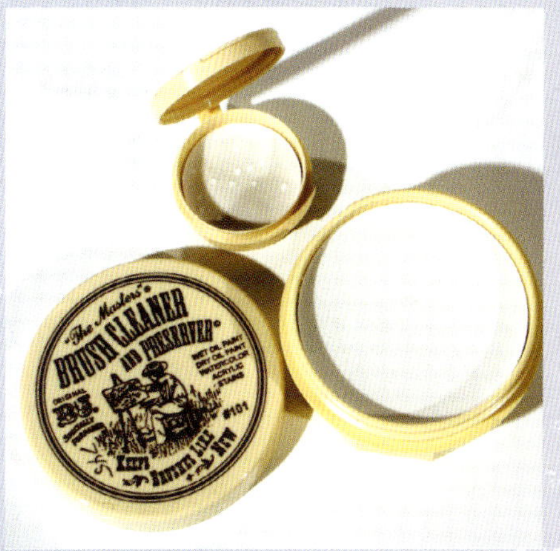

My Favorite Brush Cleaner
I've used "The Masters" Brush Cleaner for many years and swear by it. It's helped me remove some pretty stubborn paint from old brushes before. Before throwing a brush away, I always try to rescue it with the soap first. A good paintbrush will have a very long life if taken care of properly.

Painting Surfaces

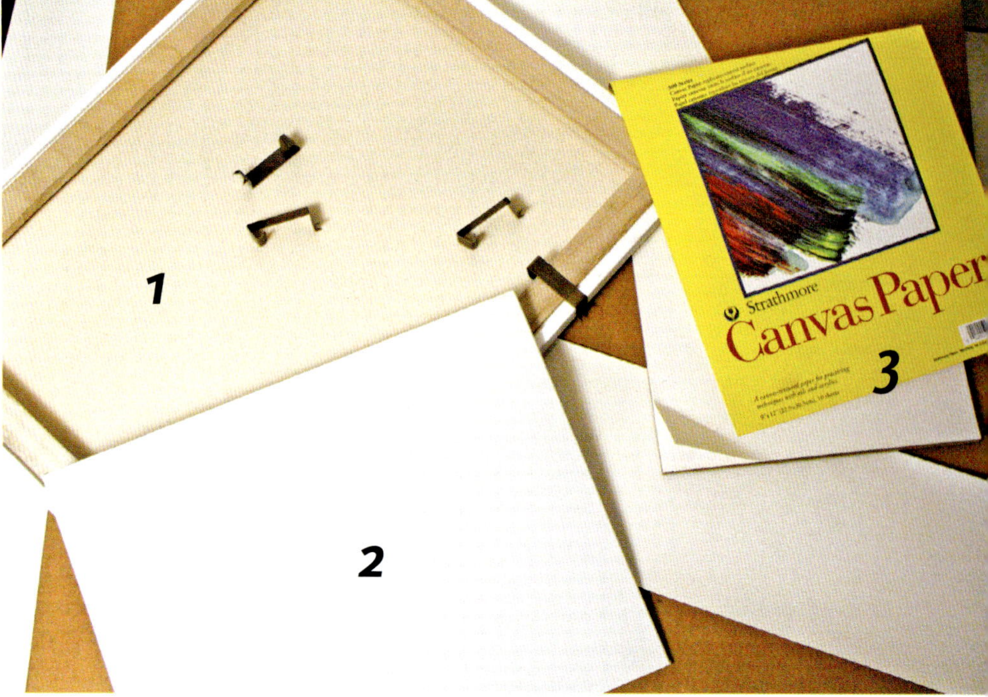

Painting Surfaces

Stretched canvas (1) is the most popular surface for fine art painting. It must go into a frame "as is" and is held into place with frame clips. These are metal brackets that snap over the wooden stretcher frames and grip the inside edge of the frame with sharp teeth.

Canvas panels (2) consist of canvas on cardboard backings. They are more rigid than stretched canvas, and the finished piece can be matted and framed.

Canvas sheets (3) can also be matted and framed. They are found in single sheets, packages and pads.

Many students ask me what the best painting surface is. That depends on your preference and what kind of painting you are doing. Acrylic paint can be used on everything from fine art canvases to wood, fabric, metal and glass. For the sake of this book, I will concentrate on surfaces normally used for paintings.

Stretched Canvas

Stretched canvas provides a professional look, making your work resemble an oil painting. It is easily framed and comes in standard frame sizes from mini (2" × 3" [5cm × 8cm]) to extra large (48" × 60" [122cm × 152cm] or larger). You will notice a bit of "bounce" when applying paint to stretched canvas.

Stretched canvas comes "primed," which means it is coated with a white acrylic called *gesso* to protect the raw canvas from the damaging effects of paint.

Stretched canvas can be regular cotton duck, excellent for most work; extra-smooth cotton, often used for portrait work; or linen, which is also smooth.

Canvas Panels

Canvas panels are canvas pieces glued onto cardboard backings. They are a good alternative to stretched canvas if you would prefer to spend less. A canvas panel is very rigid and will not give you the bouncy feel of painting on stretched canvas.

With canvas panels, unlike stretched canvas, you have the option of framing with a mat. A colored mat can enhance the look of artwork. A canvas panel also allows you to protect your painting with glass.

Canvas Sheets

Another alternative is canvas sheets. Some brands are pieces of actual primed canvas, not affixed to anything. Others are processed papers with a canvas texture and a coating that resembles gesso. Both kinds can be purchased individually, in packages or in pads.

With canvas sheets, as with canvas panels, framing can be creative. Sheets are lightweight and easy to mat and frame. For the art in this book, I used mostly canvas sheets.

Palettes and Other Tools

The last few items to gather to make your painting experience more organized and pleasurable are not expensive, and can usually be found around the house.

Palettes

I prefer a plastic palette with a lid, multiple mixing wells, and a center area for mixing larger amounts of paint. Because acrylic paint is a form of plastic, dried acrylic can be peeled or soaked from a plastic palette. I find this more economical than disposable paper palettes.

Many artists make their own palettes using old dinner plates, butcher's trays or foam egg cartons. Use your creativity to make do with what is around you.

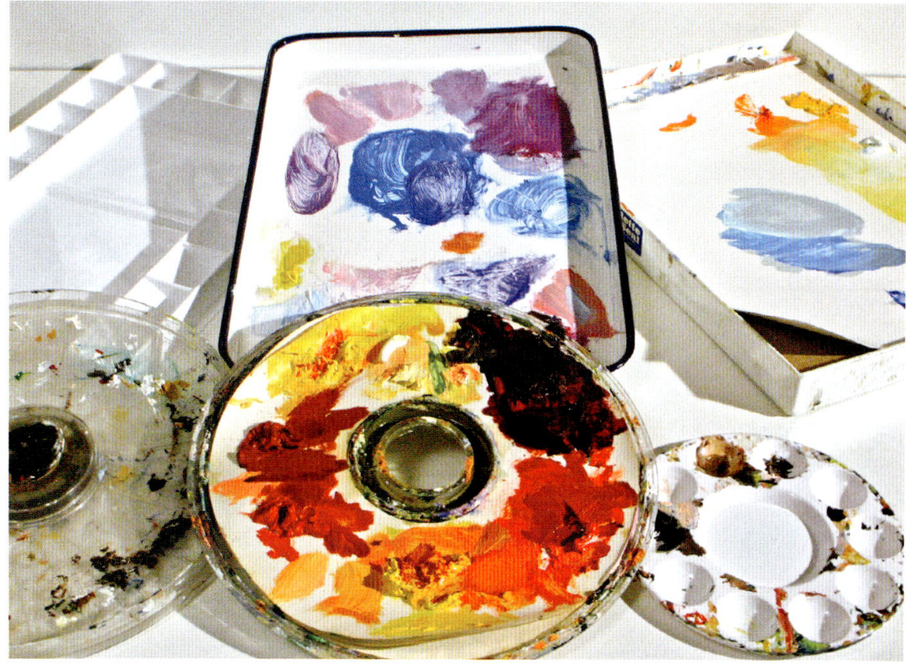

Palette Choices
Palettes come in many varieties. It is easy to make your own with plates, egg cartons or plastic containers. Be creative!

Other Tools of the Trade

Cloth Rags. Keep plenty of these handy. Keep one near your palette to wipe excess paint from your brush. You also need one to wipe excess water from your brush on. Paper towels work too, but they can leave lint and debris.

Containers. Collect jars, cans and plastic containers to use as storage for brushes or as water containers as you work.

Spray Bottles. You'll need a spray bottle to mist your paints to prevent them from drying out as you work. These paints will "skin over" in no time at all.

Palette Knives. You need a palette knife to remove or return acrylic paint from a jar, and to mix the paint on the palette.

Lighters. Sometimes acrylic paint dries inside the cap of a tube of paint. (Another reason I prefer jars!) To loosen the paint, run the cap under very hot water. If it is really stuck, holding it over the flame of a lighter for a few seconds will loosen it enough to allow you to twist off the cap.

Masking or Drafting Tape. When painting with acrylic, I like to use a table easel. If you use the canvas sheets, you'll need to tape them to a backing board as you work. To tape the edges of your paper down, use drafting tape or easy release masking tape. This type of tape will not damage or rip the paper.

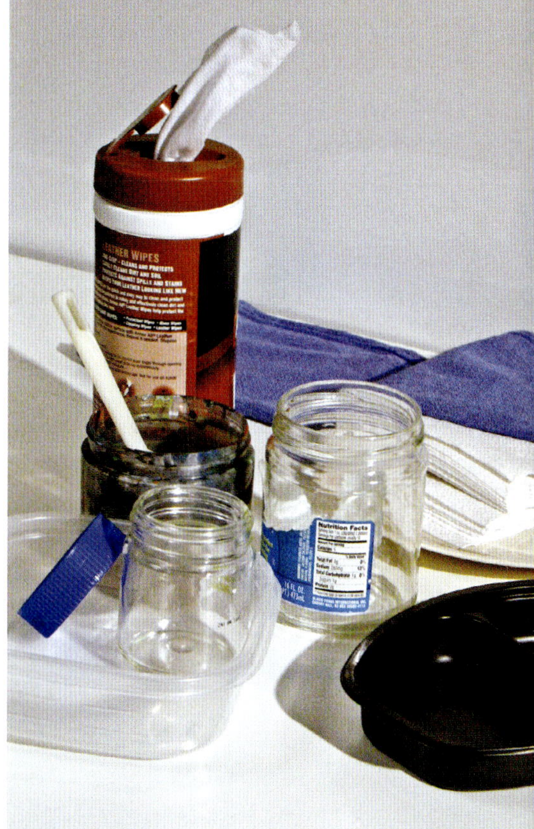

Additional Materials
Look around your house for handy items such as jars, plates, plastic trays, wet wipes and rags.

Understanding Color

Acrylic's bright, rich pigments are fun to experiment with. Artists tell a lot about themselves by the colors they choose. But color is much more than just experimenting or choosing colors based on the mere fact that you "like" them.

Colors react to each other and placing certain colors together can make quite a statement. To fully understand how colors work, the color wheel is essential.

When painting portraits in acrylic, you'll need to layer colors over one another quickly. This allows you to add highlights and shadows as you go, without having to wait for the paint to dry, like you do with oils. Also, you can experiment with background colors, simply painting over it if you do not like the outcome. Acrylic painting can be much faster and easier to make changes due to the quick drying time.

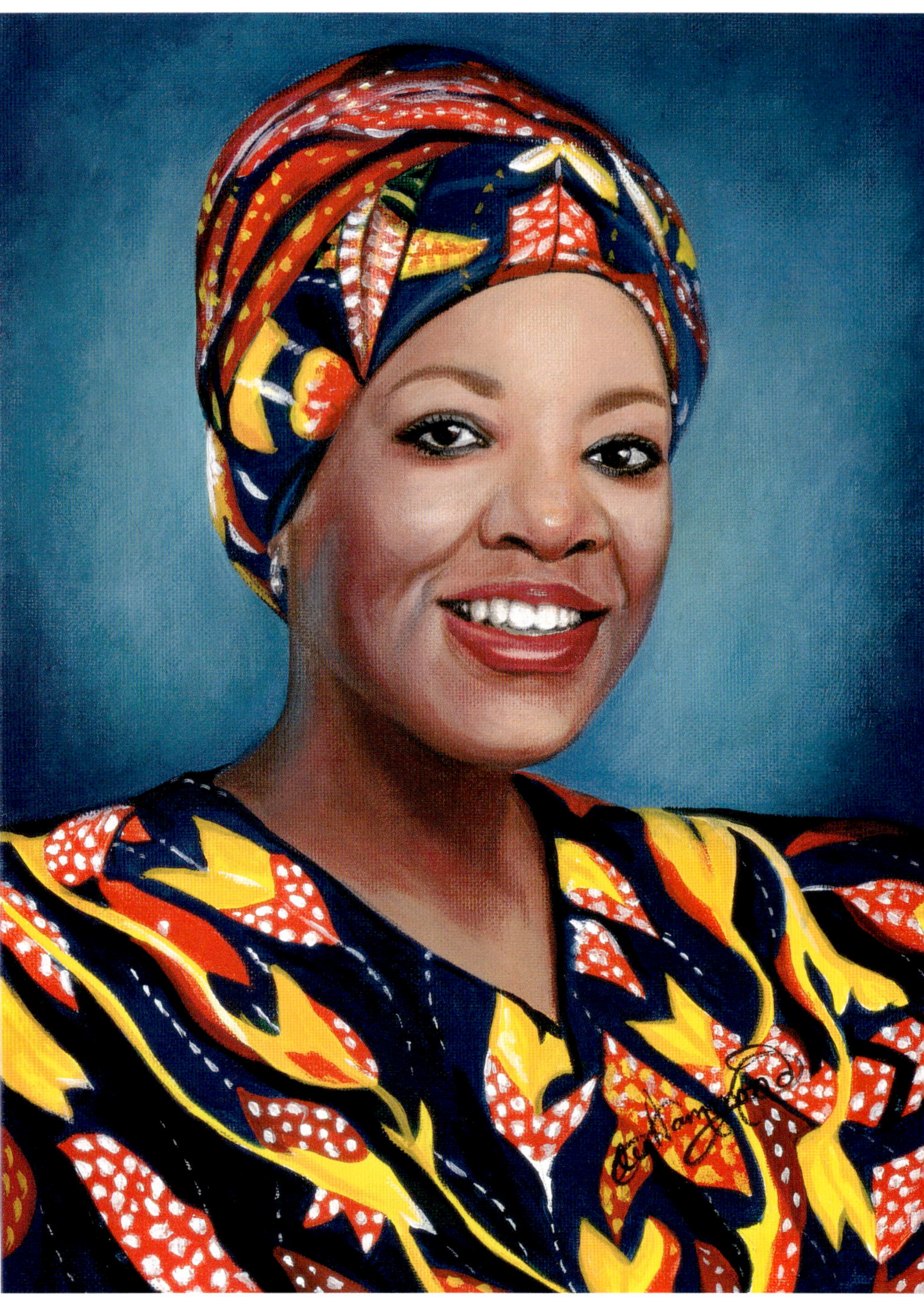

Acrylic paint is wonderful for creating bright, bold colors. This painting of my friend Stephanie is an example of a red/green complementary color scheme.

STEPHANIE
14" x 11" (36cm x 28cm)

Basics

Acrylic painting is a wonderful way to explore color theory. Its bright, rich pigments are fun to experiment with. Here are the basic color relationships to know.

Primary Colors: The primary colors are red, yellow and blue. They are also called the "true" colors. All other colors are created from these three. Look at the color wheel and see how they form a triangle if you connect them with a line.

Secondary Colors: Each secondary color is created by mixing two primaries together. Blue and yellow make green; red and blue make violet; and red and yellow make orange.

Tertiary Colors: Tertiary colors are created by mixing a primary color with the color next to it on the color wheel. For instance, mixing red and violet produces red-violet. Mixing blue with green makes blue-green, and mixing yellow with orange gives you yellow-orange.

Complementary Colors: Any two colors opposite each other on the color wheel are called complementary. Red and green, for example, are complements. The painting on the facing page is an example of a complementary color scheme used in a painting. The red and green contrast beautifully, each color making the other one really stand out.

Other Color Terms to Know

Hue: Hue simply means the name of a color. Red, blue and yellow are all hues.

Intensity: Intensity means how bright or dull a color is. Cadmium Yellow, for instance, is bright and high intensity. Mixing Cadmium Yellow with its complement, violet, creates a low-intensity version of yellow.

Temperature: Colors are either warm or cool. Warm colors are red, yellow and orange or any combination of those. When used in a painting, warm colors appear to come forward. Cool colors are blue, green and violet and all of their combinations. In a painting, cool colors will seem to recede.

Often there are warm and cool versions of the same hue. For instance, I use Cadmium Red and Alizarin Crimson. While both are in the red family, Cadmium Red is warm, with an orangey look, and Alizarin Crimson is cooler, because it leans toward the violet family.

Value: Value means the lightness or darkness of a color. Lightening a color either with white or by diluting it with water produces a tint. Deepening a color by mixing it with a darker color produces a shade. Using tints and shades together creates value contrast.

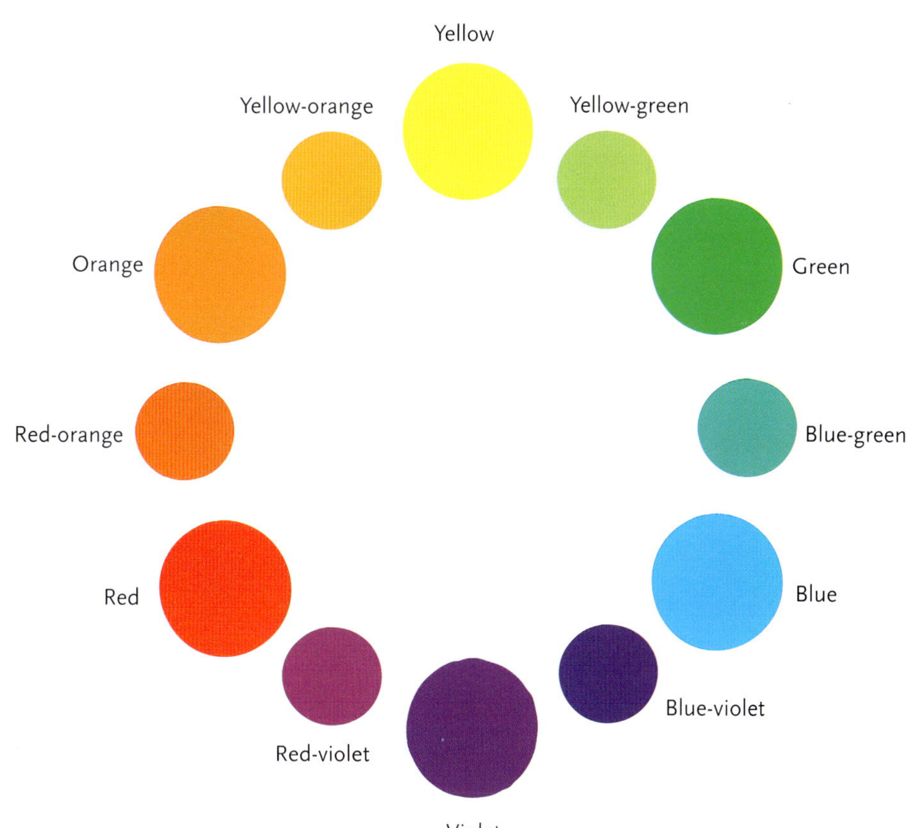

The Color Wheel
The color wheel is an essential tool to understanding the key principles of color theory. Having a color wheel handy can help you pick out color schemes and see how colors affect one another. For practice, make a color wheel of your own.

Schemes

The right color scheme is one that represents the subject, yet also adds interest for the viewer. Experiment to achieve the exact feel you want your painting to have. I'm particularly fond of complementary and monochromatic color schemes.

Complementary

Complementary colors, you'll recall, are colors that lie opposite each other on the color wheel (see page 19).

When complements are used near each other, they contrast with and intensify each other. When complementary colors are mixed, they gray each other down. You can use this knowledge to darken a color without killing it. When darkening a color to paint shadows, for example, you may instinctively reach for black. But black is a neutral color and will produce odd results in mixtures. Instead, darken a light color with its complement.

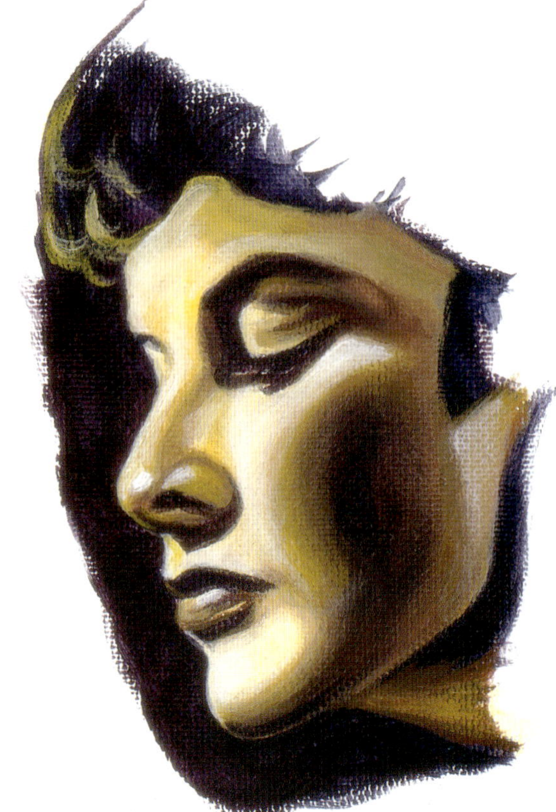

Complements: Yellow and Violet
The yellow tones of this face are complemented by violet in the background and in the shadow areas. The violet makes the yellow appear more pure and vibrant. Also, the warm yellow tones seem to come forward, while the yellow mixed with the cool violet makes the shadow areas recede. Yellow mixed with violet will give you a good shadow color. See how it is used on this face. (Yellow mixed with black would give you olive green and ruin the effect!)

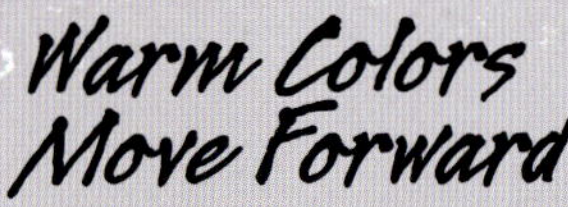

Warm colors are red, yellow and orange, and any combination of them mixed together. When used in a painting, warm colors seem to come "forward."

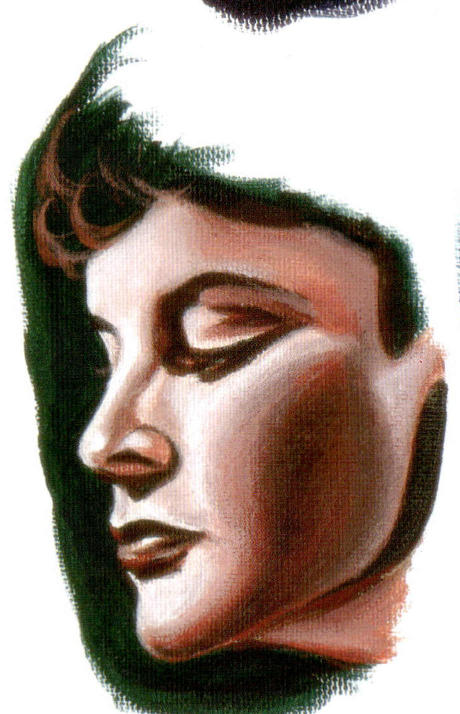

Complements: Red and Green
A red color scheme becomes more vibrant with green in the background. Adding green to the red paint gave me a good color to use in the shadow areas.

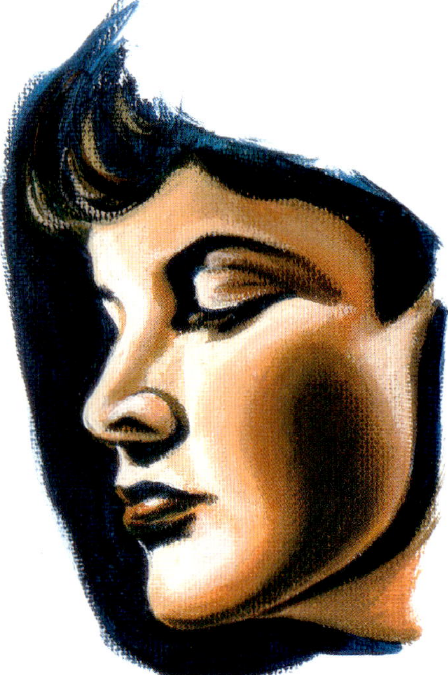

Complements: Orange and Blue
The orangey hue of this peach-complexion is made brighter when surrounded by blue. Look in the shadow areas here and you can see where I mixed the two colors together.

Monochromatic

A painting created by using variations of only one color is called monochromatic. Working monochromatically is a good way for a new student to begin painting. A monochromatic painting can look very dramatic.

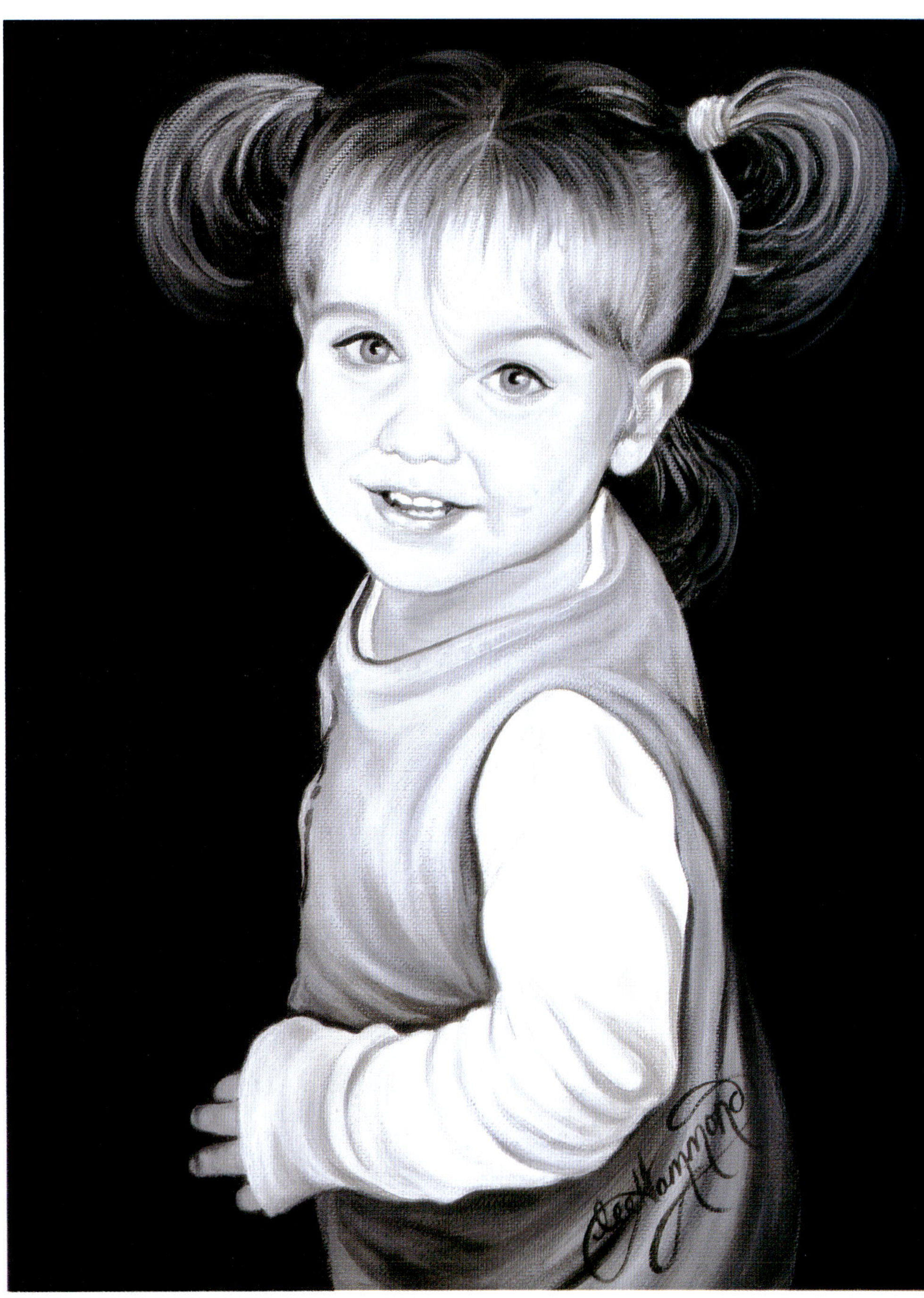

Monochromatic: Black and White

This black background makes the subject of the painting, my granddaughter, stand out.

CAITLYNN

16" x 12" (41cm x 30cm)

Working With Your Palette

Most artists love to have all of the toys associated with their craft and I am no different. I love nothing more than a set of art supplies with a hundred different colors to choose from. But while it sounds like artistic nirvana, it's really not necessary. Mixing the colors you need from just a few pigments is much more rewarding, educational and economical.

I use a very small palette of only seven colors; I create the rest of the colors on my own. By altering value and intensity with this small palette, there is no limit to the thousands of colors you can create!

The color swatches on page 23 will show you how to create a variety of skin tone colors in order to paint beautiful portraits.

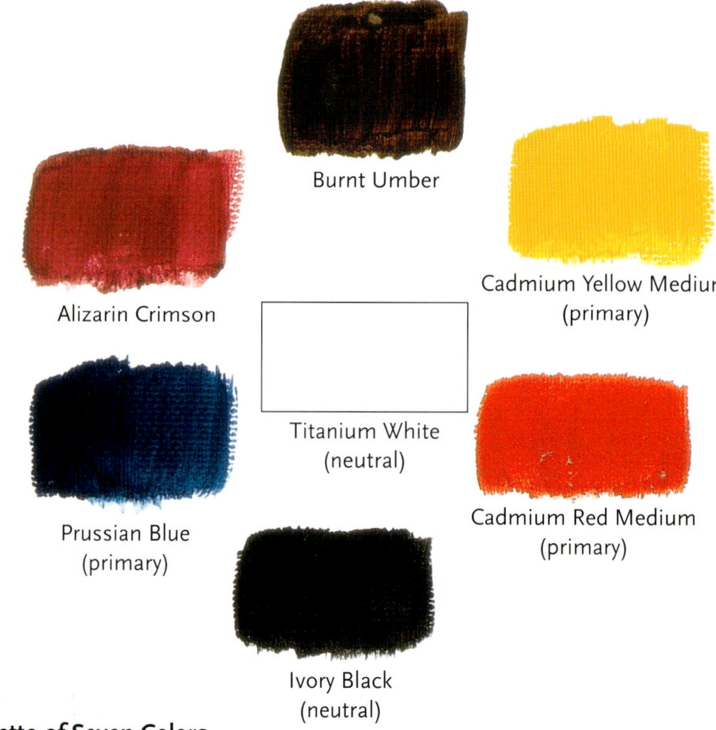

My Palette of Seven Colors

I like to use acrylic paint in jars so I can put pigment back if I don't use it all. I like the Da Vinci and Golden brands the best, and use them exclusively. You should experiment to see what works best for you.

With the primary colors (Cadmium Red Medium, Cadmium Yellow Medium and Prussian Blue), I can create all hues. I include Alizarin Crimson because when mixed with white it produces a beautiful pink. Cadmium Red has an orange quality, and when mixed with white, turns into a coral color.

Burnt Umber is a rich brown that, with the addition of other pigments, can create all of the earth tones and an abundance of skin tones.

With black and white, you can create gray.

Red Can Be Cool

Colors will often have both a warm and cool version of themselves. For instance, I use Cadmium Red and Alizarin Crimson. While both are in the red family, Cadmium Red is warm because of its orangey look. Alizarin Crimson is cooler because it leans toward the violet family.

Just a Few Colors...

A hue refers to the name of the color.

Beginning with a hue, such as Cadmium Yellow Medium

Get a Shade...

A color deepened by mixing it with a darker color is called a shade.

Cadmium Yellow Medium + Ivory Black gives you Olive Green

Or a Tint...

Colors lightened with white, or by diluting with water, are called tints.

Cadmium Yellow Medium + Titanium White or water gives you a lighter yellow

Or Interesting Shadows...

Alter intensity to dull colors by adding their complements.

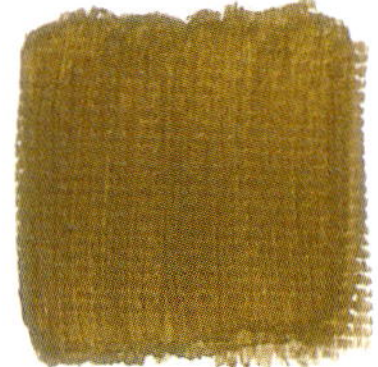

Cadmium Yellow Medium + Violet (an equal mix of Alizarin Crimson and Prussian Blue)

Mixtures for Skin Tones

There is a myriad of skin colors in the world, each one made up of highlights and shadows. Study your picture carefully to see how colors change depending on the lights and shadows. Each picture and each face is different.

The swatches on this page will give you some of the most common skin tones and the formulas to use to paint them. Don't limit yourself to these; experiment. These swatches merely represent a few of the different hues often seen in skin tones. Remember what we said about all people being unique—that goes for skin too!

All these colors have a million variations from light to dark within them. The corresponding swatches show a value scale approach, illustrating the wide range of color created by adding lights or darks.

Light Complexion Cool
Create this very pink tone often seen in pale skin by mixing Titanium White with Alizarin Crimson, and a touch of Cadmium Red Medium. Simply add more white to lighten the values further. Because of the Alizarin Crimson, the hue has a cool tone.

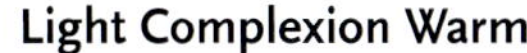

Light Complexion Warm
This mixture is used for many Caucasian skin tones. It is similar to the basic pink color, but it has more yellow, making it more of a warm peach. Mix Titanium White, Cadmium Red Medium, and a touch of Cadmium Yellow Medium. Create the wide range of values by adding more white to get lighter or more red to get darker.

Dark Complexion Warm
This skin tone is very deep. It is similar to the basic peach color, but the brown makes it darker. Mix Titanium White, Burnt Umber, Cadmium Red Medium, and a touch of Cadmium Yellow Medium. The Cadmium Red Medium keeps the tones warm.

Brown Complexion Warm
This skin tone is very brown and warm. Mix Titanium White, Burnt Umber, and a touch of Cadmium Red Medium.

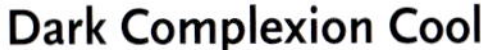

Dark Complexion Cool
This is a cool version of a deep skin color. Mix Titanium White, Alizarin Crimson, Burnt Umber, and a touch of Prussian Blue. The addition of blue cools the mixture.

Shadows
This is a shadow color used with all of the skin tones. It is created by mixing Burnt Umber and Alizarin Crimson.

Basic Techniques

Learning something new is always a bit intimidating. As with anything else, the best teacher is plain experience—trial and error. This chapter will show you how to grab a brush, dip it in the paint and experiment. In no time you should feel comfortable enough to do the projects to come. Remember, acrylics are highly forgiving. If you don't like something, you can simply cover it up!

The exercises in this section will give you a feel for flat, filbert, round and liner brushes and how they are used. You'll learn the five elements of shading and how to use them to create the illusion of form on a flat canvas. Finally, you'll learn the grid method of drawing, which will enable you to draw any subject.

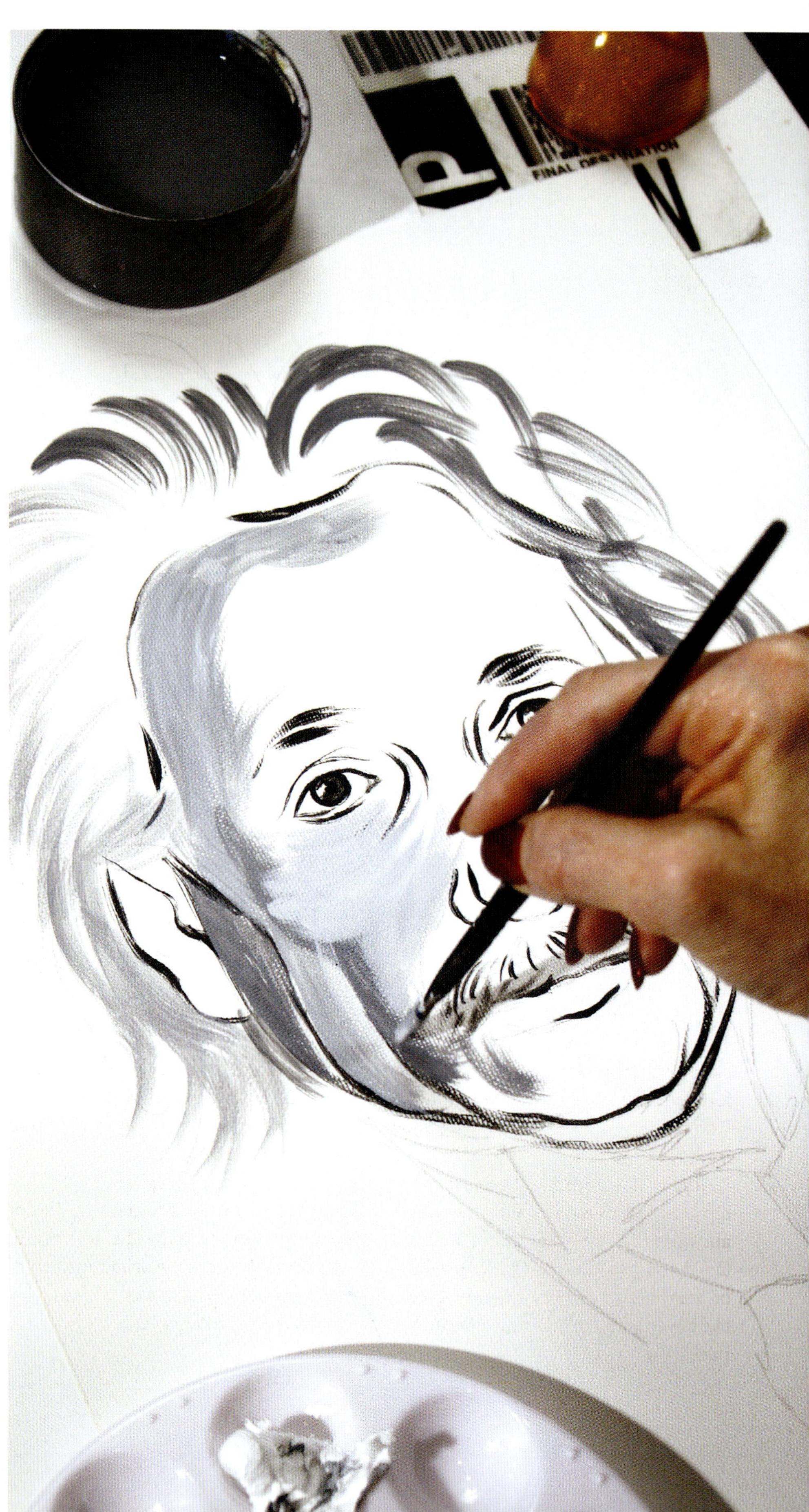

Practice holding each type of brush and learn the type of stroke it is designed for. Practice is essential and will give you the confidence you need to move into a finished piece of art.

Blending With a Flat Brush

PIGMENTS
Prussian Blue, Titanium White

BRUSHES
Any flat brush

Flat brushes are most commonly used for applying large areas of color and for creating blended backgrounds. I've done this blending exercise with Prussian Blue and Titanium White. Try it again with different colors.

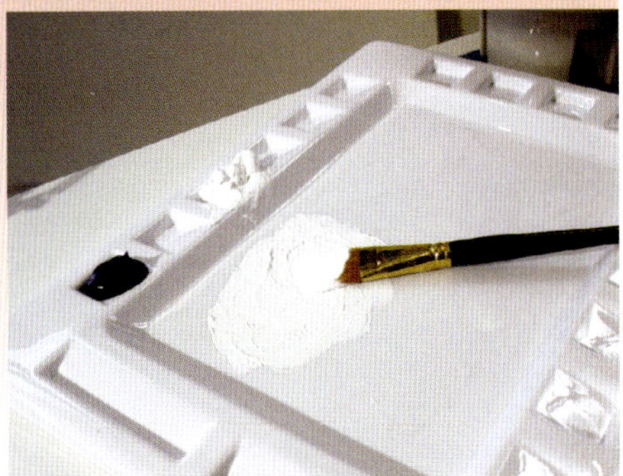

1 Set aside a blob of Titanium White about the size of a quarter.

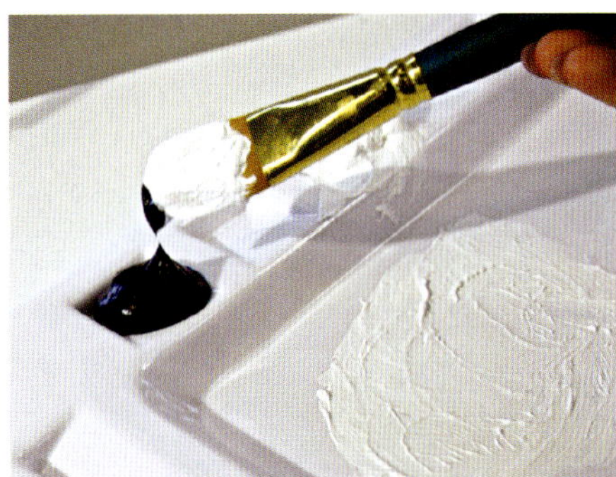

2 Add just a touch of Prussian Blue to the white.

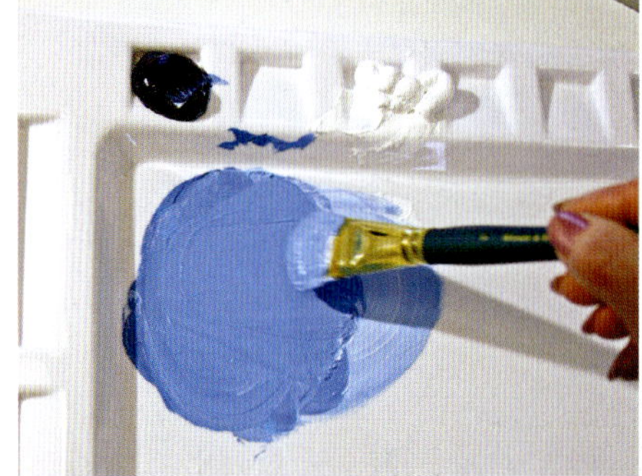

3 Mix another blob of paint that is twice as dark as the first.

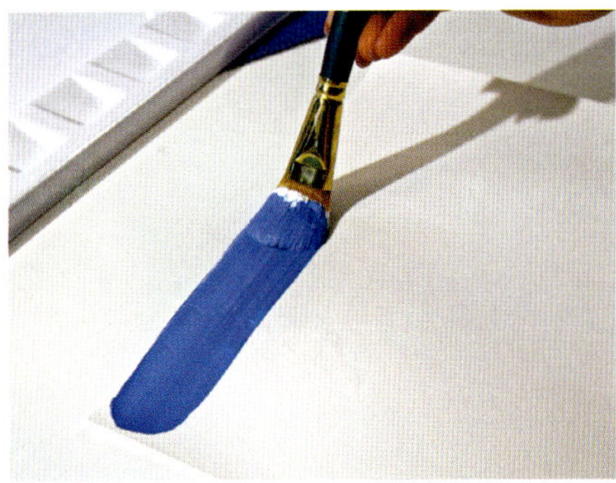

4 Dip your brush into the darker of the two blues you mixed in steps 2 and 3. Hold the brush flat against the canvas and evenly distribute the paint with long, sweeping strokes. Quickly go back and forth until the paint covers the canvas. Don't leave any of the white canvas showing through the paint.

If your paint feels stiff and hard to move, dip just the tip of the brush in the water and mix the paint until it is creamier. Don't add too much, or the paint will be too thin and appear transparent. I like to get my paint the consistency of thick hand lotion.

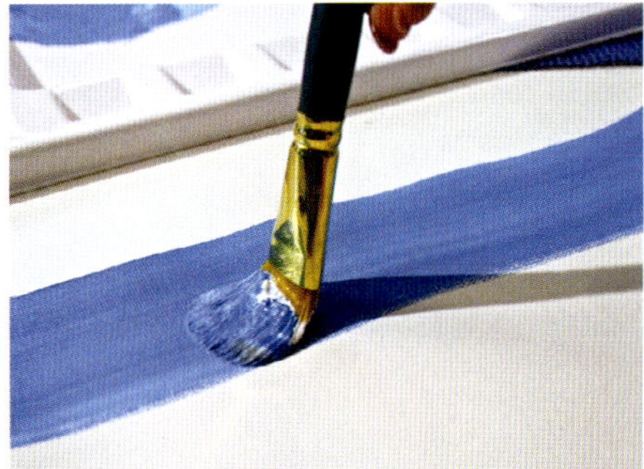

5 When you have a wide stretch of dark blue, dip into the lighter blue and apply it to the canvas slightly below the first stripe using the same stroke. Stroke back and forth to quickly blend the two blues. Blend as evenly as possible. Use a clean, dry flat to further blend and soften. This blending takes practice.

To create a photographer's type of background, you can add areas of light and dark and blend them together to create a mottled look. Scrub the paint together in a circular fashion to get the swirled look often seen in photographs.

A Dab and a Touch Will Do

When mixing paint, I will often refer to two terms: a dab and a touch. A dab is a good-sized dip into the darker paint, which will usually cover the tip of the brush. A touch is a gentle dip of the corner of the bristles, picking up a slight amount.

Always start with light pigment.

Using a Filbert Brush

A filbert brush is very similar to a flat, but the tip is rounded off much like the shape of a tongue. That's why it's sometimes called a "cat's tongue."

I like to use these brushes for almost everything that requires filling in. The rounded edges are comfortable when going along curved edges. In portraiture, the filbert is excellent for adding the colors and contours of the face.

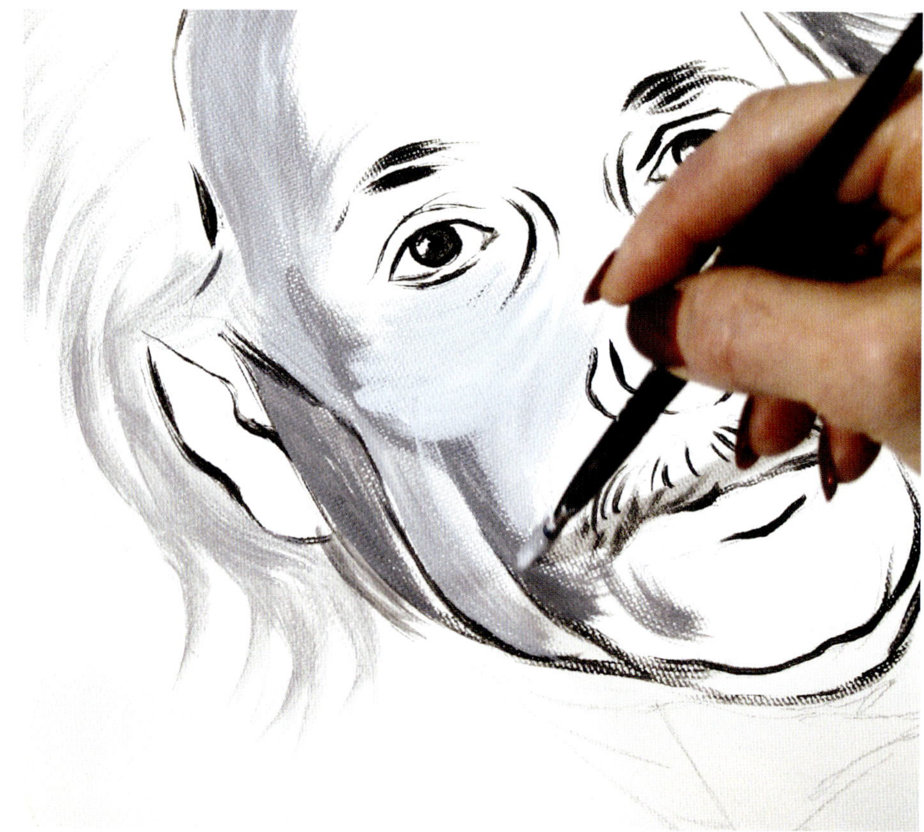

A filbert brush makes filling in a face much easier.

Paint Mixing Tip

When mixing paint, always add the darker color slowly into the lighter color. It doesn't take much to deepen a light color.

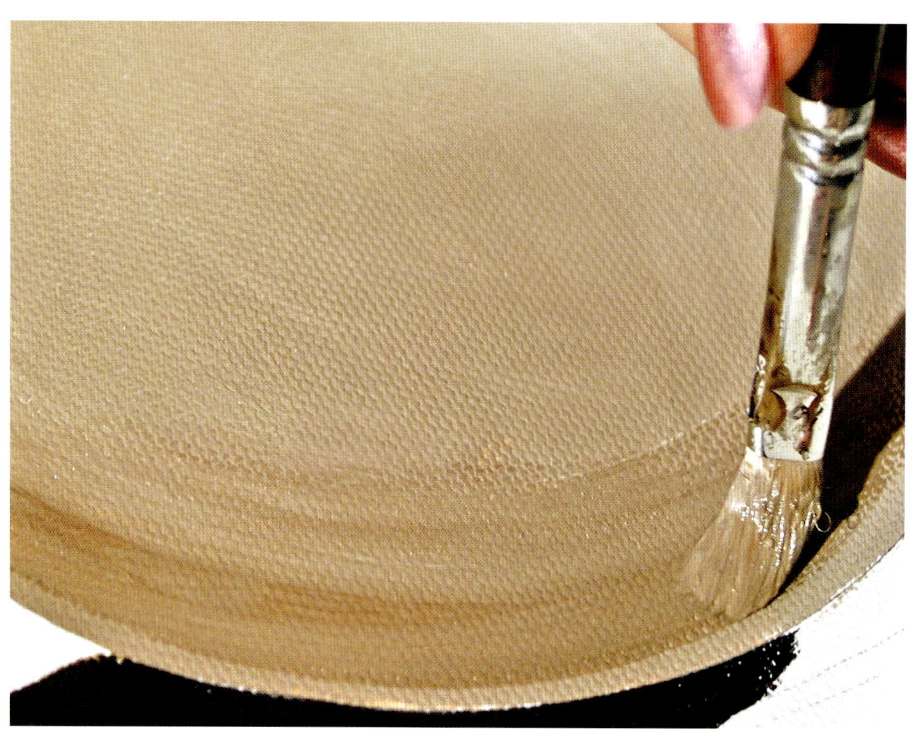

Practice using your filbert to fill in a simple circle of color.

Using Round and Liner Brushes

Pointed brushes such as round and liner brushes are excellent for creating lines and small details. They come in a variety of sizes and are essential for painting hair and fur. They are also good for making small dots for highlights and textures. I use the soft synthetics or sable brushes for these techniques.

Use round brushes and liner brushes on their tips. Don't place a lot of pressure on them or you'll cause the bristles to bend over. Here are some tips to guide you in using liner and round brushes:

- To fill in large areas, such as a head of hair, use a brush with a full head, like a no. 6 round. It will give you the width to fill an area without repeated brushstrokes.
- Switch to a smaller brush, such as a no. 1 round, to create the strands of hair. Add enough water to your paint to give it the consistency of thick ink. It needs to be fluid, but not transparent. After loading your brush with paint, quickly add the hair strands with long strokes, lifting the brush slightly as you go. This will make the line taper at the end, and the hair strands will get smaller and smaller, just as in nature.
- You can create the look of hair and fur with various sizes of liner brushes. The length of your brushstroke will represent the length of the hair. Many quick, overlapping strokes will create the illusion of layers. Keep your paint fluid by adding a few drops of water as you work.

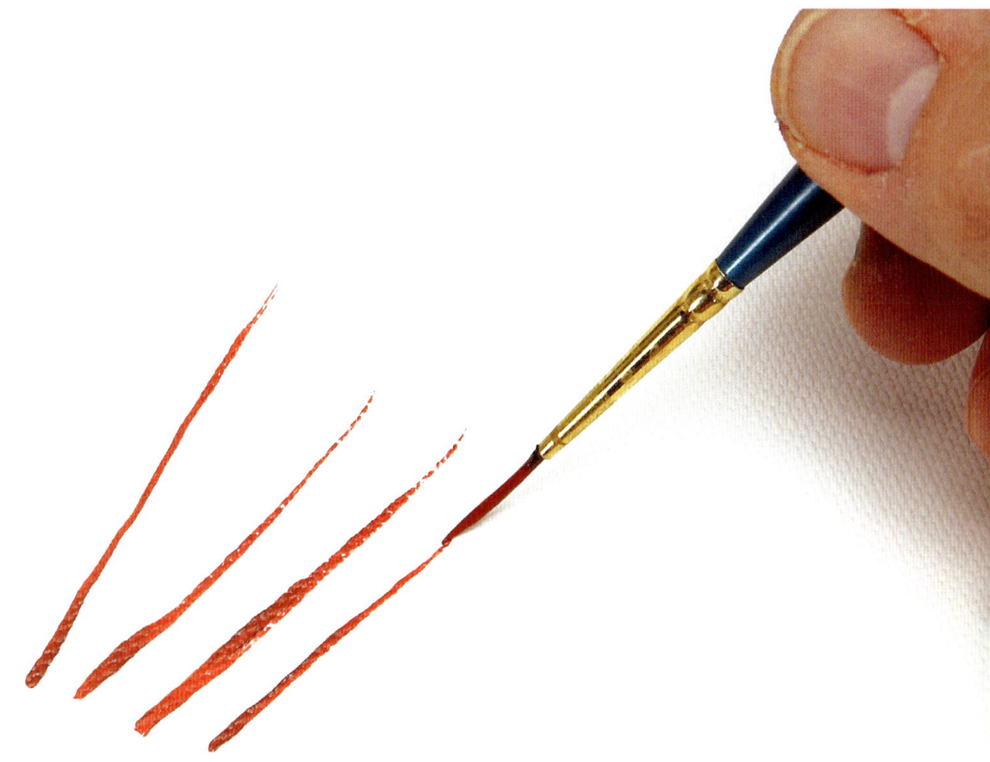

Quick strokes with smaller brushes such as liners can be used to create layered areas like hair and fur.

Note

Use soft sable or synthetic brushes for these exercises.

Drybrushing and Scrubbing

So far you've been using paint that has been thinned to make it more fluid. This time you will be using very dry paint with a technique called drybrushing. It creates a rough, textured appearance because the paint is so dry and is used so sparingly that it doesn't fully cover the canvas.

You can also drybrush to add a small layer of color to an already painted area to subtly change the look. I use this technique a lot in portraiture to add a hint of color to cheeks or a glisten of a highlight. I sometimes refer to this as *rouging* because you rub or scrub into the surface much like you would with makeup.

For this technique, use a sable or synthetic filbert or flat brush. Their shapes work well for both scrubbing and drybrushing. Once the shape and foundation of the face are painted and filled in, I drybrush in the small details of color and tone.

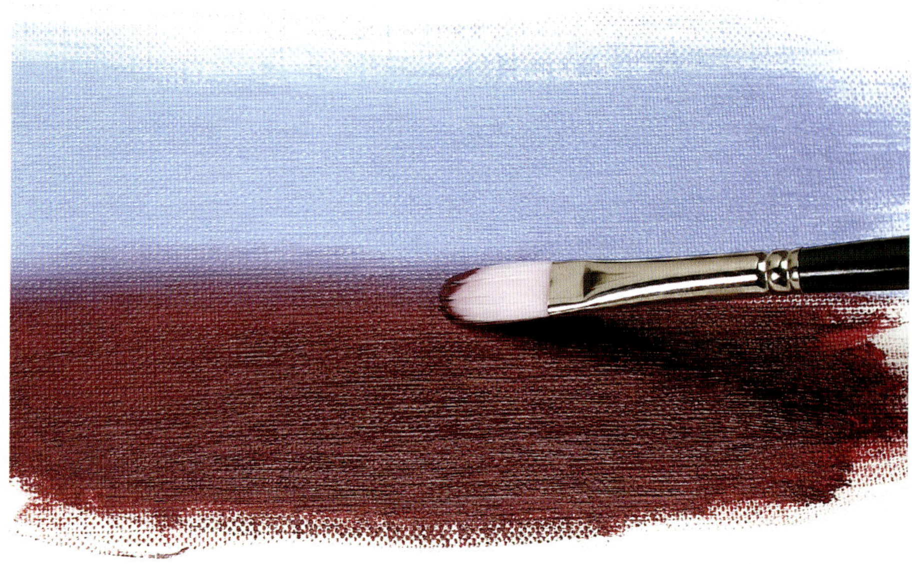

Drybrush to Add Glisten and Highlight
Lightly dip the edges of the bristles of whatever brush you're using into full-strength paint. Wipe it back and forth on the palette to remove any excess, then lightly scrub the color onto the painting surface with short strokes. Because there is barely any paint on the brush, the paint will fade into what is already there.

A Closer Look

Analyze this portrait for the techniques and brushstrokes we have covered so far. Each area of the painting was created in a unique approach due to its varied textures and surfaces. Some surfaces are smooth, while some are richly textured.

I used my entire color palette for this piece. Refer to the skin tone swatches on page 23 to see how I mixed the pigments.

IDENTIFYING BRUSHES AND STROKES

This painting has a lot of interesting qualities due to its range of colors and contrasting textures. Identify the type of brush used and which type of stroke created each area.

1. **Feathers**: Round brush, drybrushing with quick strokes for texture.
2. **Swirled background**: Flat brush, scrubbing with thinned, wet paint in a circular motion.
3. **Facial highlights**: Filbert or flat, a combination of the two techniques above. Drybrushing in a swirling motion to scrub the colors together like you would apply makeup.
4. **Adornment**: Round or liner brush, dotting or stippling where you use the very tip of your brush to create small dots for details.

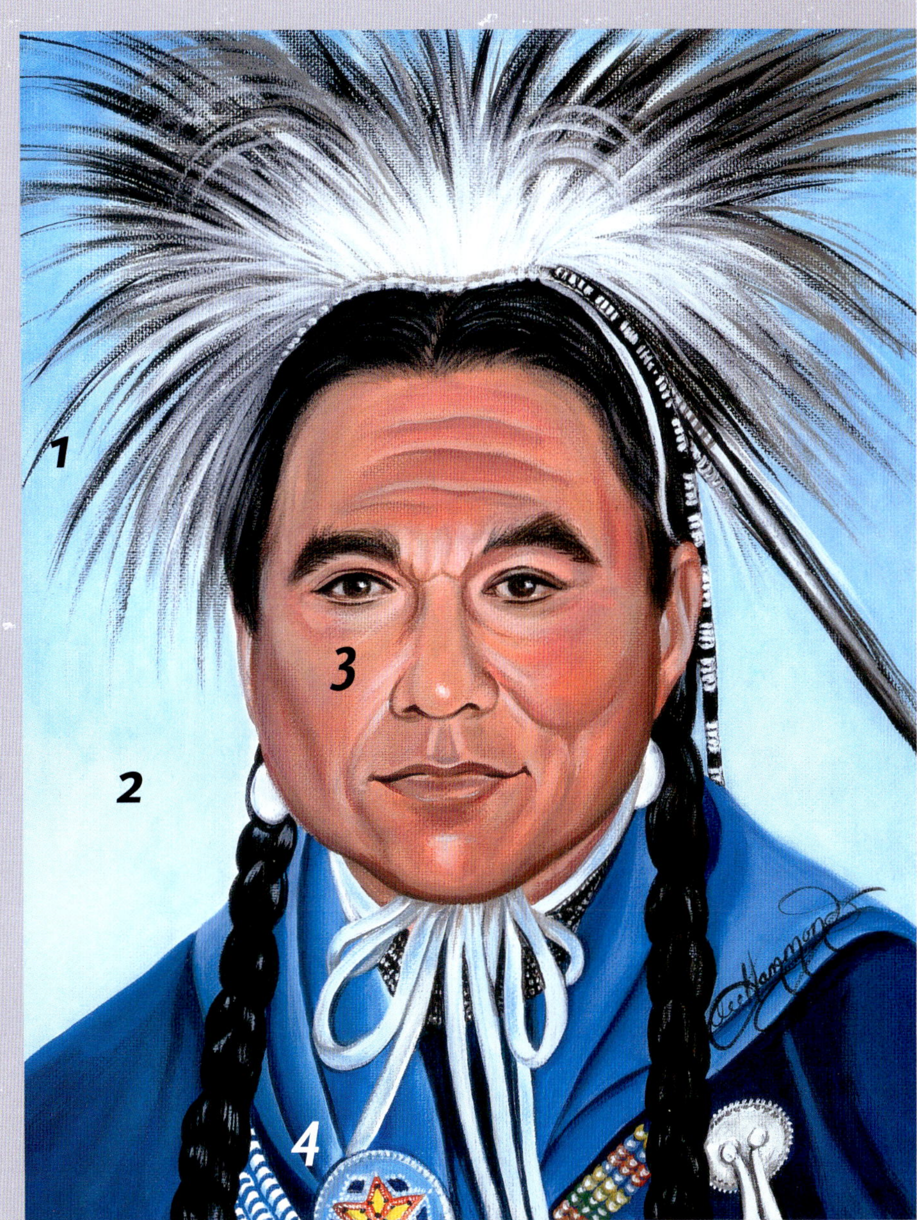

AMERICAN INDIAN IN FULL COSTUME
14" x 11" (36cm x 28cm)

The Five Elements of Shading

I start every new student with this valuable lesson. The foundation for any realistic rendering, regardless of the medium, can be found in the five elements of shading a sphere. If you can create a believable and realistic depiction of a sphere (a ball on a table), the ability to render everything else is right at your fingertips.

So why is the understanding of the sphere so important when drawing people and faces? Everything on the face is curved and rounded, and replicates the surface of the sphere.

1 **Cast Shadow:** This is the darkest tone on your drawing. It is always opposite the light source. In the case of the sphere, it is underneath, where the sphere meets the surface. This area is void of light because, as the sphere protrudes, it blocks light and casts a shadow.

2 **Shadow Edge:** This dark portion is not at the very edge of the object. It is opposite the light source where the sphere curves away from you.

3 **Halftone:** This is a medium value. It's the area of the sphere that's in neither direct light nor shadow.

4 **Reflected Light:** This is a light tone. Reflected light is always found along the edge of an object and separates the darkness of the shadow edge from the darkness of the cast shadow.

5 **Full Light:** This is the lightest area on the object, where the light source is hitting the sphere at full strength.

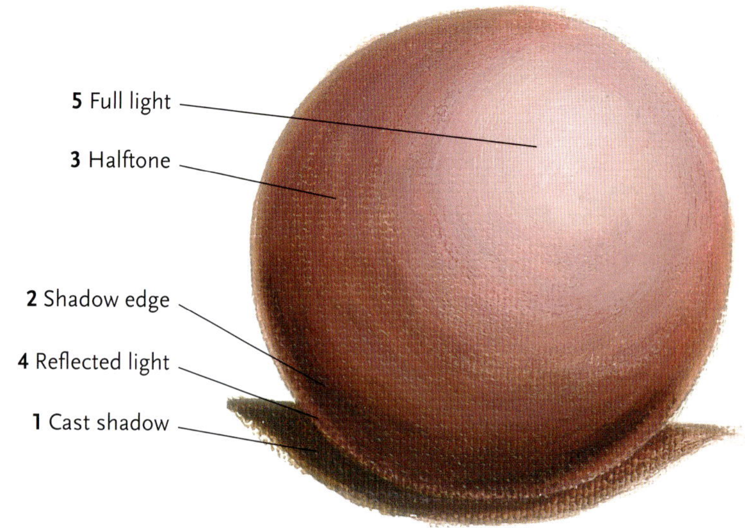

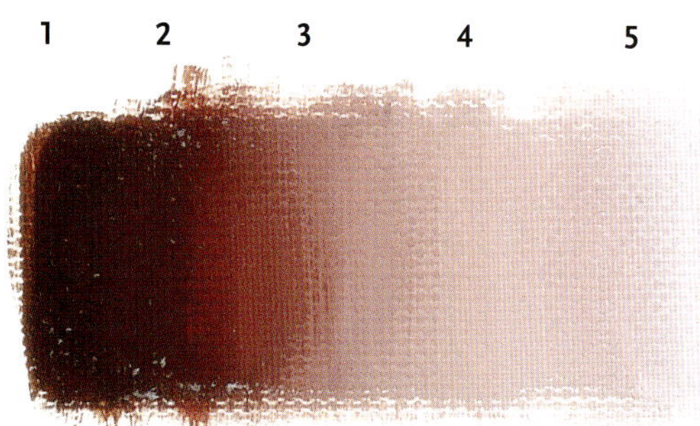

Value Scale
I typically use a value scale like this to create my paintings. Value 1 represents the darkest value and value 5 represents the lightest.

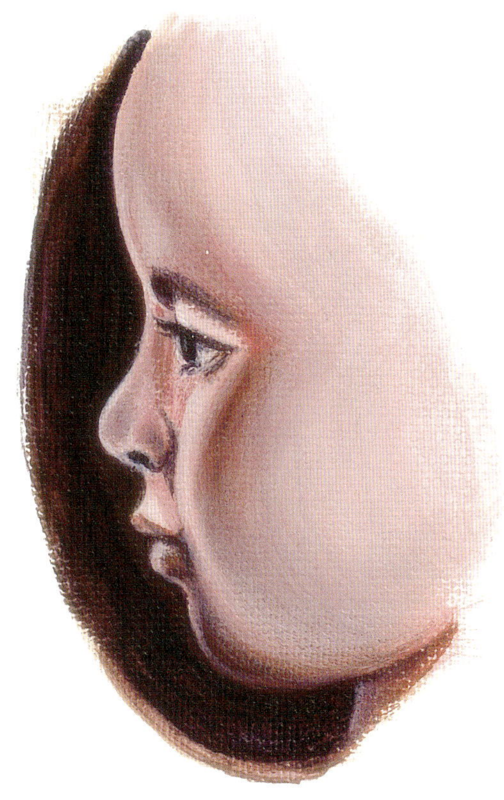

Compare this face to the sphere and you can see the similarities. Commit to memory the five elements of shading. They are essential to realistic painting.

Practice the Five Elements of Shading

PIGMENTS
Alizarin Crimson, Burnt Umber, Cadmium Red Medium, Cadmium Yellow Medium, Ivory Black, Prussian Blue, Titanium White

BRUSHES
Nos. 2 and 4 round
Nos. 4 and 6 filbert

OTHER
Mechanical pencil
Ruler

Let's paint this sphere. The first time you'll use Ivory Black and Titanium White. Keep reading for instructions for using other pigments as well.

Identify where the five elements of shading will be. In all of these examples, the light is coming from the upper right.

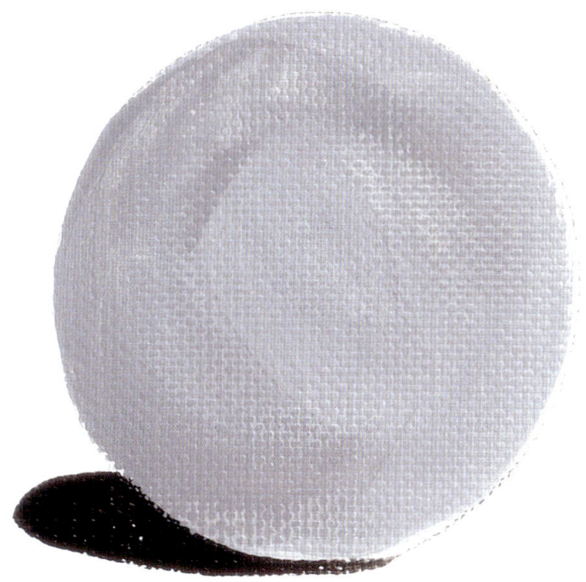

1 BEGIN THE SPHERE
With a pencil, trace a perfect circle onto your canvas paper. (You can use a stencil or simply trace around a glass or jar.)

Mix a small amount of medium gray for the base color of the sphere. Begin with a small puddle of white, then add black into it, a bit at a time until you like the color. Fill in the entire sphere with this color using the no. 6 filbert.

Use black and the no. 2 round to fill in the cast shadow below.

Lightest First

Always mix your paint beginning with the lightest pigment first.

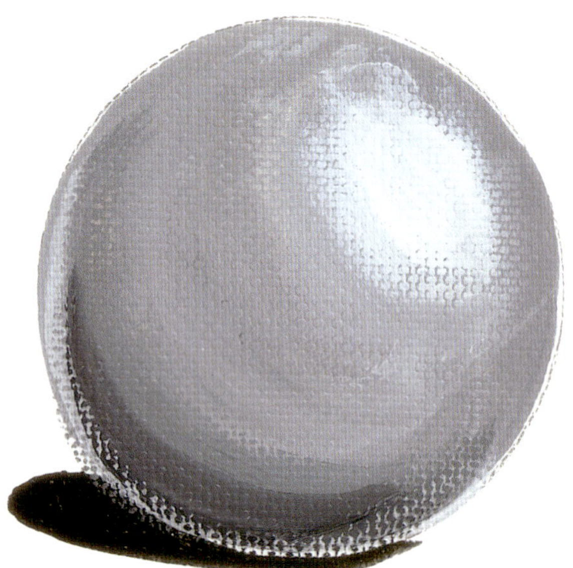

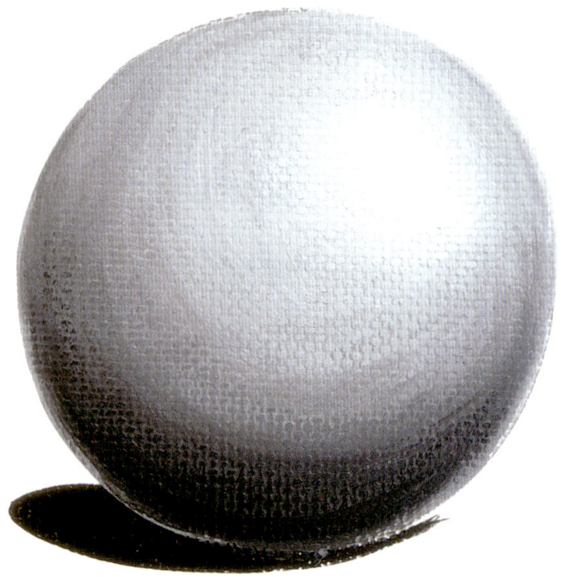

2 THE AWKWARD STAGE

You've already achieved two of the five elements of shading (the halftone and the cast shadow). Now it's time to add the rest.

Add some more black into the gray mix to create a dark gray. Apply it to the sphere with the no. 4 filbert, parallel to the edge to create the shadow edge. Keeping it parallel to the actual edge will create the reflected light area. Use pure white and the no. 4 round to add the full light area. Even though this is the "awkward stage," you have developed all five elements of shading.

3 BLEND TO FINISH

Use the dry-brush technique, small amounts of paint and the no. 6 filbert to gently scrub the tones into one another. It is like "drawing with paint," and requires the same type of blending motion. Drybrush the tones together to make them transition. Go back and forth adding and subtracting your tones until they appear smooth. Take your time.

Adjust the values as you go. For instance, when going from the pure white highlight area to the medium gray, mix an in-between color that is a smaller transition. This is not as easy as it looks, so please do not get frustrated. Remember, you can go over things as many times as you want. I often will add some paint and softly reblend into the paint that is already there.

PAINT A SPHERE USING BURNT UMBER AND TITANIUM WHITE

Now paint that sphere again, only this time add a little color. Remember, once painting spheres becomes like second nature to you, you'll be well on your way to realistic portraits.

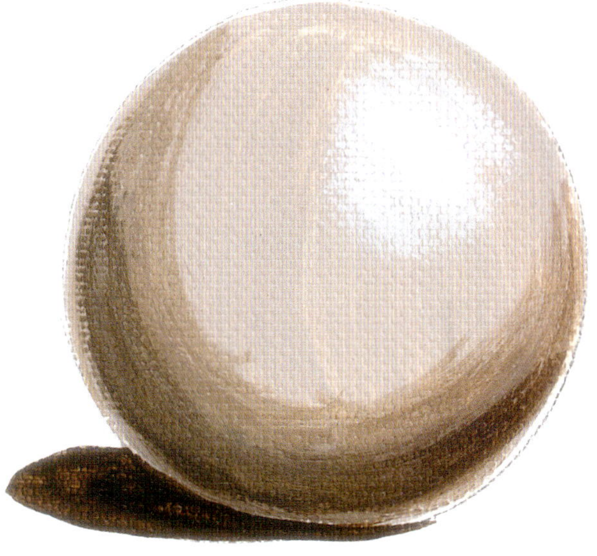

1 BEGIN THE SPHERE

Using the same process as before, create a sphere using Burnt Umber and Titanium White instead of black. Base in the entire sphere with a medium brown. Use the Burnt Umber full strength for the cast shadow.

2 THE AWKWARD STAGE

Create the shadow edge and the full light area.

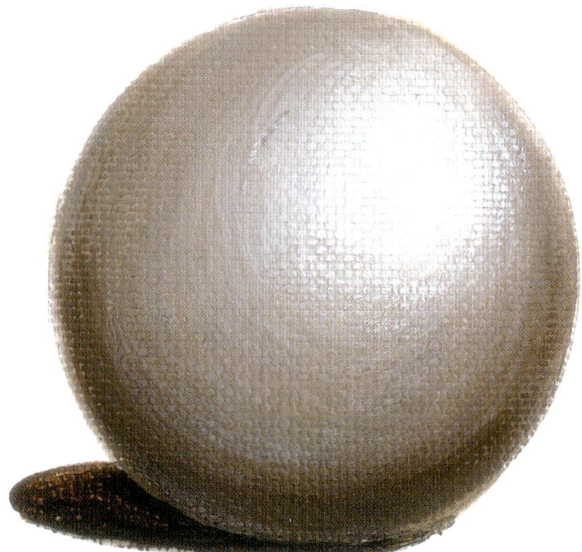

3 BLEND TO FINISH

Drybrush the colors together using the no. 6 filbert. Alter your colors a little at a time, adding and subtracting light and dark.

CREATE SPHERES USING COMPLEMENTARY COLORS

Practice painting the monochromatic sphere from the previous exercise. It really is the foundation for everything else you'll paint. When you feel you've got it, try painting spheres in color.

Remember the value scale on page 30? For spheres in color, the main color of your sphere is a 3 on the value scale. Mix the lighter values (1 and 2) by adding Titanium White. Mix the darker values (4 and 5) by adding the complement of the main color. As you learned on page 20, complements produce a pleasing grayed-down color, perfect for painting shadows.

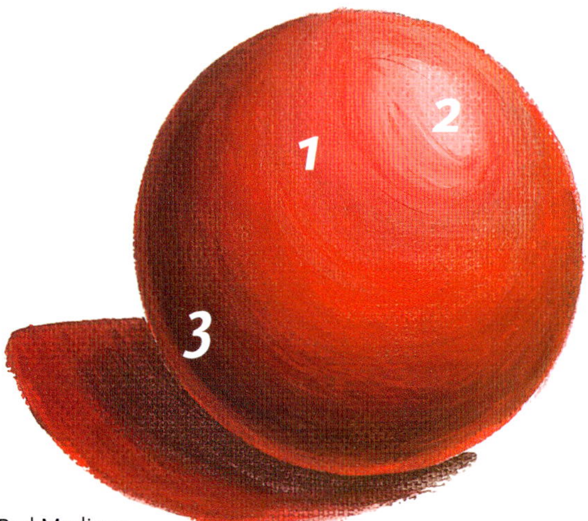

1 Cadmium Red Medium
2 Cadmium Red Medium mixed with Titanium White
3 Cadmium Red Medium mixed with green (Prussian Blue + Cadmium Yellow Medium)

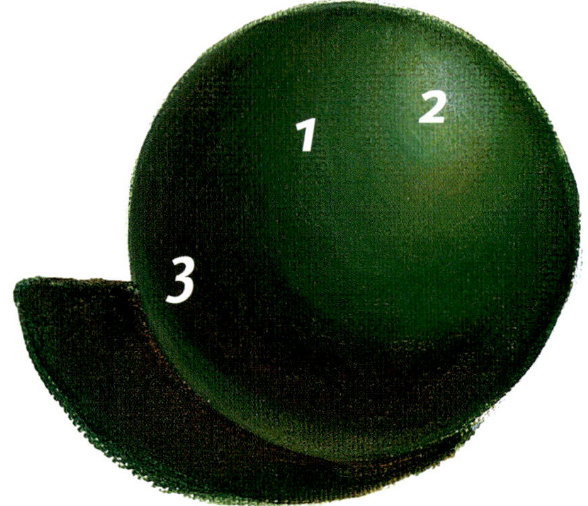

1 Green (Prussian Blue + Cadmium Yellow Medium)
2 Green mixed with Titanium White
3 Green mixed with Cadmium Red Medium

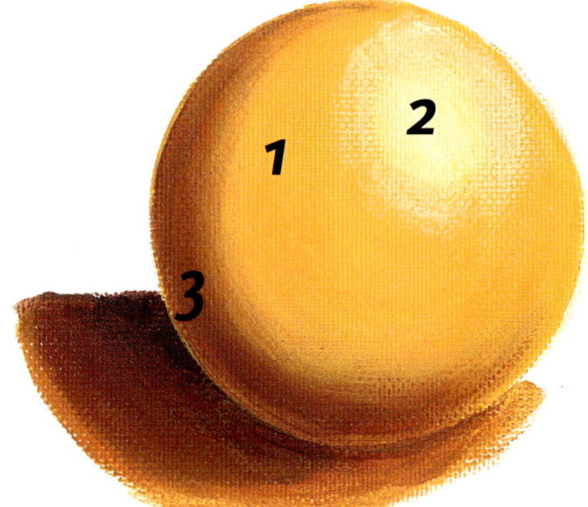

1 Cadmium Yellow Medium
2 Cadmium Yellow Medium mixed with Titanium White
3 Cadmium Yellow Medium mixed with violet (Alizarin Crimson + Prussian Blue)

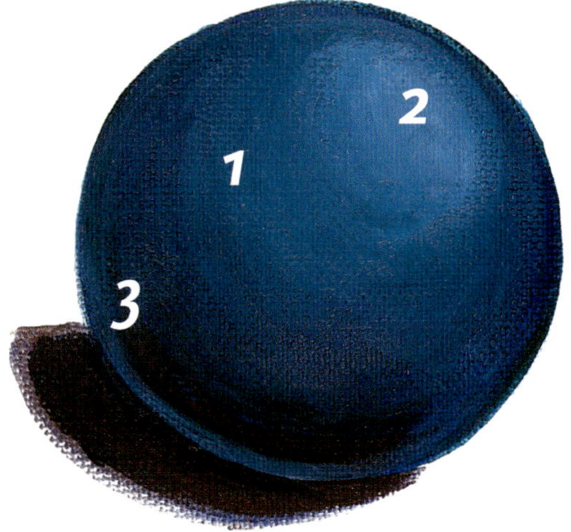

1 Prussian Blue
2 Prussian Blue mixed with Titanium White
3 Prussian Blue mixed with orange (Cadmium Yellow Medium + Cadmium Red Medium)

PAINT A SPHERE IN FULL COLOR

Now it's time to use full colors that you might be using to paint portraits.

Painting in full color requires more layers than with monochromatic. This is because full color changes more when exposed to light and shadow. The transition of color is more pronounced. You will need to alter your colors in small increments often to keep them looking smooth.

Use the no. 2 round and no. 4 filbert for this sphere.

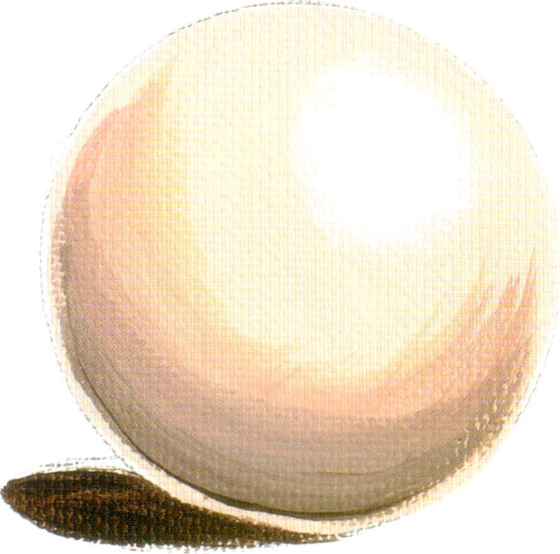

1 BEGIN THE SPHERE

Create a medium peach color using Titanium White, Cadmium Red Medium and Cadmium Yellow Medium. Base the entire sphere in this color. Paint in the cast shadow with Burnt Umber.

2 THE AWKWARD STAGE

Add a touch of Burnt Umber to the peach mixture and create the shadow edge. Add a touch of Titanium White and Cadmium Red Medium to that mixture and apply it right above the shadow edge. This will help transition the skin tones.

With pure white, add the full light area.

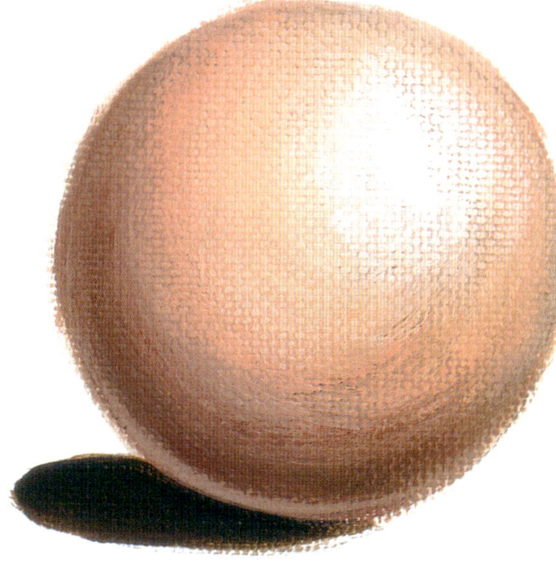

3 BLEND TO FINISH

Drybrush the colors together using the no. 4 filbert. Alter your colors a little at a time, adding and subtracting lights and darks.

Draw Using the Grid Method

To be a good painter, it is essential to learn some basic drawing skills. All paintings must have a firm foundation on which to build and the shapes of the objects you are painting must be accurate.

I take my own photo references to use in creating artwork. To accurately depict what I want to paint, I use a *grid method* to draw the shapes accurately in the beginning.

How the Grid Method Works

The grid method is excellent for breaking down a complex subject into smaller, more manageable shapes.

1 **Place a grid of squares over a photo reference.** One-inch (3cm) squares usually work well. If you have many small details to capture, you can place smaller squares over your photo.

2 **Draw an identical grid on your canvas.** The squares can be the same size, larger or smaller, but the grid on your canvas must have the same number of rows and columns as the one on the reference photo.

3 **Lightly draw what you see within each square.** This makes it easy to get the shapes right.

1	2	3	4	5	6	7	8	9	10	11	12	13
14	15	16	17	18	19	20	21	22	23	24	25	26
27	28	29	30	31	32	33	34	35	36	37	38	39
40	41	42	43	44	45	46	47	48	49	50	51	52
53	54	55	56	57	58	59	60	61	62	63	64	65
66	67	68	69	70	71	72	73	74	75	76	77	78
79	80	81	82	83	84	85	86	87	88	89	90	91
92	93	94	95	96	97	98	99	100	101	102	103	104
105	106	107	108	109	110	111	112	113	114	115	116	117
118	119	120	121	122	123	124	125	126	127	128	129	130
131	132	133	134	135	136	137	138	139	140	141	142	143
144	145	146	147	148	149	150	151	152	153	154	155	156
157	158	159	160	161	162	163	164	165	166	167	168	169
170	171	172	173	174	175	176	177	178	179	180	181	182
183	184	185	186	187	188	189	190	191	192	193	194	195
196	197	198	199	200	201	202	203	204	205	206	207	208
209	210	211	212	213	214	215	216	217	218	219	220	221
222	223	224	225	226	227	228	229	230	231	232	233	234
235	236	237	238	239	240							

The Grid Method of Drawing

Have the copy shop make acetate overlays of the grid. Then it is easy to take whatever size grid you need and tape it over any photo you want to paint. You can even number the individual boxes to help you keep track as you draw.

Puzzle Pieces

When using the grid method, remember this important idea: Everything you draw or paint should be viewed as a puzzle. And all the pieces of the puzzle are nothing more than patterns of interlocking shapes of light and dark.

Grid Practice

MATERIALS
Mechanical pencil
Ruler
Eraser

Use this exercise as practice using the grid. Draw it on a regular piece of paper first to give you some experience before you place it on canvas paper. Focus on where the shapes fill each square of the grid. This pose is a good one to start with because it eliminates the complexities of facial features.

You'll be able to complete this painting in a demonstration later in the book. For now, practice the drawing part, and put it aside.

Look only at the shapes in one box at a time. Forget you are drawing a person and see each box as a bunch of nonsense shapes.

Most of the projects in this book are started with the grid method. Practice all the drawing exercises first before you begin painting. Once you're proficient at drawing using the grid method, you'll find painting much easier.

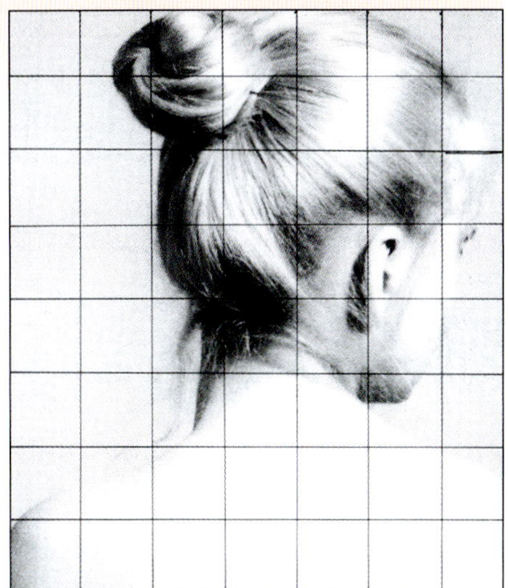

Reference Photo
A photograph of the model with one-inch (3cm) squares. Look for the nonsense shapes within each box.

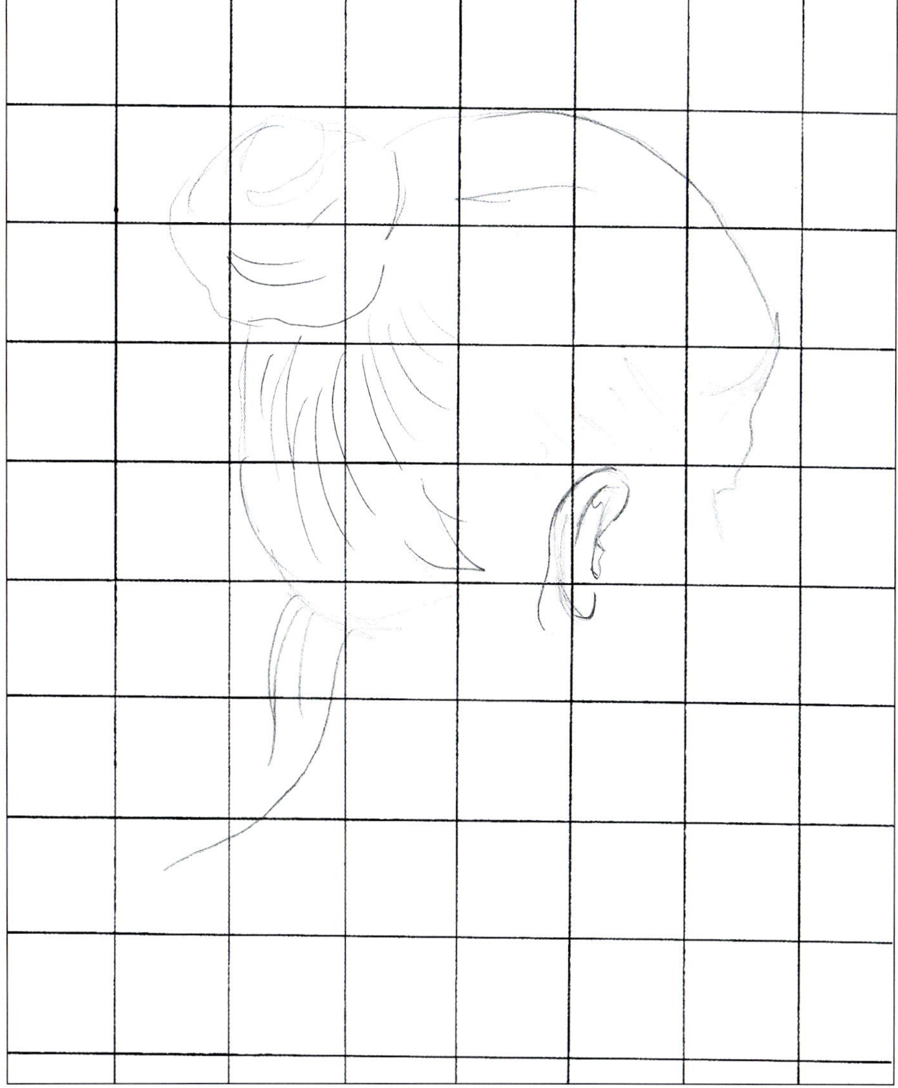

1 Lightly apply a grid of one-inch (3cm) squares to your paper with a mechanical pencil. Using the grid as your guide, begin drawing the shapes you see, one box at a time. Go slowly, concentrate on one square at a time, and forget you are drawing a person.

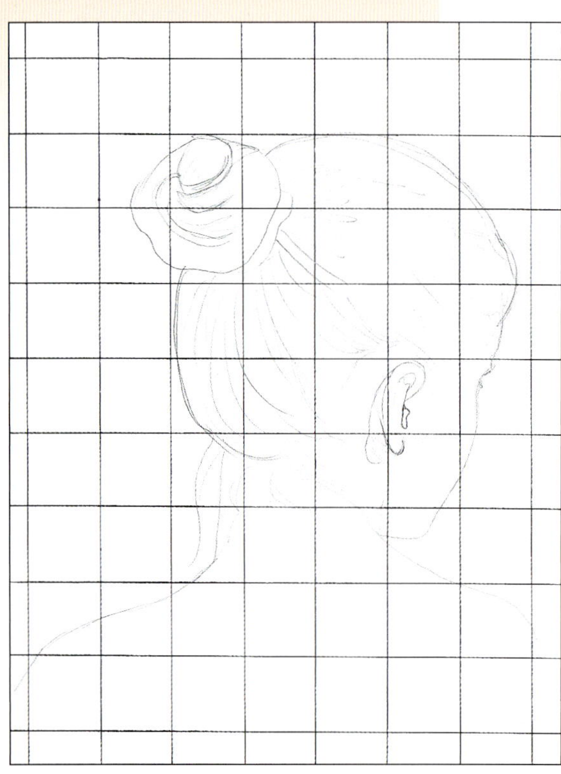

2 This is what your line drawing should look like when you are finished. Keep the small details to a minimum. Only place details that are absolutely necessary. When you start the painting process, you will cover most of it.

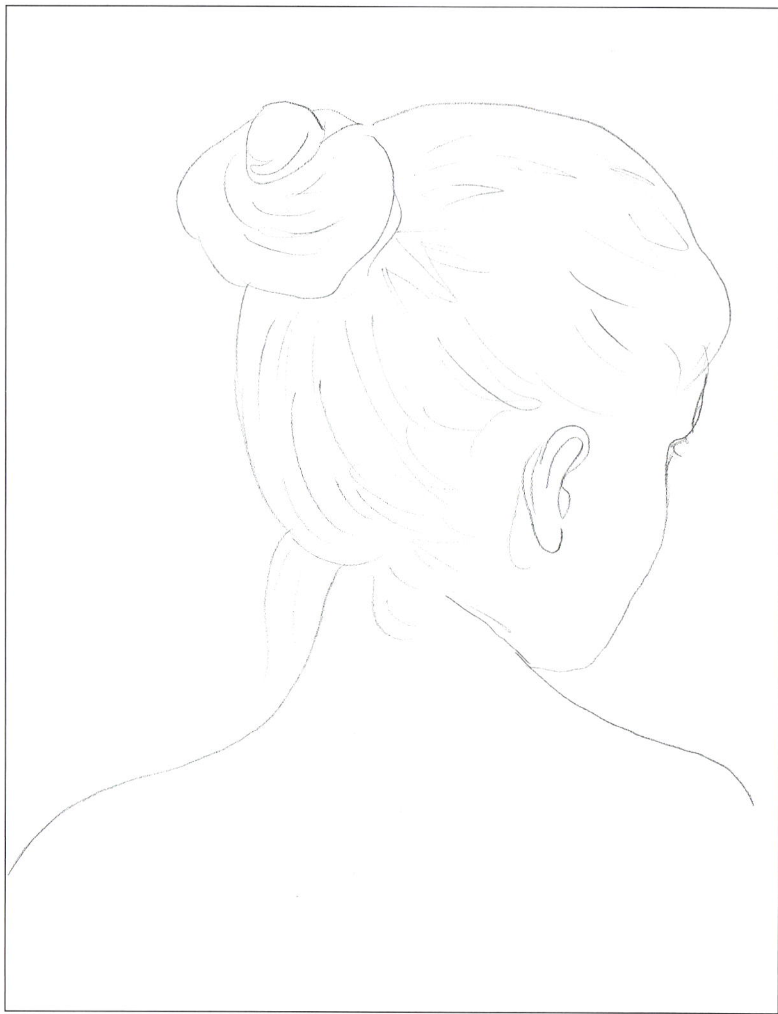

3 Use an eraser to remove the grid lines from the canvas when you are happy with the outline. Be very careful when removing the grid lines so that you do not inadvertently remove part of the subject.

Keep this line drawing for the demonstration on page 97.

More Grid Practice

Exercise your drawing skills to complete the following grid drawings.

Remember, the better you can draw, the better your painting will be. And you'll use all these drawings to complete the painting demonstrations to come!

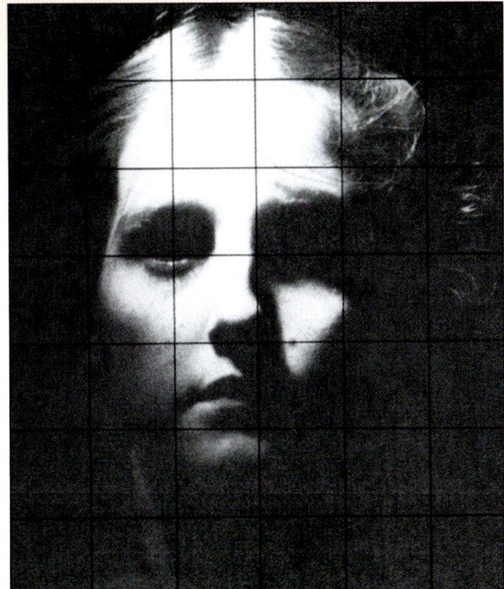

Reference Photo
The features in this subject are obscured by the extreme lighting, casting the face into a type of silhouette. When painted, it looks a bit surreal, but it has a lot of visual impact. You will paint this later in gray tones.

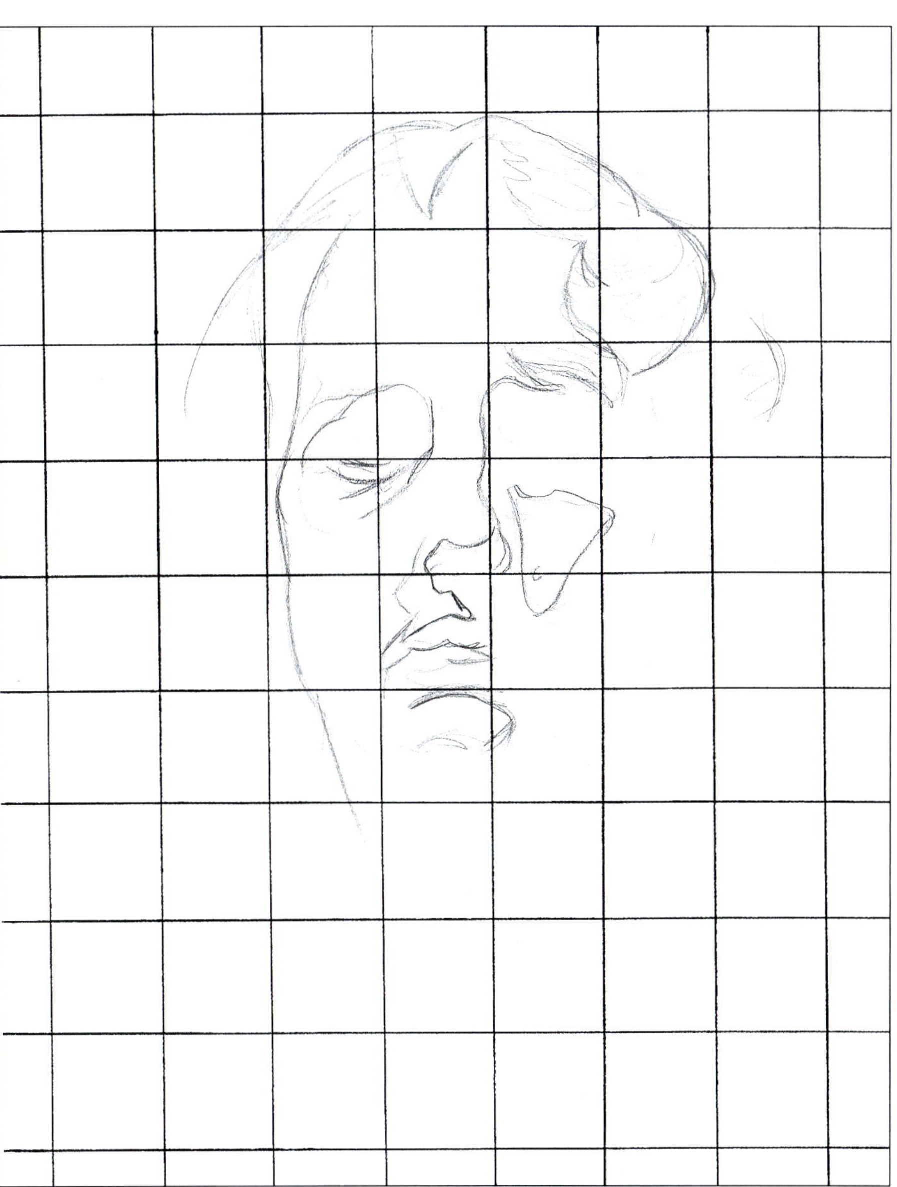

Grid Drawing
This line drawing looks very abstract. When drawing, sometimes your brain will want you to add more detail. Resist the urge. Only draw the shapes that are in each box.

The line drawing may not seem like much, but it is an essential foundation for an interesting painting later.

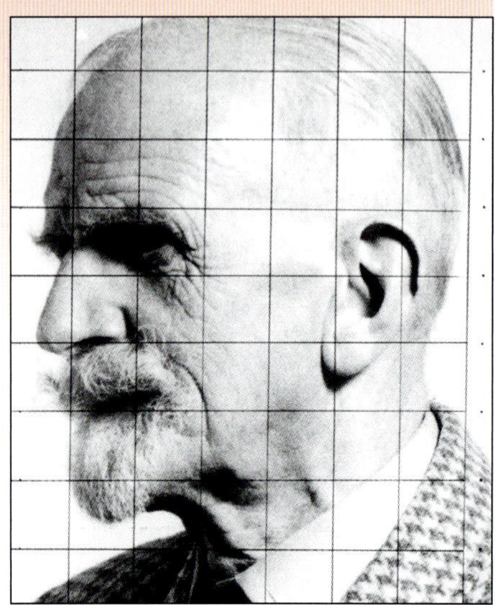

Reference Photo
This portrait is a bit more complex. Remember to draw one box at a time. Turn the photo and your drawing upside down for more accuracy as you work.

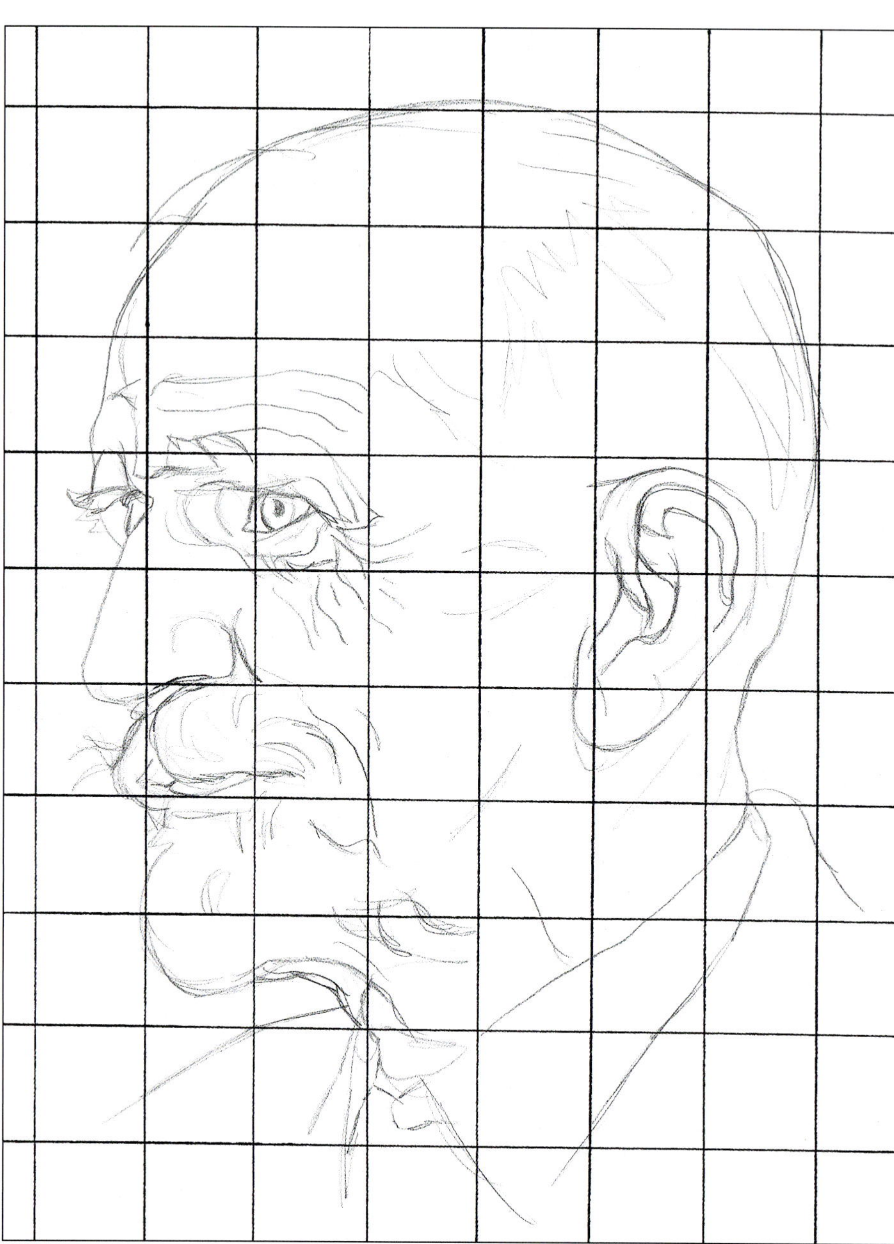

Grid Drawing
When your drawing looks like this, you can remove your grid lines with the eraser. Be careful. Do not accidentally erase any of the details in the process.

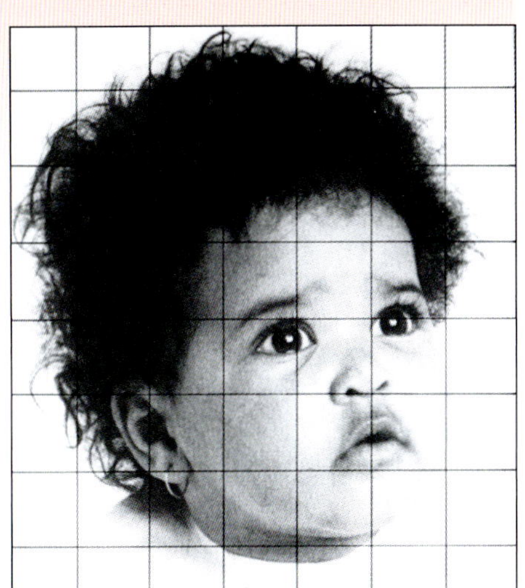

Reference Photo
I love this simple little portrait of a baby face. This will be the first full-color painting you do later on in the demonstrations. The skin's rich colors and the softness of the hair are fun to paint. It will also give you practice turning a black-and-white photo into a full-color painting.

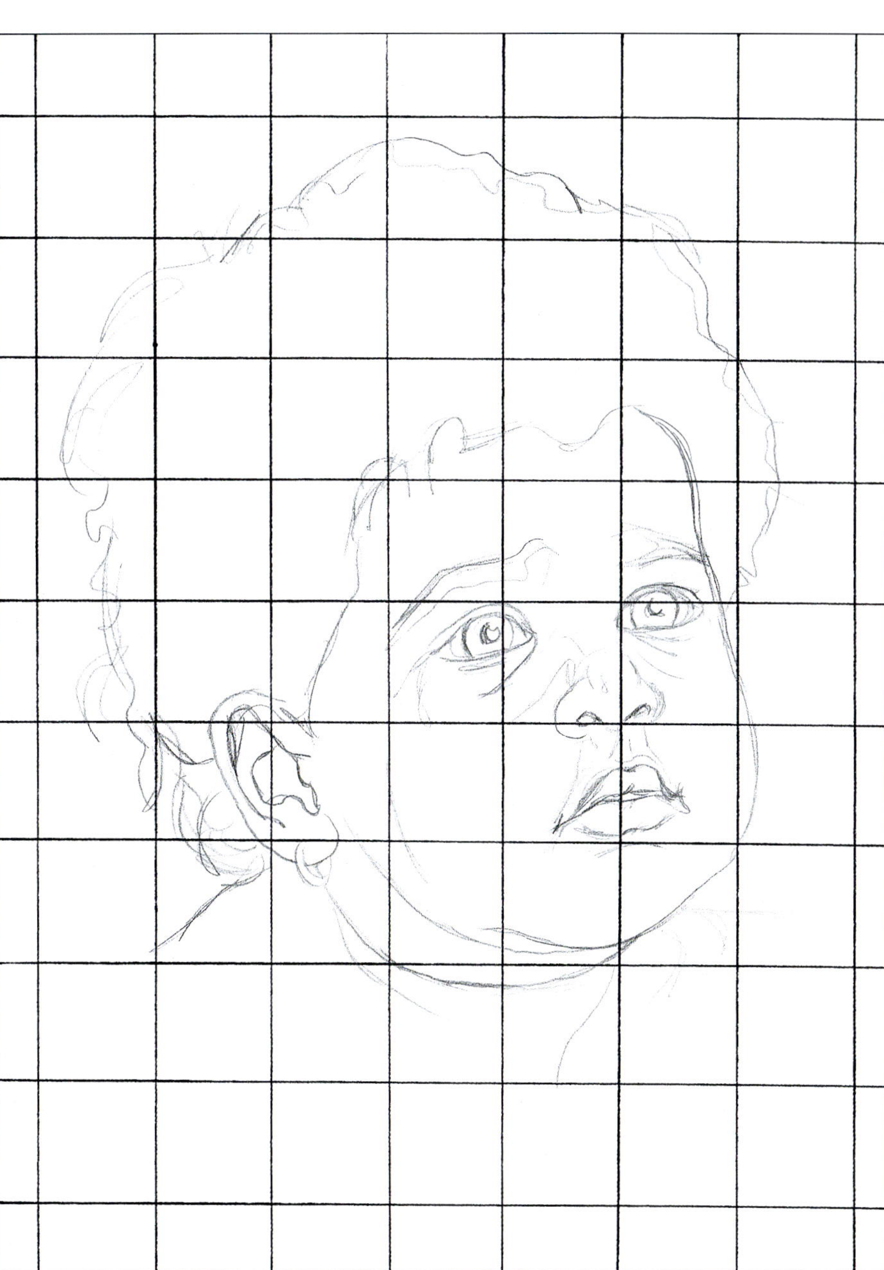

Grid Drawing
Use the grid method to capture this cute little face.

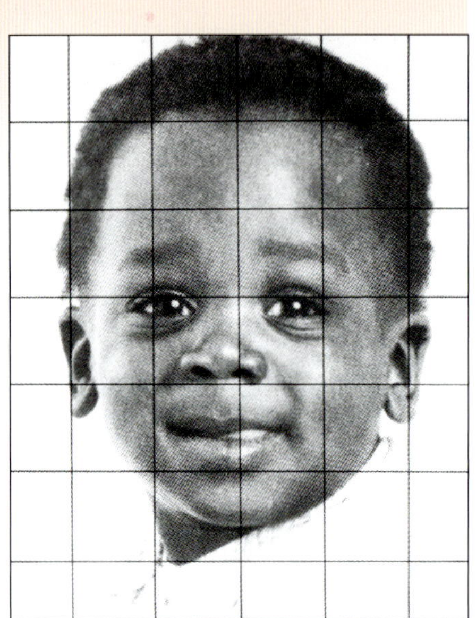

Reference Photo

The expression of this little guy is adorable and it creates a wonderful painting. This expression is a little more difficult to capture than the baby in the previous exercise due to the slant of the mouth. Study the shapes carefully.

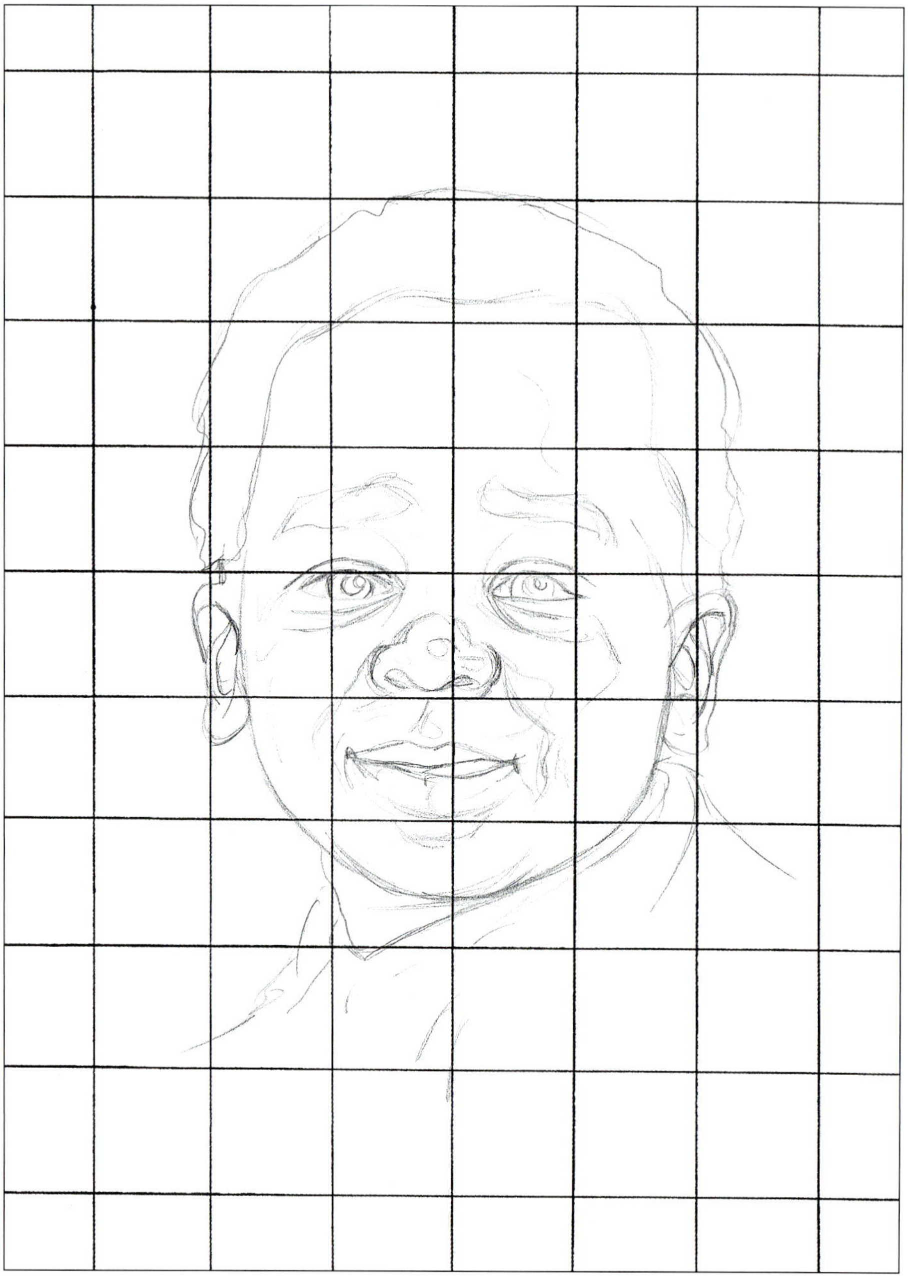

Grid Drawing

Remember to simplify the details at this stage. The drawing should look like a "map."

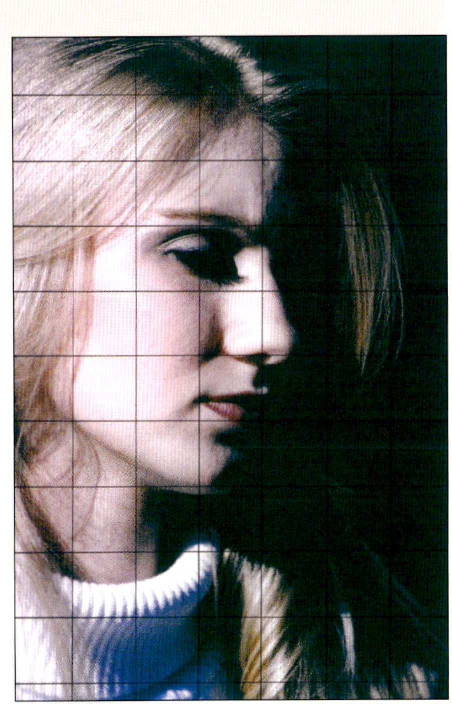

Reference Photo
This is an example of a ¾-view portrait.

The slight turn of the head changes the perspective in which we are viewing the face. It is considered one of the most difficult poses to capture because our brain wants to straighten everything out and make it symmetrical.

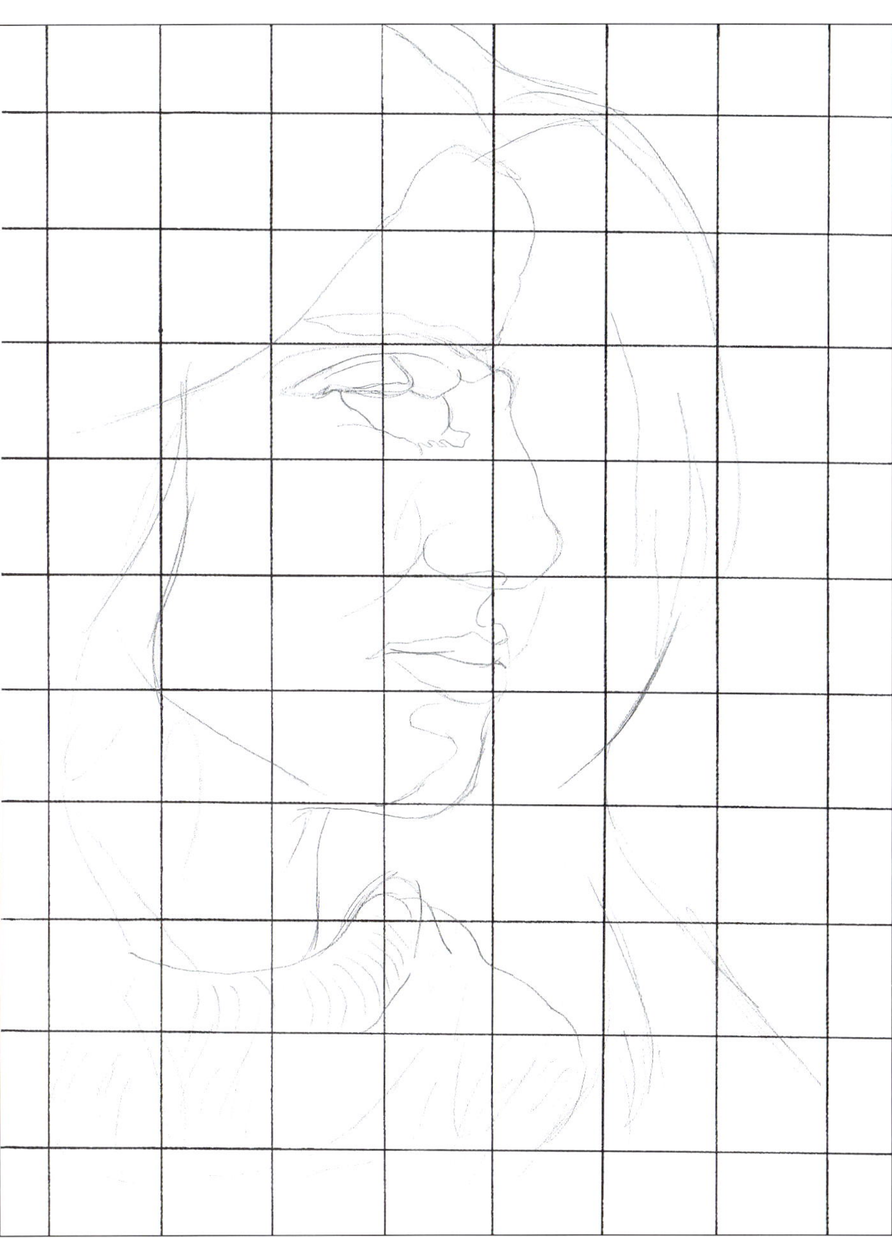

Grid Drawing
When drawing this pose, take extra care in capturing what you see, and not what you remember. This vantage point combined with the lighting hides one eye altogether. You will only see one side of the nose. And, from the center of the mouth, you will see much more on the left side than the right. Carefully draw within each square of your grid for accuracy.

This portrait is a good example of how the exercises in the previous chapter apply to portraits. His round face, along with the extreme lighting, creates wonderful sphere-like impressions. The color scheme is very similar to the flesh-colored sphere, and the technique is identical. It just takes a lot more time and layers to do a portrait because of the more complex shapes.

GAVYN
14" x 11" (36cm x 28cm)

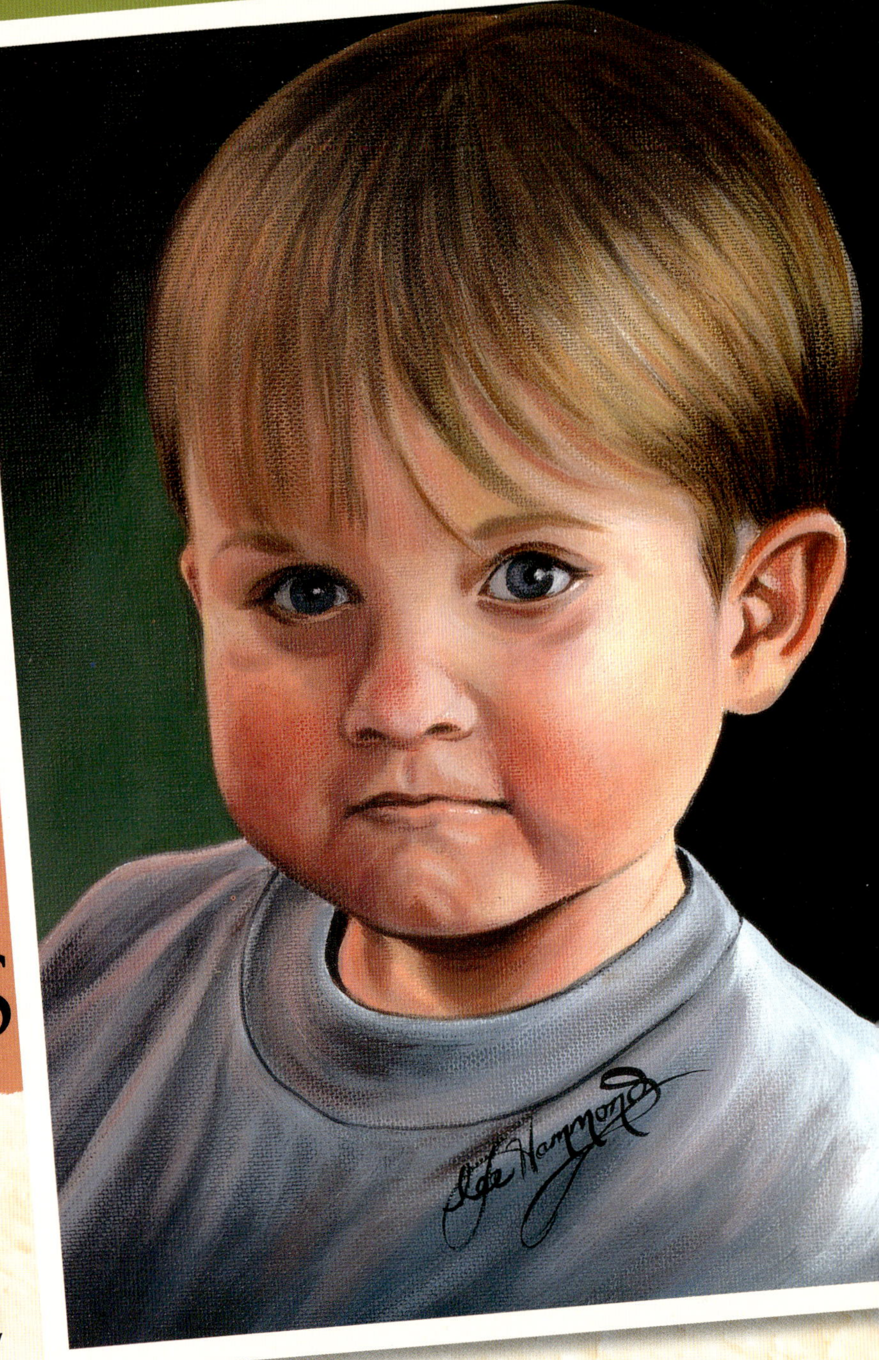

PART 2

PAINTING FACIAL FEATURES

To become proficient in painting portraits, it is important to have a good understanding of each of the facial features. Practicing painting the features individually before attempting to create an entire portrait will make your journey much, much easier. Painting the individual features is just simpler. This means you'll experience success faster. The result of that is confidence! When I was first learning, I went page by page through magazines and drew and painted every feature I could find.

Begin With the Nose

The nose is the simplest of all the features, so let's start there.

Once again, we can turn to the sphere. It shares many of the same elements.

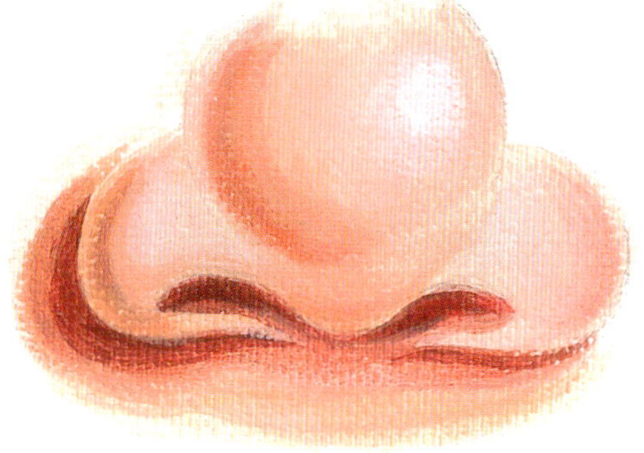

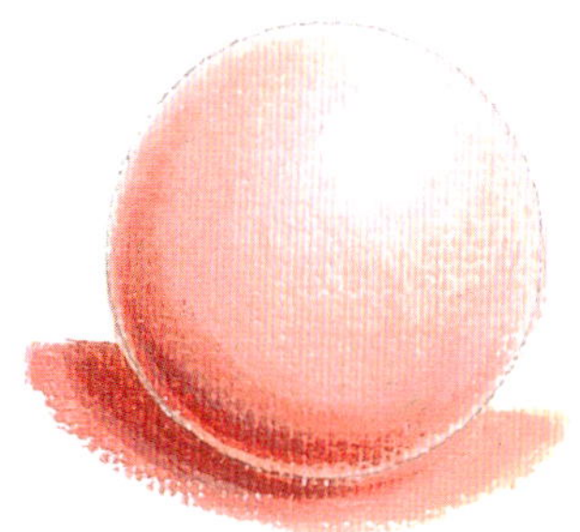

Look at this baby nose. The nose of a baby is so round, the sphere is actually replicated in the tip.

Nose Profile

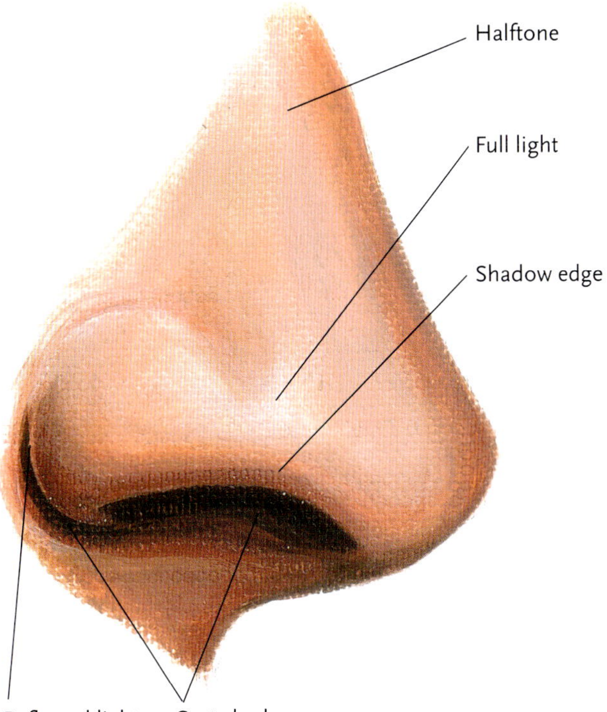

Nose, Front View

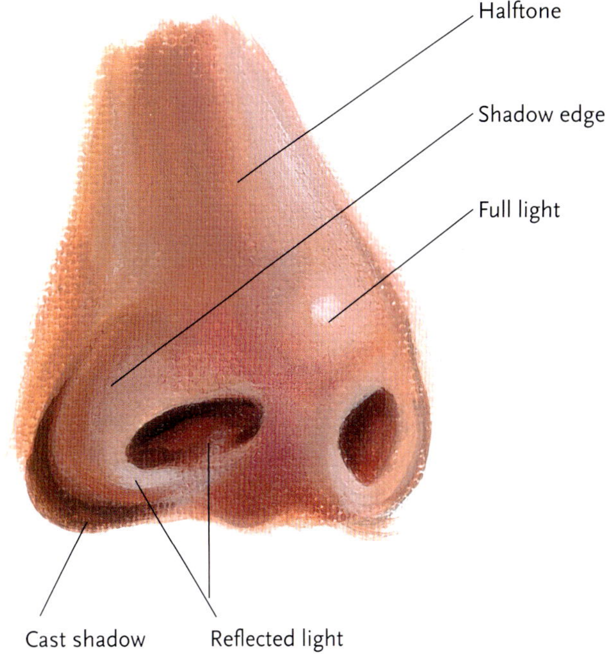

While adult noses are not generally as round as the example of the baby's nose, they still have all the five elements of shading.

Monochromatic

PIGMENTS
Ivory Black, Titanium White

BRUSHES
Nos. 1 and 4 round

It is easier to learn to paint in a monochromatic color scheme, so you can concentrate strictly on blending tones.

Gray Scale
Match your tones to this gray scale.

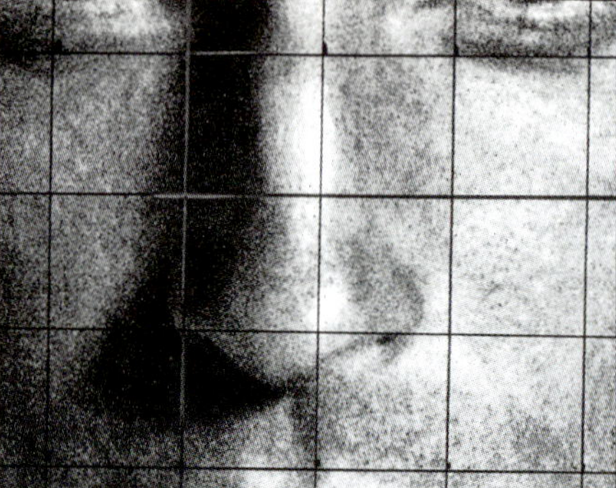

Reference Photo
Study this nose carefully for shape and shading. Use the grid method to draw the nose on your canvas paper. Remove the grid lines with an eraser when it is accurate.

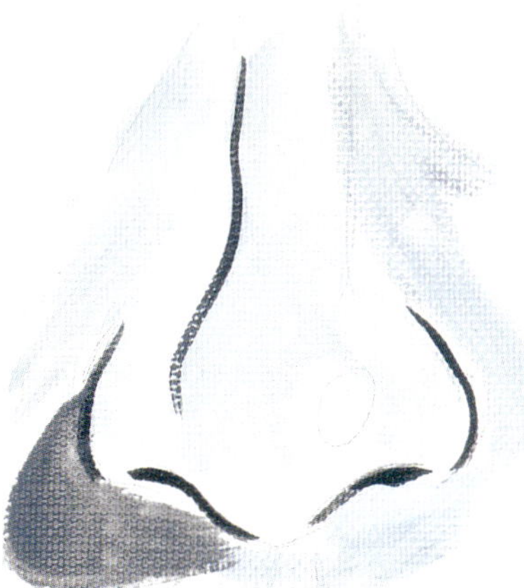

1 BEGIN WITH HALFTONES

Place dime-sized blobs of black and white paint on your palette. Add a touch of black to a small amount of white to get a light gray. Basecoat the entire nose with this mixture and the no. 4 round.

Add a touch more black to deepen the gray and fill the cast shadow on the left.

With the no. 1 round, add more black to make a dark gray for the nostril area, the edges of the nose, and the contour of the bridge.

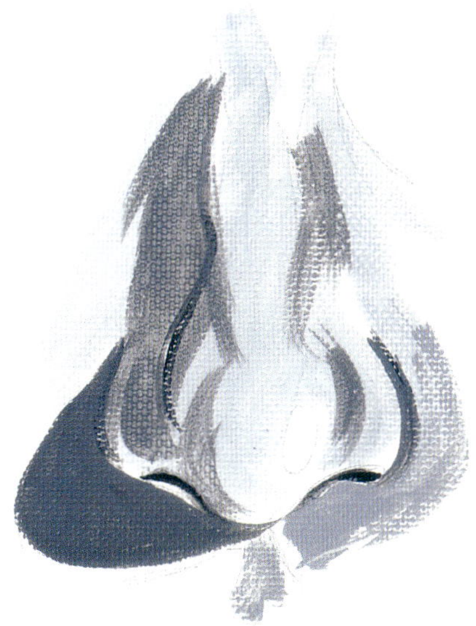

2 THE AWKWARD STAGE

With the no. 4 round, add the shadow areas of the nose with a medium gray. The paint can be a little transparent. It looks a bit sloppy at this stage, and this is where many beginners put the brush down and quit. But don't! All paintings go through this stage. Continue adding tones to build the layers and create the form.

3 FINISH

Use thicker paint and the dry-brush technique to rub in different gray tones. It may take many layers to get it to look like this example. It is merely a process of adding light, medium and dark gray tones to the painting, and fading them into one another. Place each tone according to the light source and the five elements of shading.

Light Complexion

PIGMENTS
Alizarin Crimson, Burnt Umber, Cadmium Red Medium, Cadmium Yellow Medium, Titanium White

BRUSHES
Nos. 1 and 2 round

Now let's follow the same process using a full-color photo. This example is a very light skin tone. Your values will be very light with little contrast. The edges of the nose are difficult to see. This quality is important to capture in your painting. If you exaggerate the tones and edges, your painting will look cartoonish.

Light Complexion Warm
Follow the instructions on page 23 to mix light, medium and dark versions of this peach color.

Add Burnt Umber and Alizarin Crimson to the mixture to create the shadows.

Reference Photo
Use the grid to capture the shape of the nose on your canvas paper. Remove the grid lines with an eraser when you are finished.

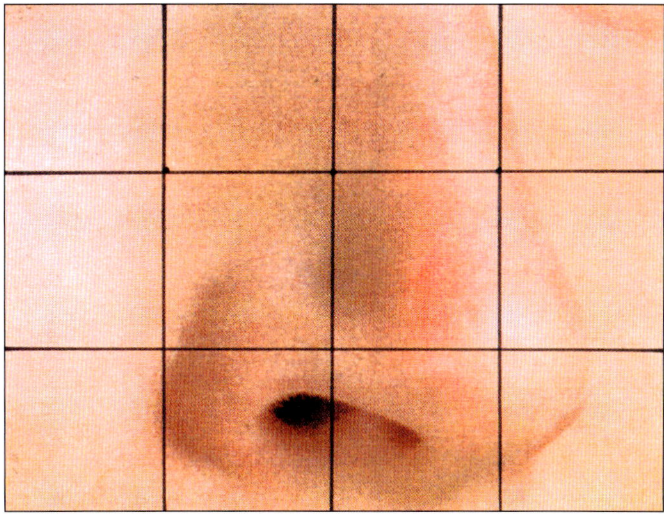

Paint Mixing Hint

To match your paint, place a clear piece of glass or acetate over the swatch and dab your paint mixture next to it. You can see how close you are to matching it this way. Keep in mind that acrylic paint will become a bit darker when dry.

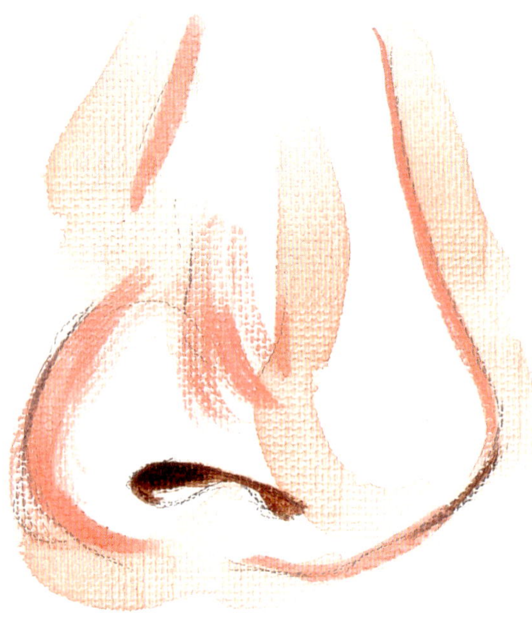

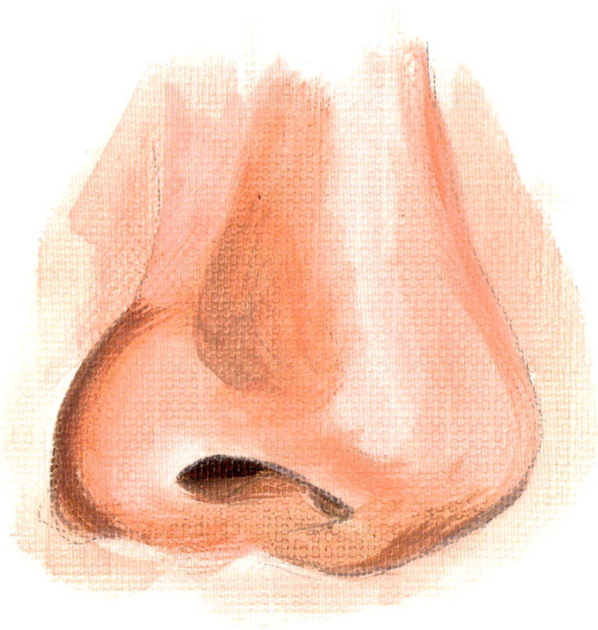

1 BEGIN THE HALFTONES
Add water to the medium peach color and wash in the basic shapes of the nose contours using the no. 2 round. Use the shadow mixture and the no. 1 round to add the nostril area.

2 THE AWKWARD STAGE
Continue adding tone with the no. 2 round using the light, medium and dark colors. Keep the paint very thin. All the darker shadow areas are on the left side and under the tip of the nose.

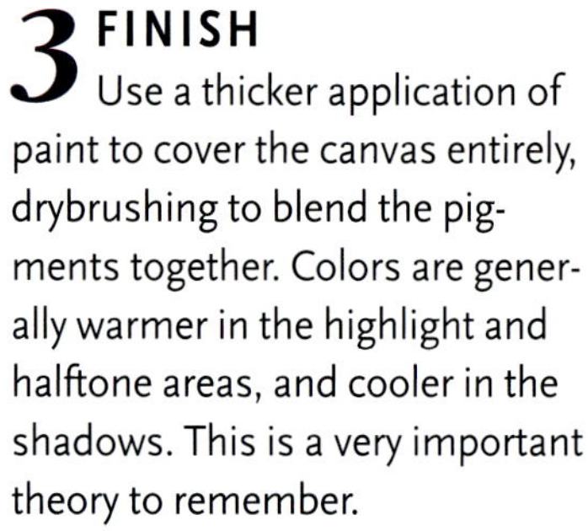

3 FINISH
Use a thicker application of paint to cover the canvas entirely, drybrushing to blend the pigments together. Colors are generally warmer in the highlight and halftone areas, and cooler in the shadows. This is a very important theory to remember.

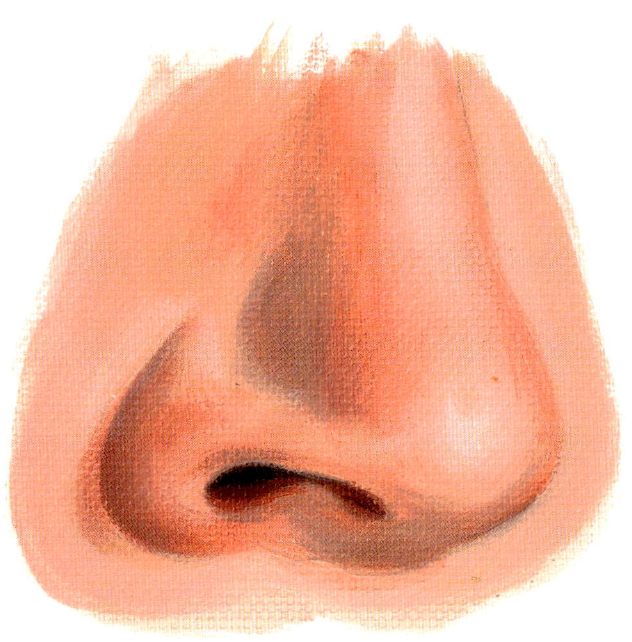

Dark Complexion

PIGMENTS
Burnt Umber, Cadmium Red Medium, Titanium White

BRUSHES
Nos. 1 and 2 round

The process of working with darker skin is exactly the same.

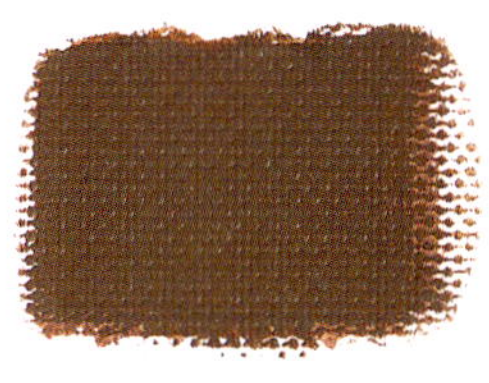

Brown Complexion Warm
Follow the instructions on page 23 to mix a light, medium and dark version of this color by altering the amount of white. Use pure Burnt Umber for the nostril and shadow.

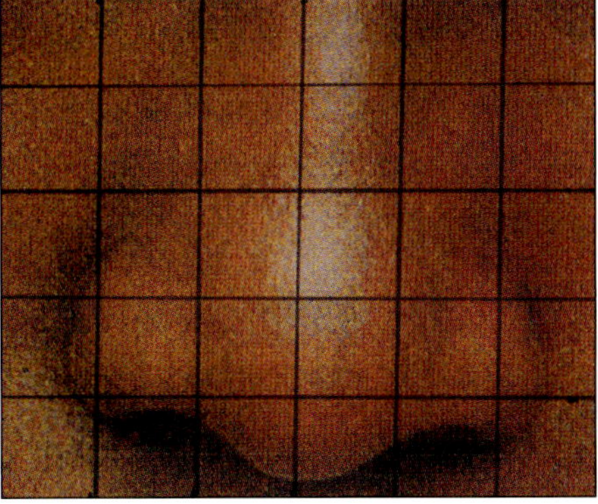

Reference Photo
Use the photograph to make an accurate line drawing. I used half-inch (13mm) squares to make the accuracy and symmetry of this front view easier.

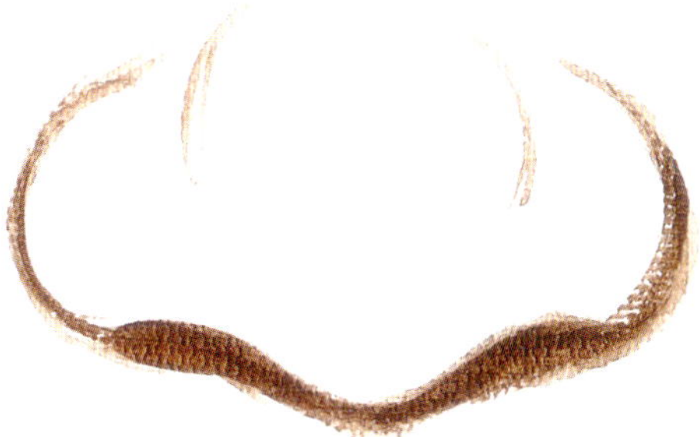

1 BEGIN WITH HALFTONES

Dilute the warm brown mixture and wash in the basic shapes of the contours with the no. 2 round. With pure Burnt Umber and the no. 1 round, add the dark color to the nostril area.

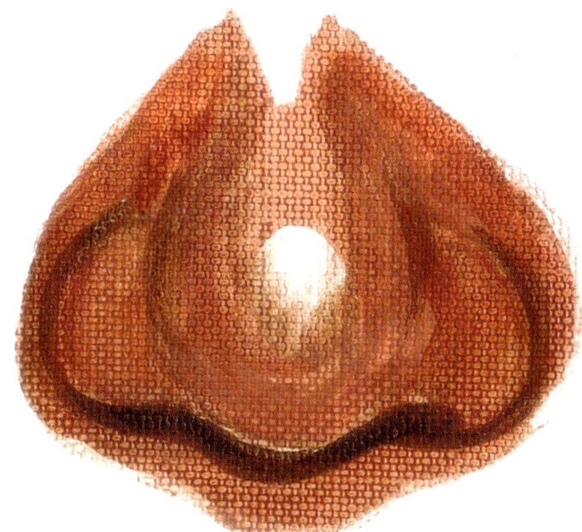

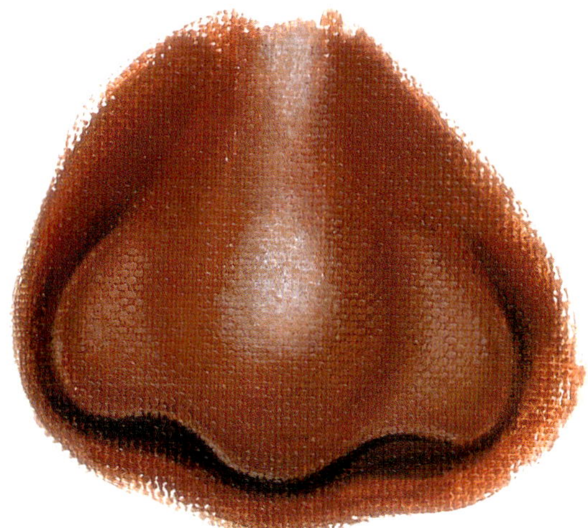

2 THE AWKWARD STAGE

Continue adding tone to the canvas paper with the no. 2 round using the light, medium and dark colors. Your paint should still be very thin with water. Watch for the five elements of shading. All the darker shadow areas are on the sides and under the tip of the nose.

3 FINISH

Use a thicker application of paint to cover the canvas entirely. Drybrush to blend all the colors together. Notice how the colors are warm in the highlight and halftone areas. Cool down the shadows using Burnt Umber, as Burnt Umber has blue in it.

Profile

PIGMENTS
Burnt Umber, Cadmium Red Medium, Cadmium Yellow Medium, Titanium White

BRUSHES
Nos. 1 and 2 round

This is a wonderful nose to paint due to the lighting and the effects of age. The contours of the nose are exaggerated due to the aging, and the lights and darks make very distinct patterns. The dark background illuminates the light edge along the front of the nose, making the light source from the left very obvious.

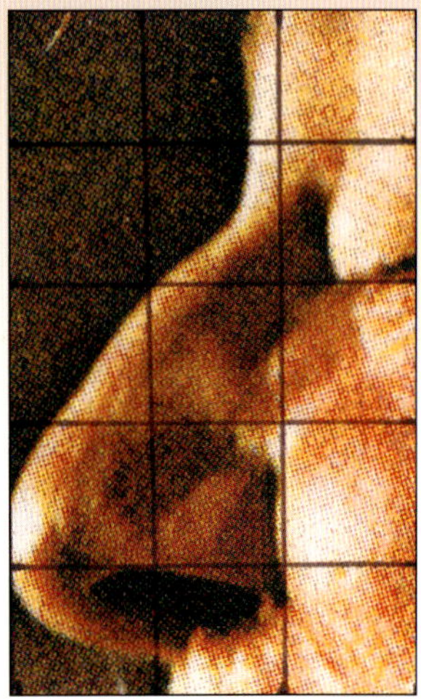

Reference Photo

Light Complexion Warm
Follow the instructions on page 23 to prepare light, medium and dark versions of this color. Use pure Burnt Umber for the nostril and shadow areas.

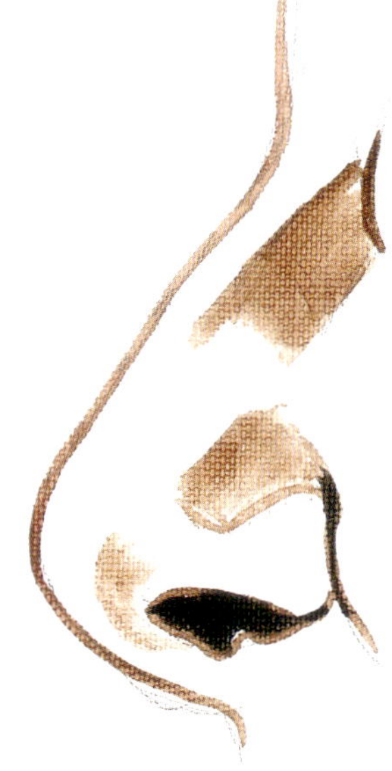

1 THE OUTLINE AND DARK PATTERNS

With pure Burnt Umber and the no. 1 round, outline the shape of the nose and fill in the nostril area. With a diluted application, fill in the dark patterns on the nose.

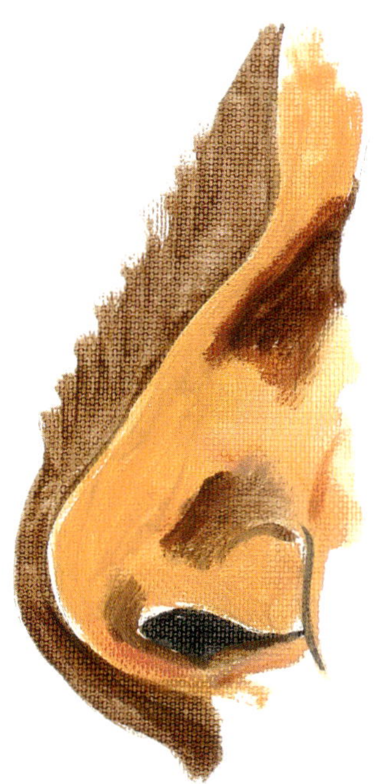

2 THE AWKWARD STAGE

Wash in the basic shapes of the nose with the no. 1 round and a diluted application of the middle skin tone mixture. This skin tone has a lot of yellow in it, so you may need more Cadmium Yellow Medium and a little Burnt Umber. Create the light edge by filling in the dark background with pure Burnt Umber and allowing the white of the canvas to show through. Create the shape of the nose using the different tones as illustrated. Keep the paint still very thin. Watch for the five elements of shading. The reflected light along the nostril edge is very distinct.

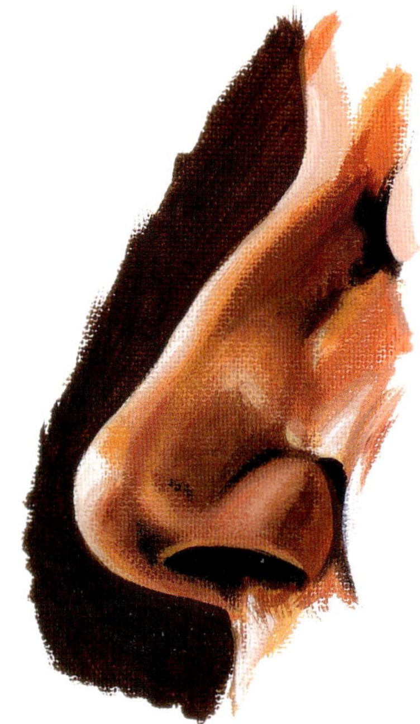

3 FINISH

Use a thicker application of paint and the no. 2 round to cover the canvas entirely. Use the rouging technique, drybrushing and blending all the colors together. Notice how the colors are warm in the highlight and halftone areas. By using Burnt Umber in the shadows, they appear cool.

The Mouth

The mouth is the feature that most expresses the mood of the individual, offering the smile for happiness and the frown for sadness. It also can exude anger, surprise, hesitance and joy. For an artist, the mouth can hold many challenges because of its structure.

Painting a Closed Mouth

To paint the closed mouth remember two things:

- The upper lip is generally darker than the bottom because of the angle of the lips and the way they reflect light.
- The corners of the mouth create a dark comma shape called the "pit" of the mouth. It is important to capture this to keep the mouth from looking flat.

Painting the Open Mouth

The open mouth is full of complexities due to the teeth. It is crucial to capture the size, shape and placement of that person's teeth. If not, the likeness will be lost.

The position of your subject, as well as the mood, will alter the way the mouth is viewed. A mouth from the side has a protruding shape created by the teeth. The upper lip angles in and the lower lip angles out. This is what makes the upper lip appear darker. The angle of the bottom lip gathers more of the light source.

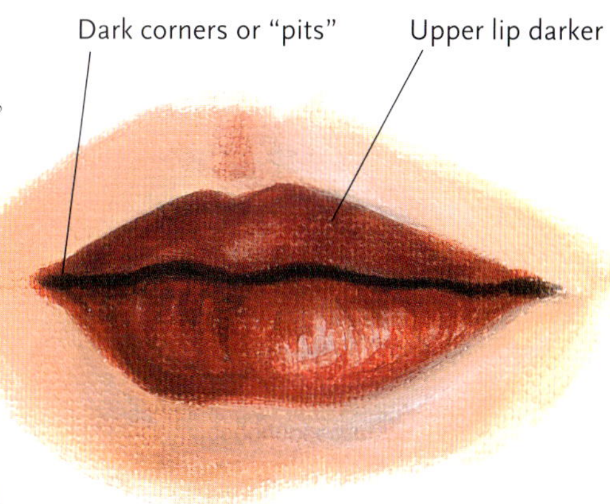

Closed Mouth

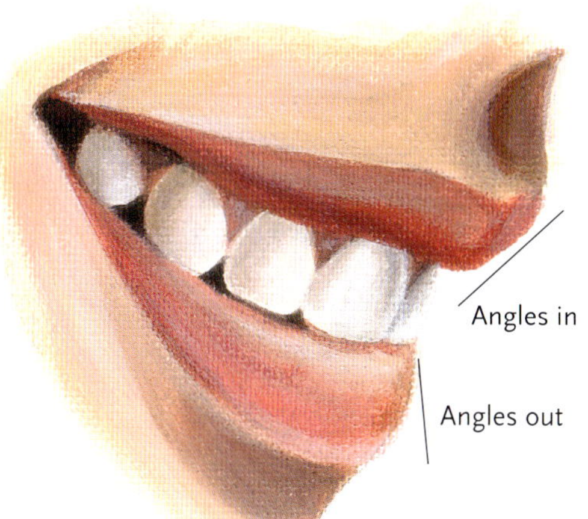

Side View

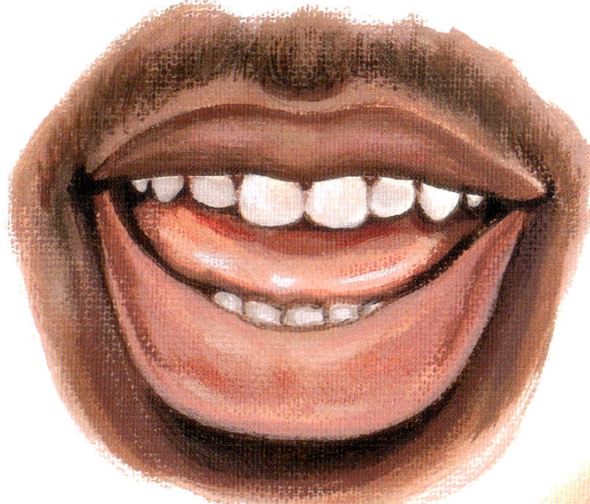

Open Smile
Each person's teeth are unique. Capturing their exact form is essential to a realistic portrait.

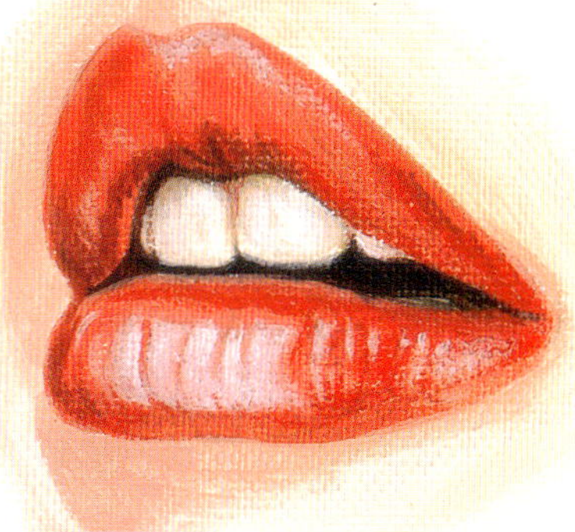

Do's and Don'ts of Painting Teeth

- **Don't paint them white.** Teeth, no matter how many treatments the dentist has applied, are not white! Even if they were, they are inside the mouth, and are altered by the affects of shadows and reflected color. Most teeth will have a yellowish and gray cast to them.
- **Don't paint a hard line between each tooth.** A dark line actually represents space. A hard, dark line would mean the teeth were not touching, and you were seeing between them. Use a soft color where the teeth touch.
- **Do** keep the bottom teeth in shadow. They are farther behind, so they will always be shadowed.
- **Do** give each tooth a unique shape.
- **Do** create the gum line and the dark shapes below the teeth as shapes as well. This helps maintain the tooth shape as you draw.

Monochromatic

PIGMENTS
Ivory Black, Titanium White

BRUSHES
Nos. 1 and 2 round

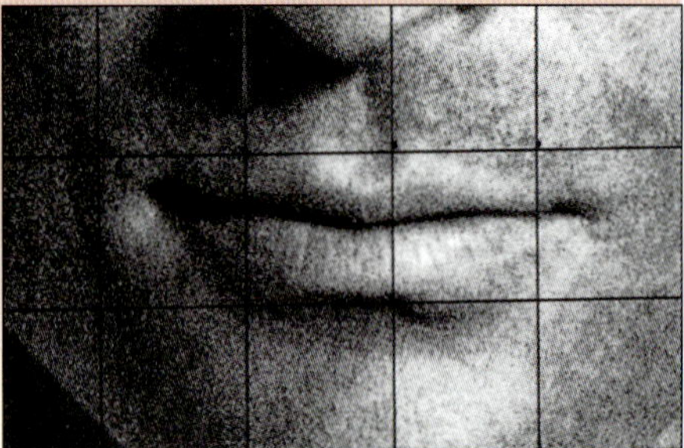

Reference Photo
Notice how the upper lip and the pits on the sides appear darker. Create an accurate line drawing using the grid method. Carefully remove the pencil lines when you are done.

Once again, we will start with a monochromatic color scheme for practice.

Gray Scale
Match your tones to this gray scale.

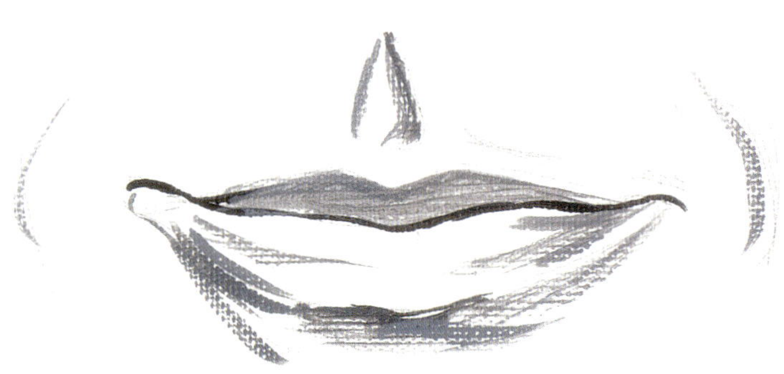

1 BEGIN WITH HALFTONES

Dilute the gray tones to mix light, medium and dark gray. Start with the white first, and then gradually add some black to achieve the right value. Use the gray scale as a reference. With the no. 1 round, capture the main shapes with some of the dark gray. Add some of the medium gray to the upper lip.

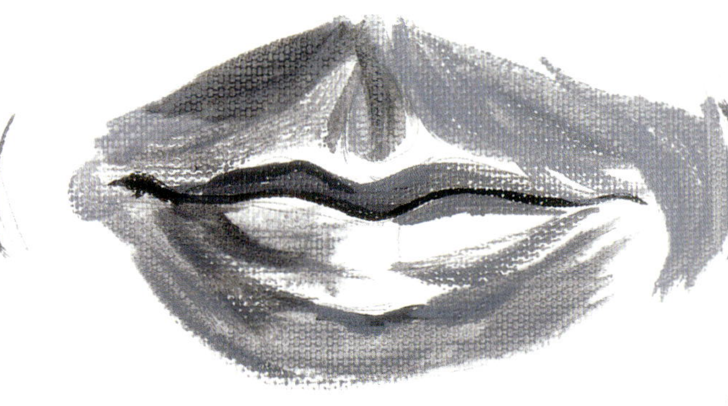

2 THE AWKWARD STAGE

Continue adding tone with the no. 2 round using the light, medium and dark colors. The paint should still be fairly thin.

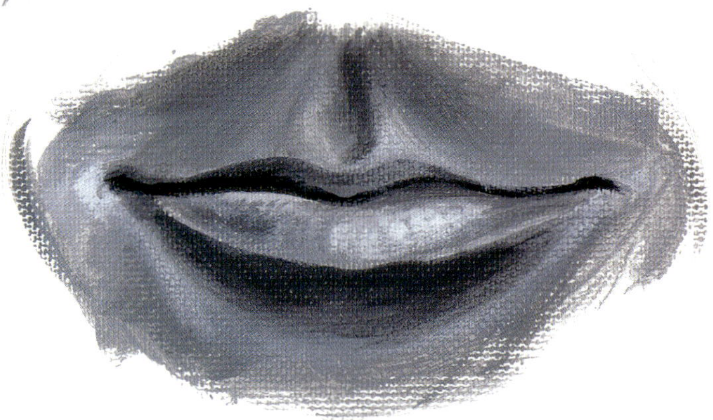

3 FINISH

Use a thicker application of paint to cover the canvas entirely. Drybrush all the tones together.

Closed, Light Complexion

PIGMENTS
Alizarin Crimson, Burnt Umber, Cadmium Red Medium, Cadmium Yellow Medium, Titanium White

BRUSHES
Nos. 1 and 2 round

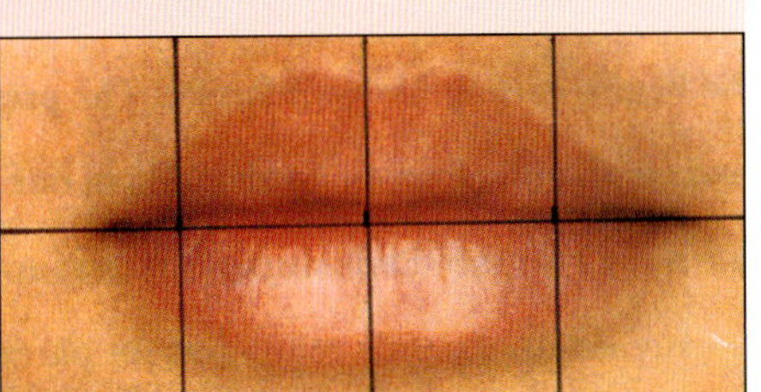

Reference Photo
Use the grid method to create an accurate line drawing. Remove the grid lines from your drawing when you are done.

Let's try another closed mouth, but this time in full color.

Light Complexion Warm
Follow the instructions on page 23 to mix a light, medium and dark version.

Add Burnt Umber and Alizarin Crimson to the mixture to create the shadows.

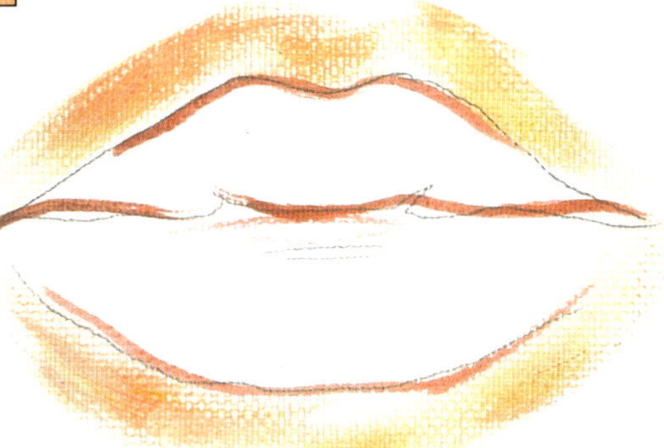

1 BEGIN WITH HALFTONES

Add some water to the Burnt Umber and Alizarin Crimson shadow mixture to paint in the basic shapes of the mouth with the no. 1 round. Create the outline of the mouth and the line between the lips.

With the no. 2 round, wash in some of the medium peach color around the mouth to represent the face.

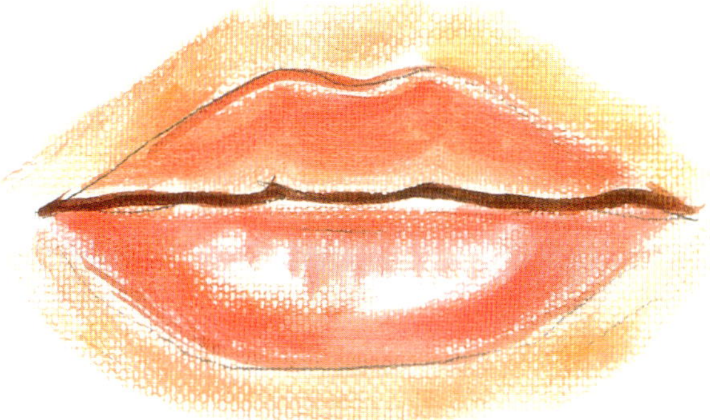

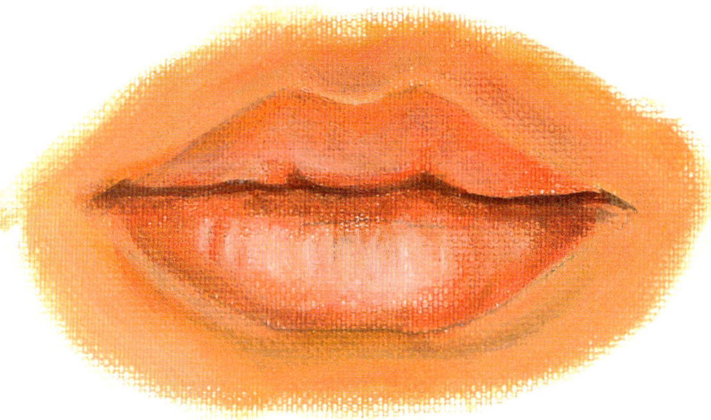

2 THE AWKWARD STAGE

Apply the color to the lips with the no. 2 round, making the upper lip darker than the bottom. Keep the paint thin. The upper lip should be more filled in than the bottom one. Leave a large highlight area on the bottom lip.

3 FINISH

Use a thicker applications of paint to drybrush the colors together.

Closed, Dark Complexion

PIGMENTS
Alizarin Crimson, Burnt Umber, Cadmium Red Medium, Titanium White

BRUSHES
Nos. 1 and 2 round

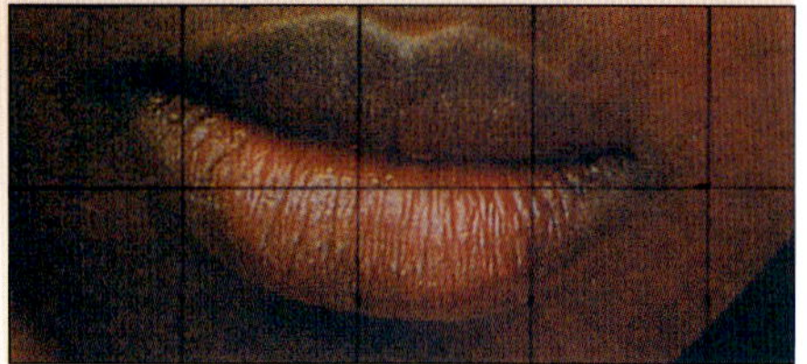

Reference Photo
When your drawing is accurate, carefully remove the grid lines with an eraser.

Let's do another closed mouth, this time using a photo of a darker complexion. While the colors are different, the painting process is the same.

Brown Complexion Warm
Follow the instructions on page 23 to mix light, medium and dark versions of this color by altering the amount of white. Add Burnt Umber and Alizarin Crimson for the darkest portions. Use a lot for the deepest tones.

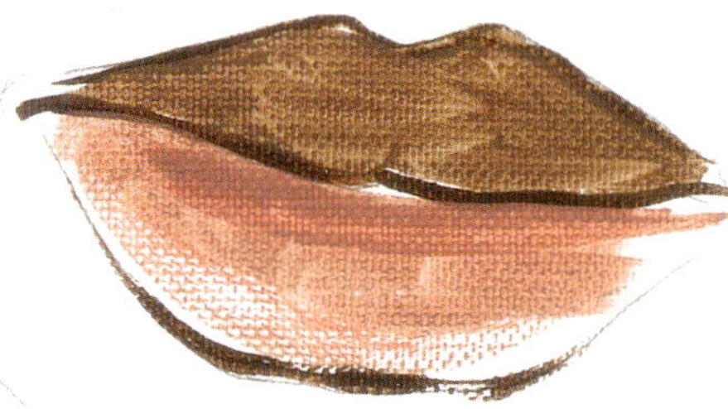

1 BEGIN WITH HALFTONES
With the no. 1 round, add the dark color around and between the lips. With the no. 2 round, add water to the midtone to wash in the color of the lips. Use pure Burnt Umber for the upper lip and the medium version of your warm brown complexion mixture for the bottom.

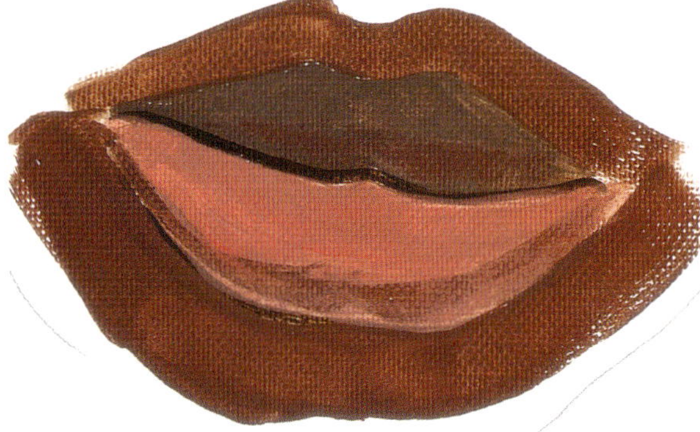

2 THE AWKWARD STAGE
Continue adding skin tone with the no. 2 round using the color swatches as a guide. Keep the paint thin. Because of the fullness of these lips, there is a distinct shadow edge on the bottom lip. Apply this with Burnt Umber and a small amount of white. This creates the look of reflected light along the bottom edge of the lip.

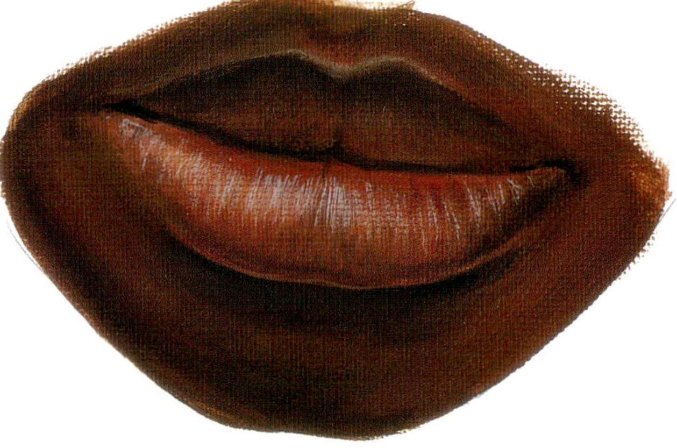

3 FINISH
Use a thicker application of paint to drybrush the colors together. Make the colors warmer in the highlight and halftone areas. Add highlights to the bottom lip with the no. 1 round and quick strokes with Titanium White. This gives the illusion of the lip creases some mouths have. There is also an edge of reflected light along the upper lip. Apply that with the no. 1 round and white as well.

Slight Smile: Begin Painting Teeth

PIGMENTS
Alizarin Crimson, Burnt Umber, Cadmium Red Medium, Cadmium Yellow Medium, Titanium White

BRUSHES
Nos. 1 and 2 rounds

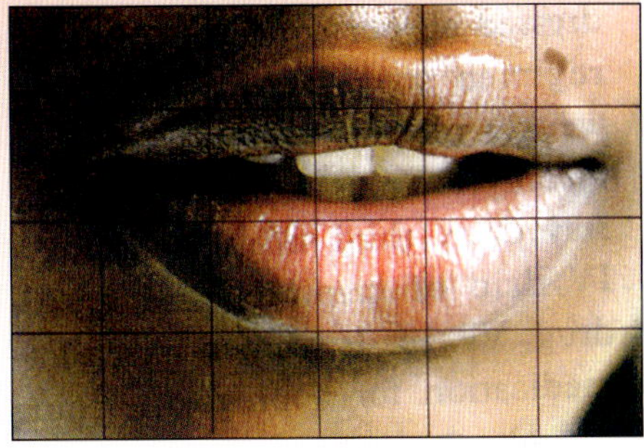

Reference Photo
Use the grid method to create an accurate line drawing on your canvas paper. The teeth must be absolutely exact in their size, shape and placement. When you are sure of the accuracy, remove the grid lines with an eraser.

This is very similar to the mouth you just finished, but it is slightly opened, revealing the teeth. It will give you an introduction to painting teeth, a little at a time.

Dark Complexion Warm
Follow the instructions on page 23 to mix light, medium and dark versions of this color. Use pure Burnt Umber or add more Burnt Umber to this mixture for the shadow areas.

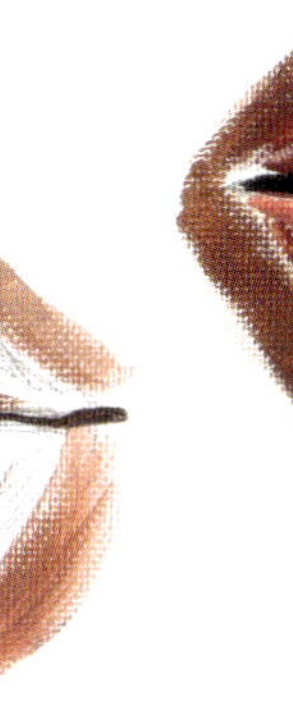

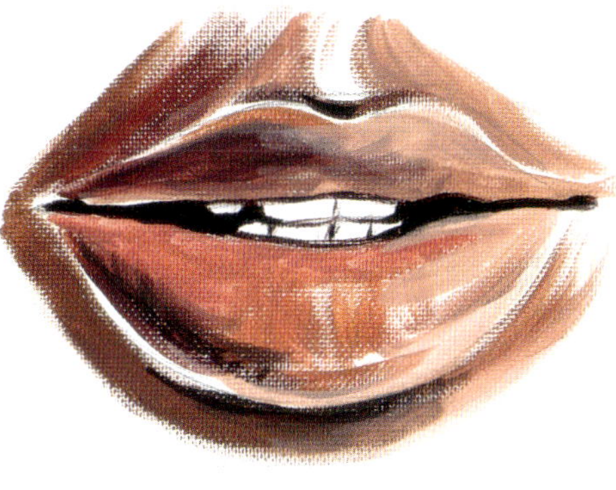

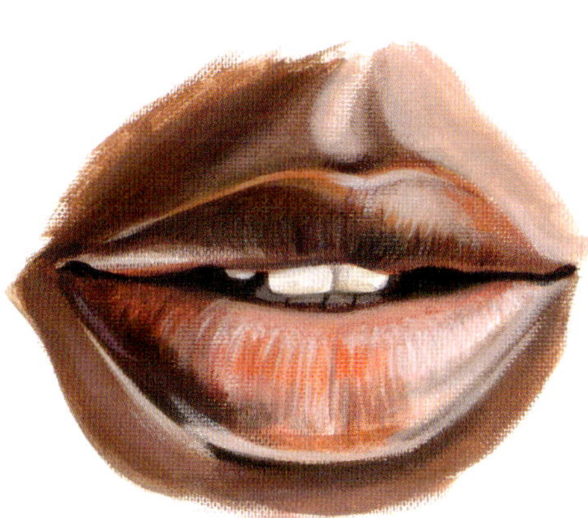

1 BEGIN WITH HALFTONES

Fill in the area inside the mouth with Burnt Umber and the no. 1 round. This will help create the shape of the teeth. Create the corners (the pits), too.

With a mixture of white, Burnt Umber and Alizarin Crimson, block in some of the color around the mouth and upper lip.

Begin to block in the skin tones to the lips and face.

2 THE AWKWARD STAGE

Create a lighter value by adding some white to the mix, and continue filling in the lips using the no. 2 round. With Burnt Umber, add some shadow under the bottom lip and along the upper lip, and shape the teeth.

3 FINISH

Drybrush using thicker applications of paint to build and blend the colors together. Add highlights to the bottom lip with the no. 1 round and quick strokes. Apply the edge of reflected light along the upper and lower lip as well.

In this example, the teeth are a very light brown. Mix a dab of Burnt Umber with white and fill in the teeth. Add a touch of Cadmium Yellow Medium, too.

Full Smile, Female

PIGMENTS
Alizarin Crimson, Burnt Umber, Cadmium Red Medium, Cadmium Yellow Medium, Titanium White

BRUSHES
Nos. 1 and 2 round

A full smile can be one of the most challenging things to paint. As I mentioned before, every tooth must be perfect. If I painted a portrait of you, but painted the teeth in a general way, not paying attention to your unique tooth shape, the portrait would look similar to you, nothing more.

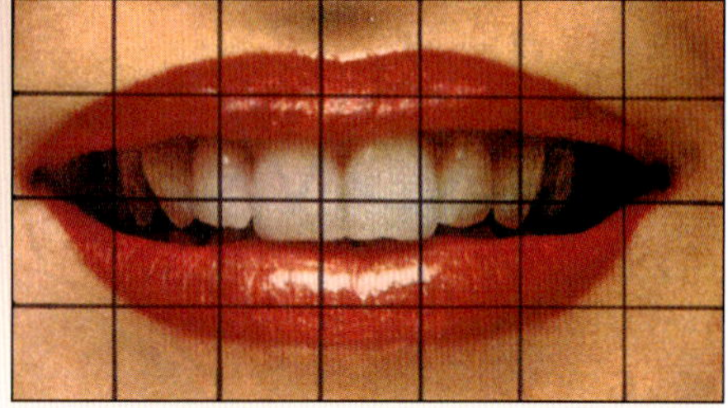

Reference Photo
Use the grid method to capture this open mouth smile on your canvas paper. Be careful to see how each tooth is placed inside of its corresponding box. I used a half-inch (13mm) grid to tighten up the accuracy. Take your time. When you are sure of the accuracy, carefully remove the grid lines with an eraser.

Light Complexion Warm
Follow the instructions on page 23 to mix a light, warm complexion.

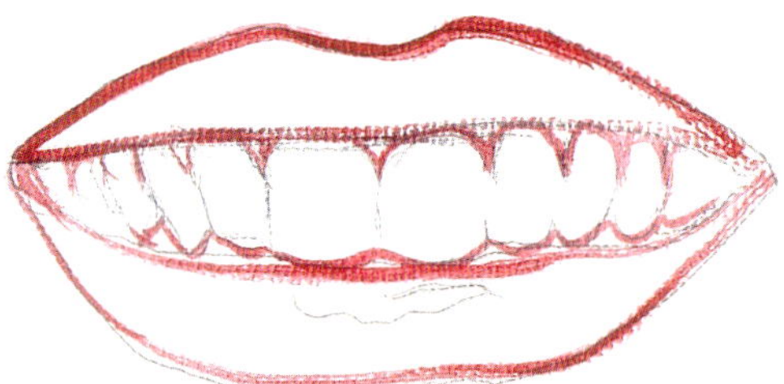

1 BEGIN WITH AN OUTLINE

With Alizarin Crimson and the no. 1 round, outline the lips, the gum line, and the shapes of the teeth.

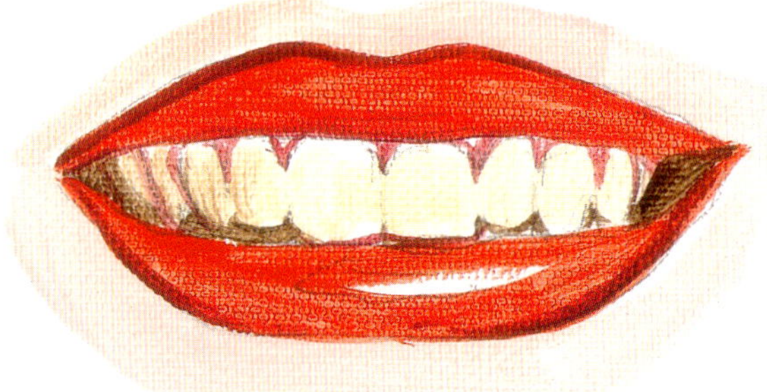

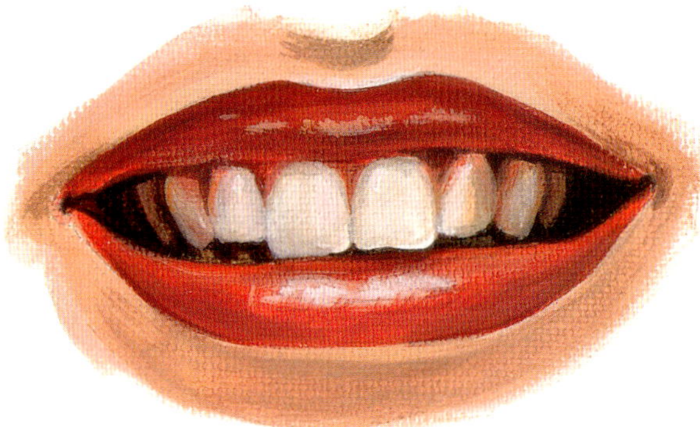

2 THE AWKWARD STAGE

Begin adding color to the lips with full-strength Cadmium Red Medium to capture the color of the lipstick. Leave a small area on the bottom lip for the highlight. Use the no. 2 round and diluted light peach color to paint in the skin tone around the mouth.

Add a hint of Burnt Umber to Titanium White to get an off-white color. Basecoat the teeth with it, getting darker as they recede into the mouth. Shadow the back teeth by adding more Burnt Umber to the mixture.

3 FINISH

Add Alizarin Crimson to Cadmium Red Medium for a realistic darker color for shadow. Leave the reflected light along the lower edge of the upper lip. Add the highlight on the bottom lip with Titanium White.

Deepen the skin color of the face by adding a touch of Burnt Umber and Alizarin Crimson to the peach mixture. Drybrush over the existing application.

Add details to the teeth, one at a time. Each tooth contains many colors, so study the example carefully. Some will reflect the red of the lipstick. Some have white highlights. There are gray and brownish shadows, too. Work on them for as long as it takes to replicate this example.

Full Smile, Male

PIGMENTS
Alizarin Crimson, Burnt Umber, Cadmium Red Medium, Cadmium Yellow Medium, Titanium White

BRUSHES
Nos. 1 and 2 round

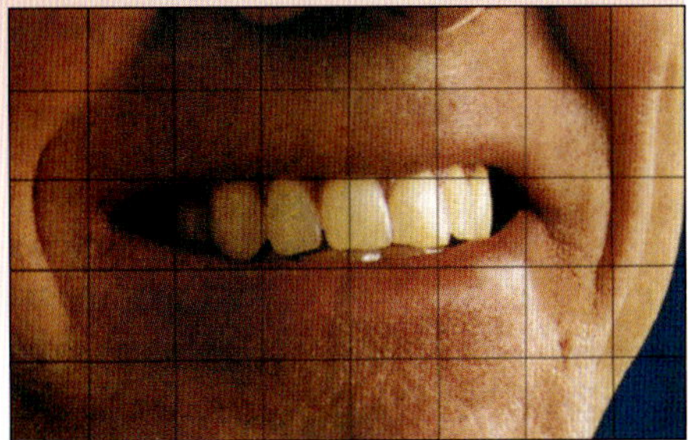

Photo Reference
This man's mouth is slightly turned and the light source is not straight on like the example on page 56.

The more you practice the better you will become. You may still feel clumsy, but do not quit. It takes time to become proficient with anything. This will give you more practice painting teeth.

Light Complexion Warm
Follow the instructions on page 23 to mix a light, warm complexion.

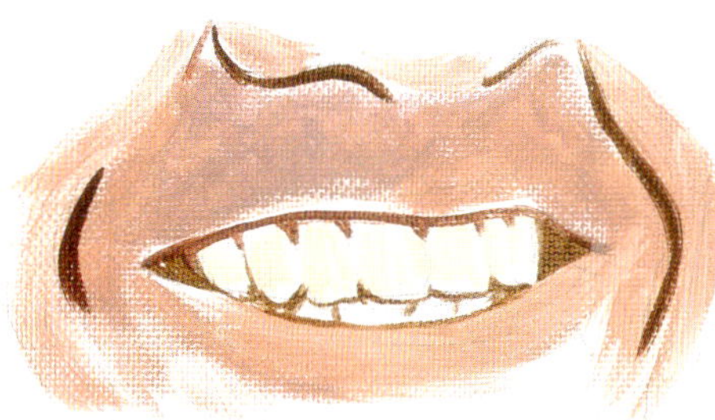

1 PAINT HALFTONES AND OUTLINE THE GUM LINE

With Alizarin Crimson and the no. 1 round, outline the lips, the gum line, and the shapes of the teeth. Be sure to maintain their accuracy. With an off-white color that leans towards yellow, base in the teeth.

Basecoat the skin tones with a medium peach mixture using the no. 2 round.

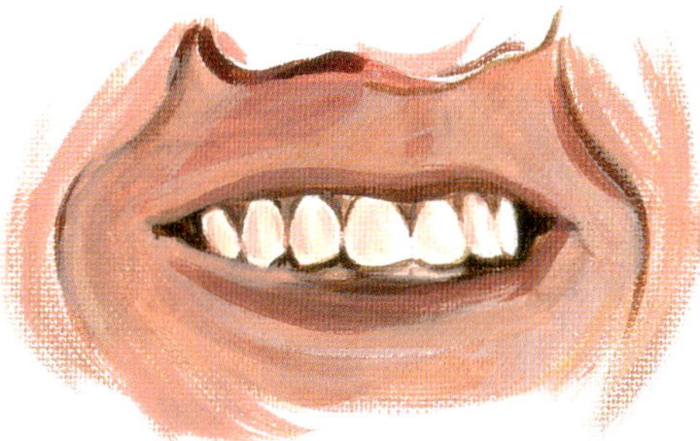

2 THE AWKWARD STAGE

Use the no. 2 round. Add a touch of Alizarin Crimson and Burnt Umber to the medium skin tone mixture and add color to the lips. Continue to build up the skin tone around the mouth. The colors are darker on the left side due to the light source; use more of the Alizarin Crimson and Burnt Umber mixture here.

Begin adding gray and brownish shadows to the teeth. The teeth are darker on the left side, reflecting the skin color. Add white highlights to the teeth on the right using the no. 1 round. Do not quit early; the more you do, the more realistic the teeth will look. Continue to build up the skin tone around the mouth.

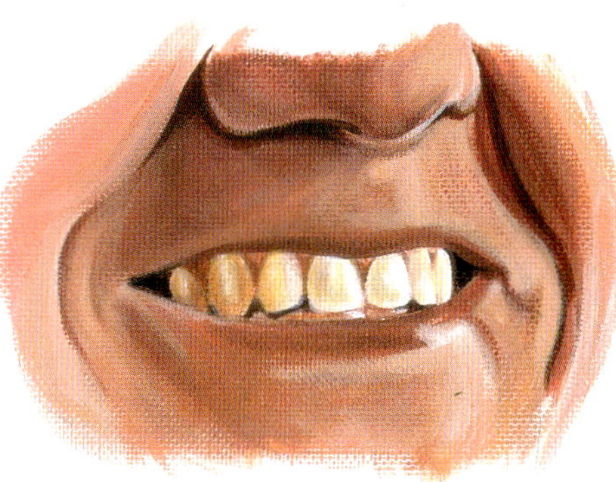

3 FINISH

Drybrush to build up the skin tones and refine the painting. Use Titanium White to add highlights showing light is coming from the right.

Profile

PIGMENTS
Alizarin Crimson, Burnt Umber, Cadmium Red Medium, Cadmium Yellow Medium, Titanium White

BRUSHES
Nos. 1 and 2 round

Each of the facial features connects to the others. You have practiced drawing both the nose and the mouth separately. Now it is time to put the two together. This exercise will give you practice painting a profile and the natural connection of the nose to the mouth. Resist the urge to do an entire face at this stage. It is much better to learn the features a little at a time before trying to capture an entire likeness.

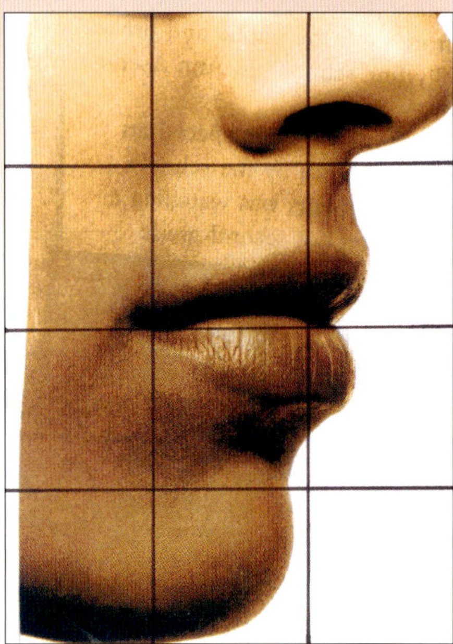

Reference Photo
Use the grid method to capture these shapes on your canvas paper. When you are sure of the accuracy, remove the pencil lines with an eraser.

Light Complexion Warm
Follow the instructions on page 23 to mix a light, warm complexion. This skin has a touch more Burnt Umber to it, with not as much of the red tones. Each face is different. Adjust your paint mixtures accordingly.

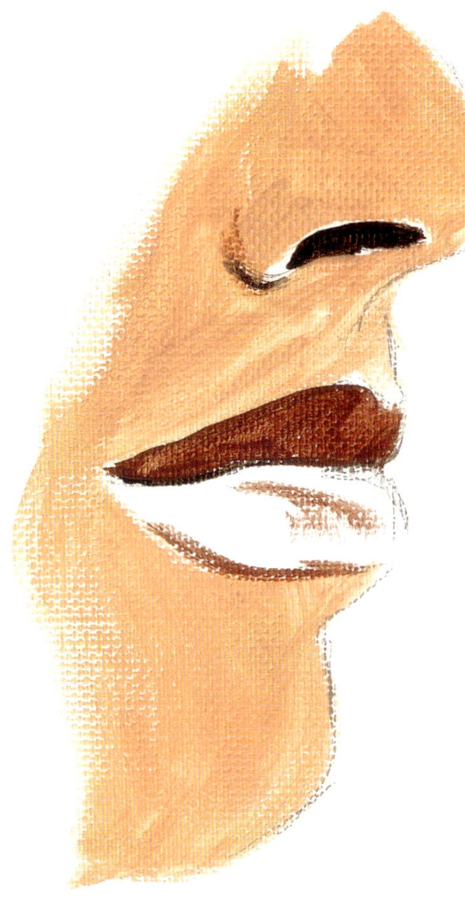

1 BEGIN HALFTONES

With the light peach mixture, basecoat the skin tone using the no. 2 round. Fill in the nostril area with Burnt Umber and the no. 1 round. Fill in the upper lip with a diluted mixture of Alizarin Crimson and Burnt Umber. Leave the white of the paper on the majority of the bottom lip.

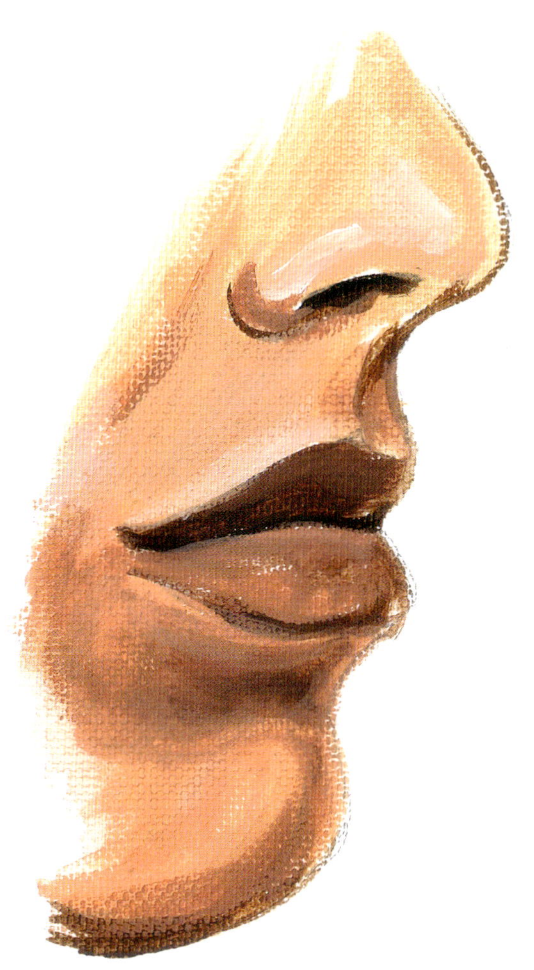

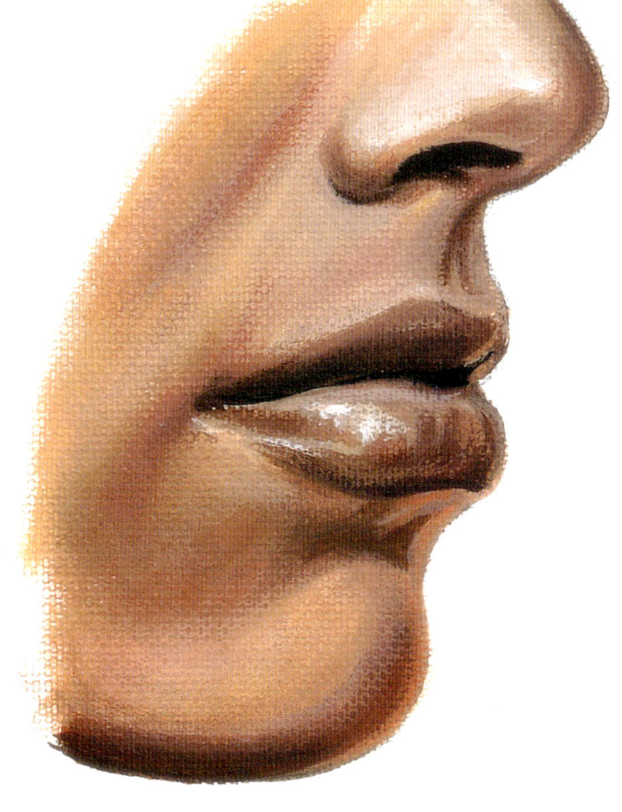

2 THE AWKWARD STAGE

Lighten the upper lip mixture with some Titanium White. Use it to fill in the bottom lip and drybrush into the skin tones to develop the face. Pay particular attention to the area between the nose and the mouth. This area connects the nose to the lips, and is a part of the lips' overall shape. It differs from one face to the next as far as how pronounced it will appear. In most cases, it resembles the shape of a teardrop. Here, it looks like an upside down V-shape due to the angle. Add a little more Burnt Umber to your mixture and begin the shadows.

3 FINISH

Drybrush with a thicker application of paint to build the skin tones. Look for the five elements of shading in the rounded areas such as the nose, lips and chin. Remember the reflected light around the rim of the nostril.

Use white for the highlights on the nose and lower lip and apply them with the no. 1 round.

Painting Eyes

Eyes hold the essence of the portrait. It is essential to draw and paint eyes accurately. Any distortion or lack of detail will interrupt the believability of your work.

The eye can be a difficult thing to paint. Breaking down and memorizing the eye's separate, puzzle-like shapes will make it easier to include them in your work.

Twelve Crucial Eye Shapes

These shapes must always be included in your portraits.

1. The iris
2. The pupil
3. The sclera
4. The catchlight
5. The corner membrane
6. The upper eyelid
7. The lid crease
8. The lower lid thickness
9. The lash line
10. The upper lashes
11. The lower lashes
12. The eyebrow

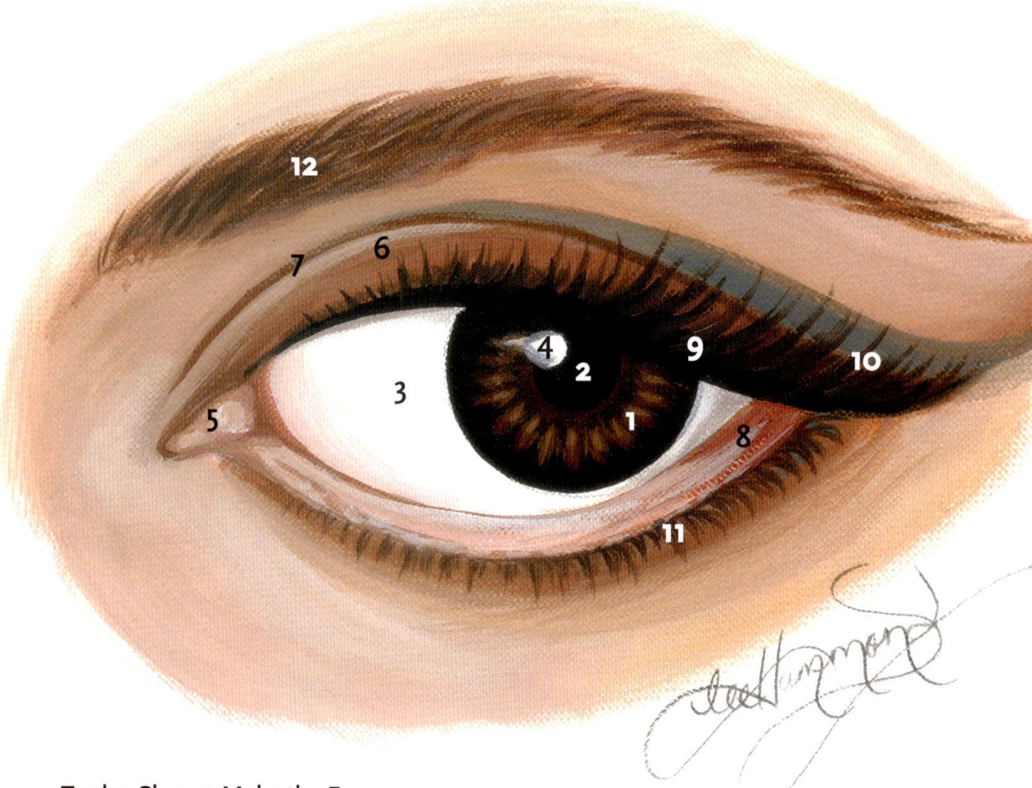

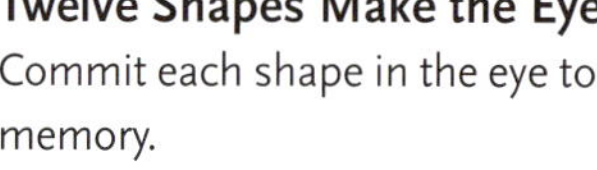

Twelve Shapes Make the Eye
Commit each shape in the eye to memory.

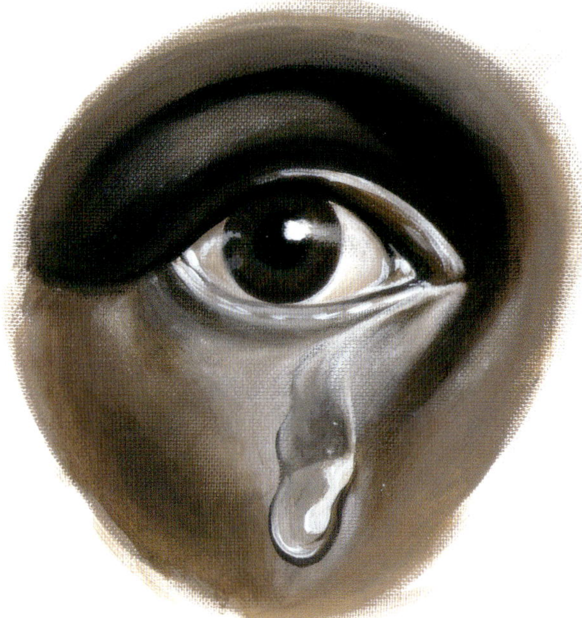

Eyes Are the Most Important Part of the Portrait
Emotion is captured through the eyes. Without seeing the rest of the face, or even the other eye, you can feel the sadness and the pain of this subject.

Basic Eye Color

One of the my favorite aspects of painting the eyes are the beautiful colors they hold. These are three examples of the most common eye colors, but there are variations of each.

Although each of these eyes is very different, they share the twelve key features explained on page 60.

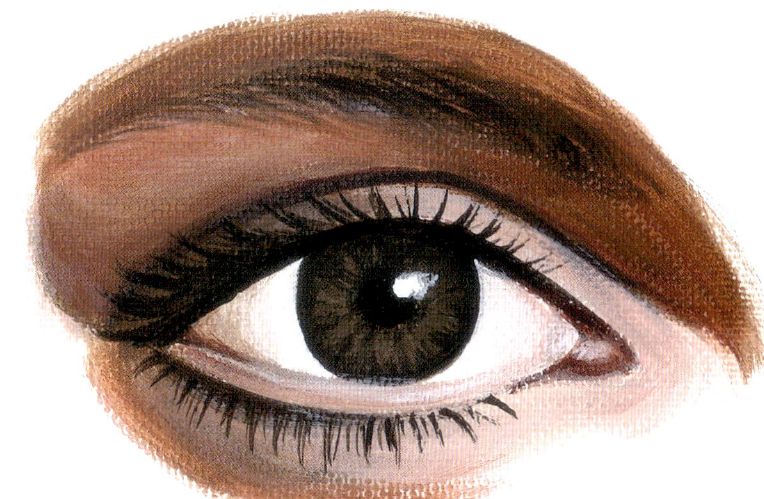

Burnt Umber Creates Brown Eyes
The iris of the eye contains patterns. The patterns radiate outward from the pupil much like a wagon wheel. Brown eyes generally take a lot of Burnt Umber.

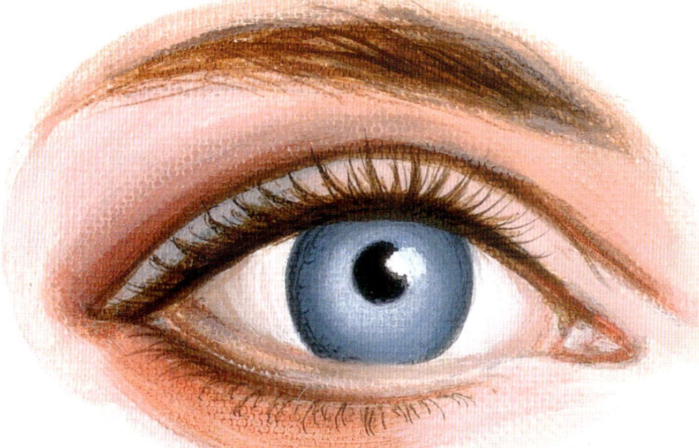

Touch Prussian Blue Into White for Blue Eyes
Blue eyes do not have the patterns like brown ones. They have a smoother, glassier appearance. A touch of Prussian Blue into Titanium White will make this shade of blue. Add a hint of Ivory Black to the mix for the darker outer rim.

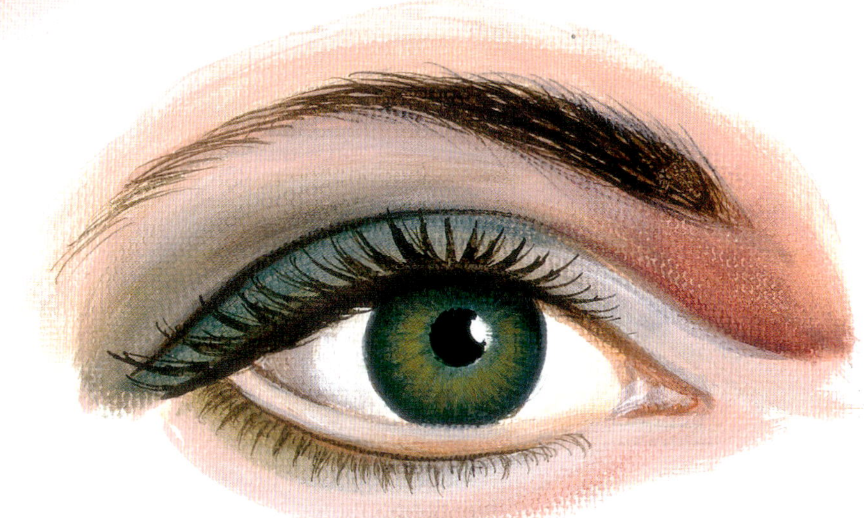

Bring Out the Palette for Green Eyes
Green eyes are the most colorful and will have many colors within the iris. Study this eye closely and you will see yellow, blue and brown within the mix. Begin with a medium green made by mixing Prussian Blue, Cadmium Yellow Medium, and a dab of Titanium White. Add some Ivory Black to the outside rim of the iris for the dark edge. Make the light patterns by adding more Cadmium Yellow Medium to the green mixture.

Eyebrows and Eyelashes

PIGMENTS
Burnt Umber, Cadmium Red Medium, Cadmium Yellow Medium, Titanium White

BRUSHES
No. 2 round
No. 3/0 liner

Any type of hair is always painted in last. This is true for facial hair, hair on the head, and the eyelashes and eyebrows. All the skin tones and detail must be complete first.

Before you begin the eye exercises, it is important to understand how to paint the lashes and brows. It is not as difficult as it seems. They are painted in layers.

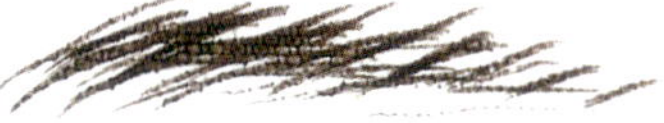

Don't
These lines are too heavy and thick. Always use a quick stroke to make the lines taper at the ends.

Do
A quick stroke makes the hair look realistic. The ends must taper.

Don't
Lashes must not be created with thick, harsh lines. Eyelashes grow in clumps.

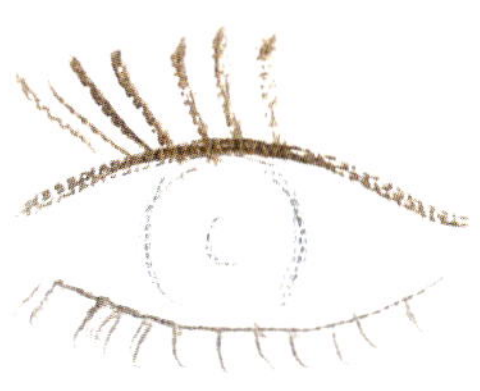

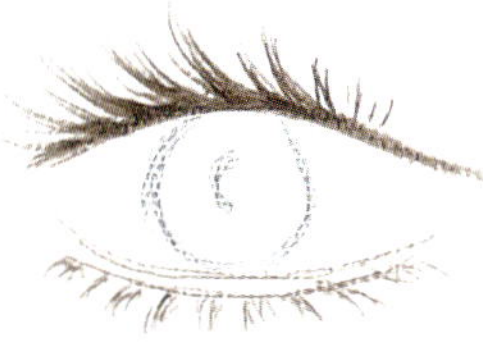

Do
Quick, clumped strokes make lashes look realistic. The ends taper, just like the brows.

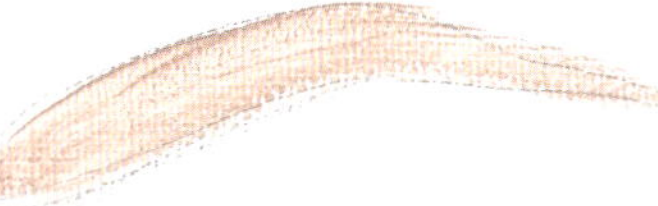

1 CREATE SKIN TONE
Skin tone must always be underneath the brow area before you apply the hairs. This is a light complexion.

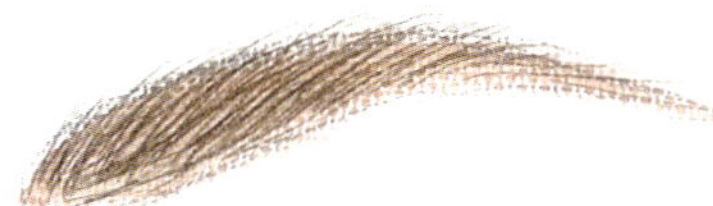

2 BEGIN STROKES
With the no. 3/0 liner, layer very quick strokes with a very diluted Burnt Umber. Follow the growth and direction of the hairs. They all grow from a different spot.

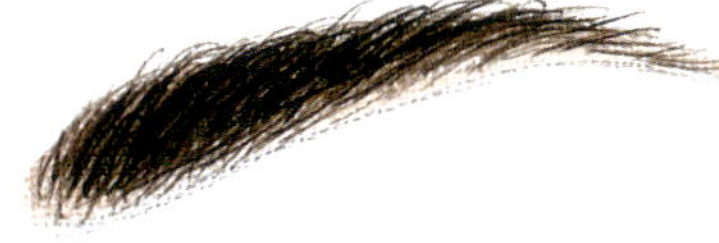

3 FINISH
Continue to build the brow with many layers.

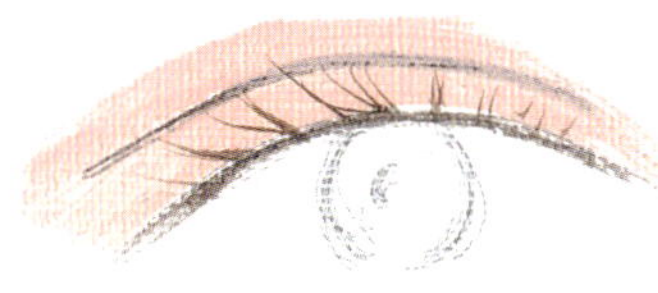

1 CREATE THE SKIN TONE
As before, apply the skin tone underneath the brow area first. This is a light complexion. The lashes grow from the lash line. Use the no. 3/0 liner, diluted paint and very quick strokes.

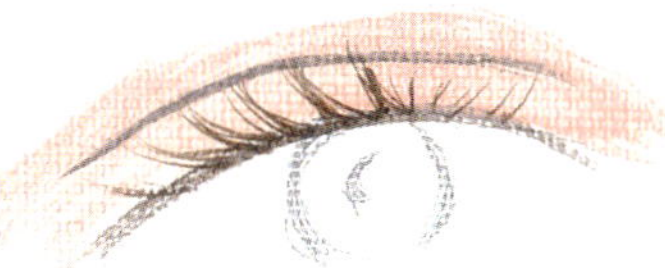

2 BUILD THE CLUMPS
Continue adding the lashes in small clumps.

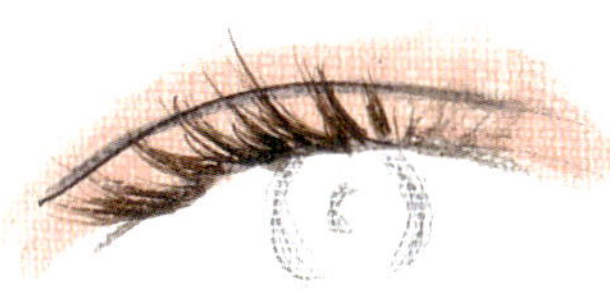

3 FINISH
Make the lashes longer on the outside edge. This is due to perspective. The ones in front seem shorter because they are being viewed from the front. We don't see the entire length.

Monochromatic

PIGMENTS
Ivory Black, Titanium White

BRUSHES
No. 1 round
No. 3/0 liner

To learn how to paint the eye, let's try one in black and white. A monochromatic scheme is always easier. It allows you to concentrate on the anatomy and details, without having to worry about color.

Gray Scale
Match your tones to this gray scale.

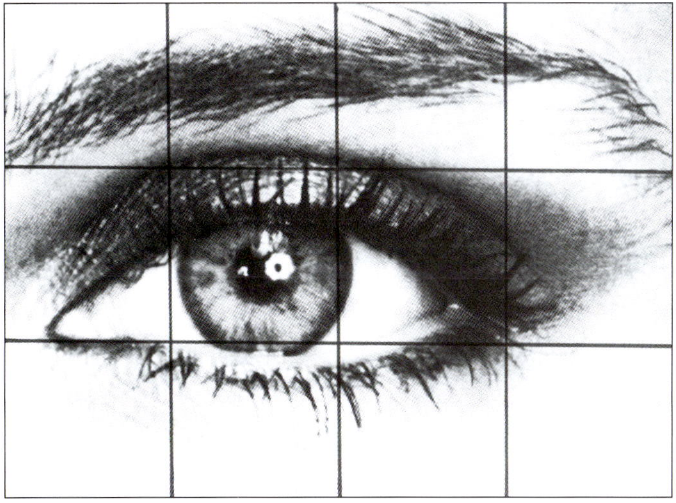

Reference Photo
Locate and identify all twelve distinct parts of the eye. Refer back to the diagram on page 60 if you need to. This is very important before you begin to draw.

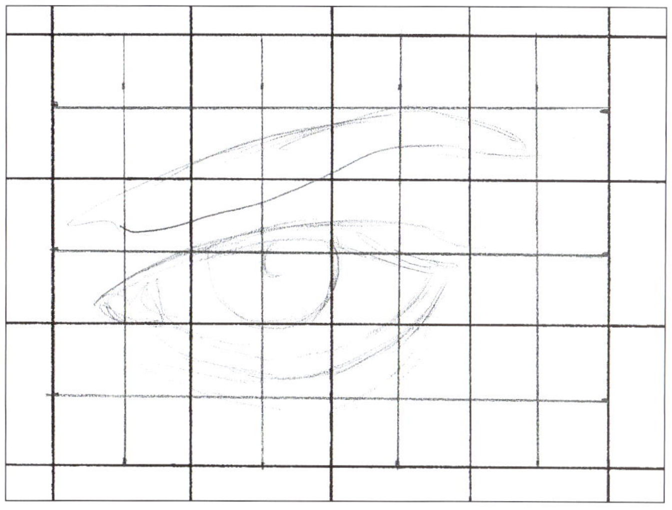

Grid Drawing
Use the grid method to draw the eye on your canvas paper. Look for all twelve shapes that make up the eye. When you are sure of the accuracy, carefully remove the grid lines with an eraser. It is very important that the iris and the pupil are perfect circles. Place a circle template over your drawing that matches the size to the circle you drew with the grid. Make the edges of the iris crisp. Do the same with the pupil.

It is also essential that the pupil is perfectly centered within the circle of the iris. Leave a small area for the catchlight. Regardless of the photo reference, I always move the catchlight over, so it is half in the pupil and half in the iris. If there is more than one catchlight in the photo, reduce it to only one.

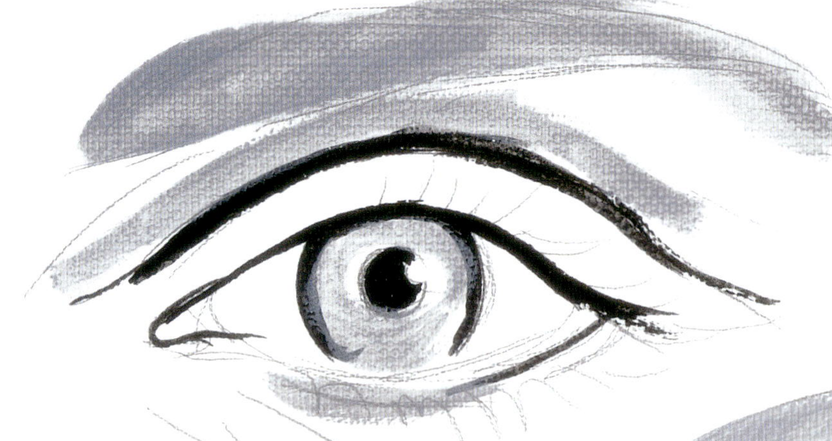

1 CREATE THE OUTLINE

With the no. 1 round, outline the iris and paint in the lash line and lid crease with pure black. Be sure to keep the iris a perfect circle. Fill in the pupil, leaving an area for the catchlight.

Refer to the gray scale to create a medium gray color and fill in the iris, above the lid crease and the eyebrow area. Add some medium gray below the eye to create the lower lid thickness.

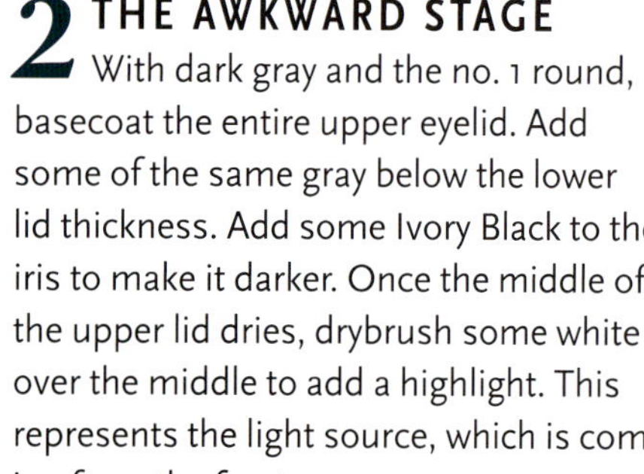

2 THE AWKWARD STAGE

With dark gray and the no. 1 round, basecoat the entire upper eyelid. Add some of the same gray below the lower lid thickness. Add some Ivory Black to the iris to make it darker. Once the middle of the upper lid dries, drybrush some white over the middle to add a highlight. This represents the light source, which is coming from the front.

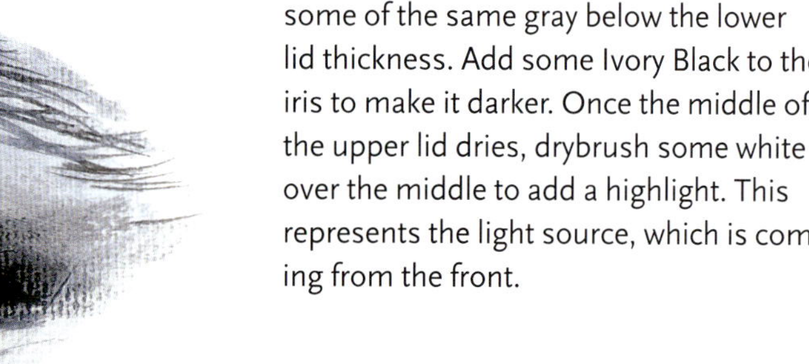

3 FINISH

With the no. 3/0 liner, detail the patterns of the iris alternating black and white paint. The pattern is darker toward the center and radiates outward like a wagon wheel. Use pure white for the catchlight.

Add some light gray around the eye to represent the skin tone before adding the eyelashes and eyebrows. Add the eyelashes and eyebrows with the no. 3/0 liner and Ivory Black. Dilute the paint with some water so you can achieve very quick strokes with the brush. Thin paint will help the lines taper at the ends.

Toddler

PIGMENTS
Burnt Umber, Cadmium Red Medium, Cadmium Yellow Medium, Ivory Black, Titanium White

BRUSHES
Nos. 1 and 2 round
No. 3/0 liner

This will give you a chance to paint an eye in full color. This is the eye of a toddler, and the eye appears very round. We are born with full-size irises. The eye and the face grow around it. That is why an infant's eye seems so large, yet small at the same time.

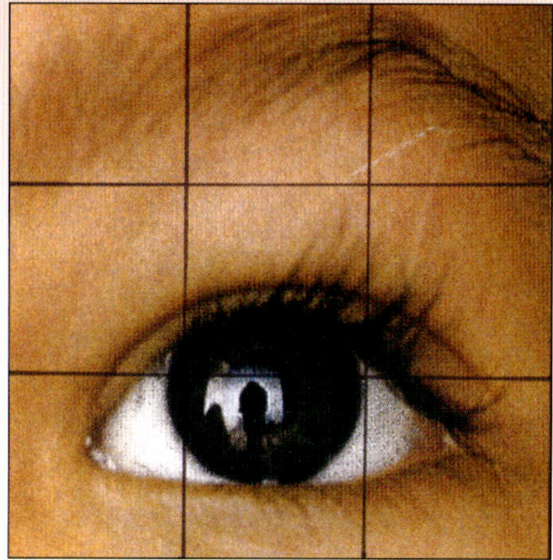

Reference Photo
The iris appears quite large, and the photographer is reflected in the catchlight. Use the grid method to achieve the shape of this eye on your canvas paper. Use the circle template to make the iris and the pupil a perfect circle.

Light Complexion Warm
Follow the instructions on page 23 to make sure to have light, medium and dark versions of this peach color.

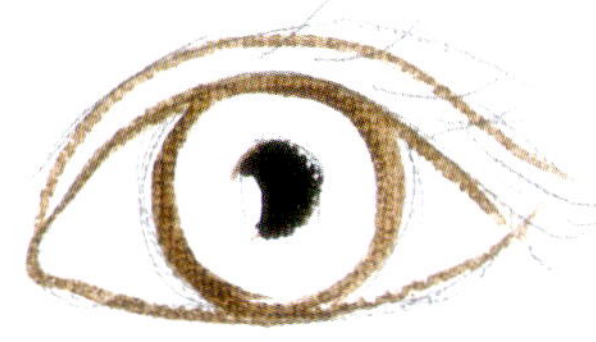

1 BEGIN WITH OUTLINES

With the no. 1 round, fill in the pupil with pure Ivory Black. With diluted Burnt Umber, outline the iris, around the eye and in the lid crease.

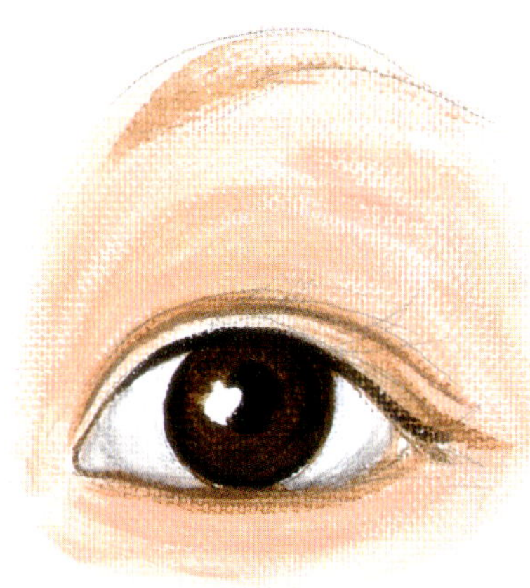

2 THE AWKWARD STAGE

Base in the skin tone with the no. 2 round. Add some thin Burnt Umber into the eyebrow area. Fill in the iris with Burnt Umber. Add white to the sclera and shadow the corners with some light gray. This makes the eyeball appear round.

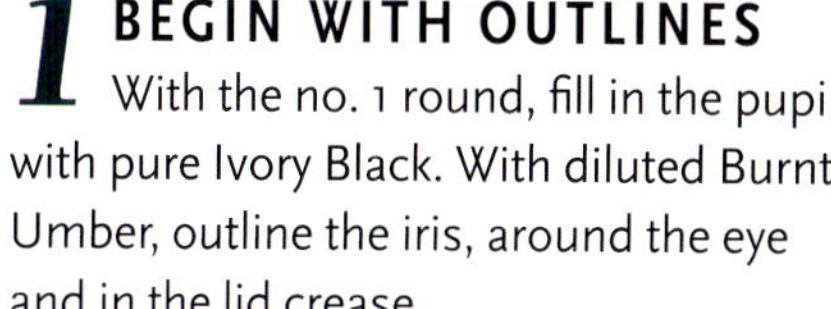

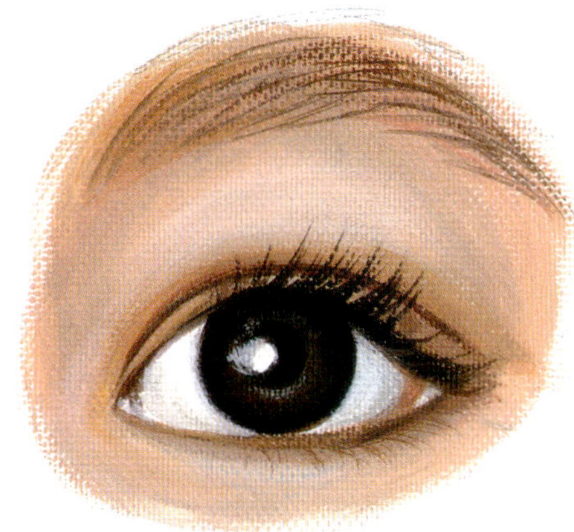

3 FINISH

Thicken the paint to drybrush and develop the tones. There is a subtle highlight above the eye. Add some more Burnt Umber to the iris and add interest to the iris by adding some Ivory Black to the outside edge. Create highlighting around the iris with some white, and fill in the catchlight.

Add the eyebrow and eyelashes with the no. 3/0 liner and diluted Burnt Umber.

Adult

PIGMENTS
Burnt Umber, Cadmium Red Medium, Cadmium Yellow Medium, Ivory Black, Titanium White

BRUSHES
Nos. 1 and 2 round

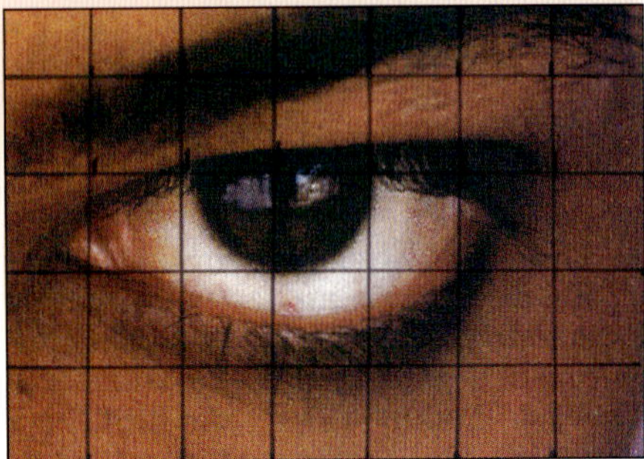

Reference Photo
Use the grid method to capture the eye on your canvas paper. Use the circle template to make the iris a perfect circle. Keep in mind, much of the circle is hidden under the upper eyelid.

This is an example of an adult eye with a dark complexion. It's viewed from slightly above and the eye is looking up. Notice the white under the iris? This is never seen unless viewed from this angle.

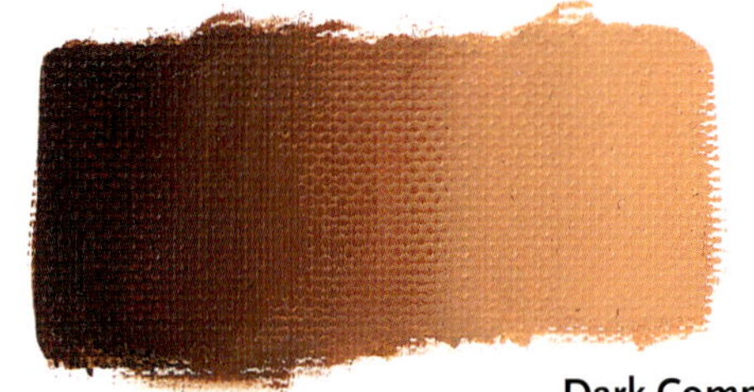

Dark Complexion Warm
Follow the instructions on page 23 to make light, medium and dark versions of this skin tone. It is warmed up with Cadmium Red Medium.

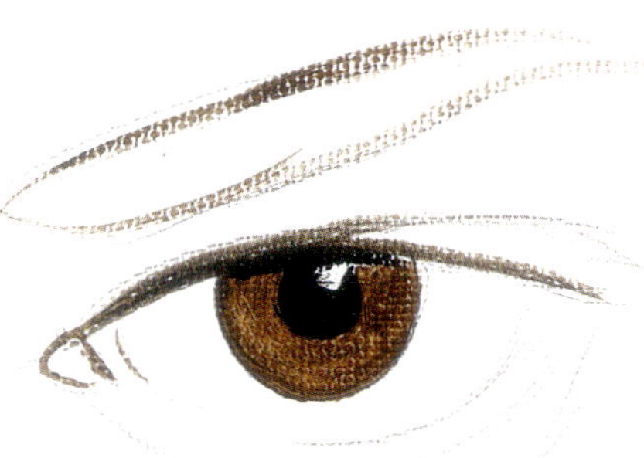

1 BEGIN WITH THE IRIS
This is a very dark eye, so fill in the iris with pure Burnt Umber. Use the no. 1 round. Fill in the pupil with Ivory Black, leaving a small area for the catchlight (half in the pupil, half in the iris). Outline the lash line and the shape of the eyebrow.

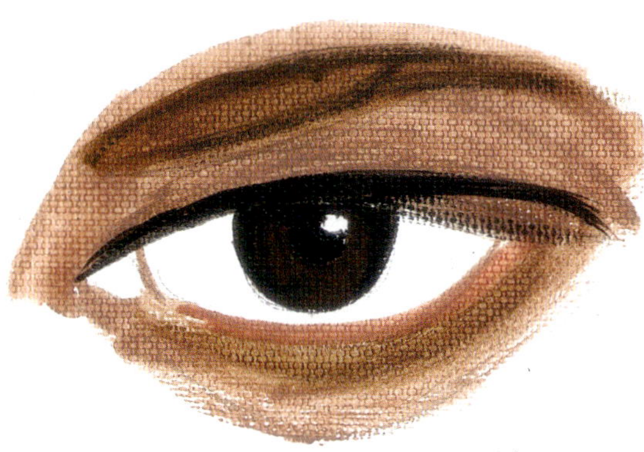

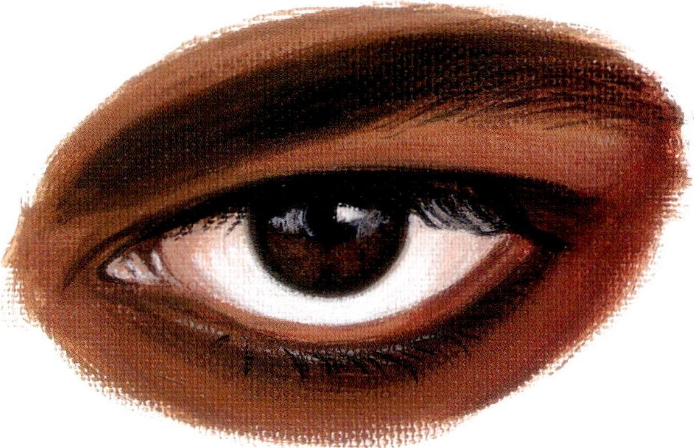

2 THE AWKWARD STAGE
Using the no. 2 round, basecoat the skin tone all around the eye, including the eyebrow area with a diluted mixture of Burnt Umber and Cadmium Red Medium. Add a little more Cadmium Red Medium to the mixture and fill in the lower lid thickness.

3 FINISH
Thicken the paint with the skin tone pigments and drybrush in the rich color of the skin using the no. 2 round. Switch to the no. 1 round and fill in the sclera with Titanium White. Add some Cadmium Red Medium into the corners for roundness. Do the same for the corner membrane. Deepen the color of the iris and add some patterning with Ivory Black. Add some white for the catchlight and highlights.

Fill in the eyebrow with Burnt Umber, and then add the hairs with Burnt Umber mixed with a touch of Ivory Black. Add the eyelashes with the same mixture. Notice how the lashes are going down in this pose.

Mature

PIGMENTS

Alizarin Crimson, Burnt Umber, Cadmium Red Medium, Cadmium Yellow Medium, Ivory Black, Prussian Blue, Titanium White

BRUSHES

Nos. 1 and 2 round
No. 3/0 liner

The previous eyes were fairly simple in their details. The skin was even and smooth and the coloration was not overly affected by bright highlights or shadows. While this certainly is an easier situation to paint, life is not always that easy. Mature faces have character and most natural situations have extreme lighting.

Light Complexion Warm

Follow the instructions on page 23 to mix light, medium and dark versions of this peach color.

Add Burnt Umber and Alizarin Crimson to the mixture to create the shadows.

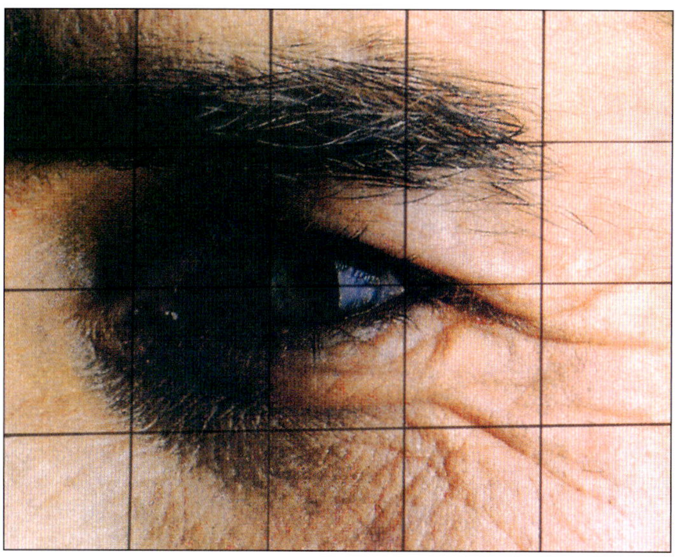

Reference Photo

The laugh lines around this eye are important to this man's face. However, you don't want to overdo it. They need to be realistic and subtle.

Use the grid method to draw the eye on your canvas paper. Capture the lines and wrinkles around the eye. When you are sure that you are accurate, remove the grid lines with an eraser. Make the iris and pupil perfect circles with a template.

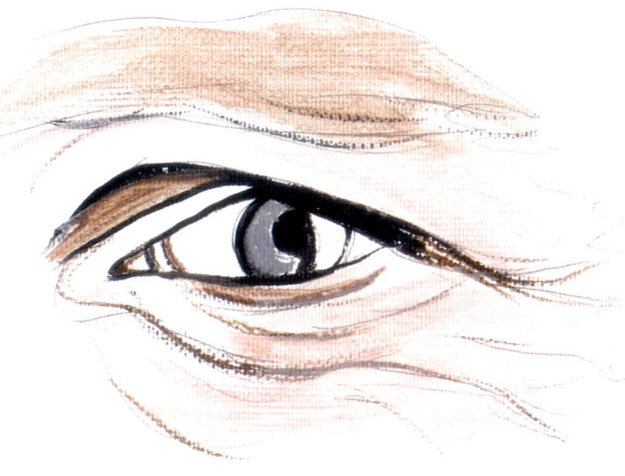

1 BEGIN WITH OUTLINES AND SKIN TONE

Use the no. 2 round to fill in the entire area around the eye with a diluted light peach mixture. With the no. 1 round and Ivory Black outline the iris, lash line and lid crease. With diluted Burnt Umber, fill in the eyebrow area and the small area above the eyelid. Outline some of the wrinkles under the eye.

Because of the extreme lighting situation and the deep shadows, the blue color of the eye is divided in half and there is no bright catchlight. Fill in the left side of the iris with a blue/gray mixture of Titanium White, Prussian Blue, and a touch of Ivory Black. Fill in the pupil with pure black.

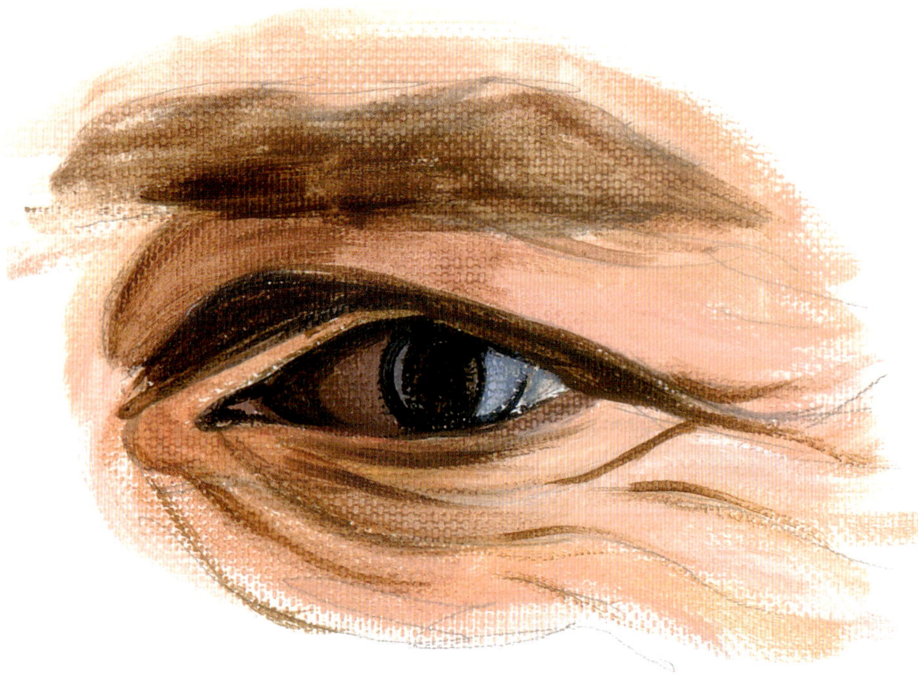

2 THE AWKWARD STAGE

Thicken the paint and drybrush to build the skin tones with the light peach mixture. Fill in the eyebrow area and the area above the lid with more Burnt Umber.

This is where the iris and the sclera become interesting. Due to the deep shadows and the reflecting color, the iris appears both blue and brown. Add some Burnt Umber with the no. 3/0 liner around the pupil. Add more of the blue/gray mixture to the right side. Add a touch of Burnt Umber and a touch of Alizarin Crimson to some white and fill in the area of the sclera left of the iris. This will make the eye appear shadowed.

3 FINISH

Using the no. 1 round, develop the deep shadows on the left side of the eye using the same mixture as the dark side of the sclera. Deepen it with more Burnt Umber and Alizarin Crimson.

Add more Alizarin Crimson in the left corner and under the eye. The rest of it is more of a brown tone. Layer your painting, drybrushing to blend the tones together.

Switch to the no. 3/0 liner and add the eyebrows with layers of Burnt Umber and Ivory Black. Make your brushstrokes go the same way the hairs are growing. Use quick strokes. Add a few white hairs on top of the eyebrow on the right side.

Add more Burnt Umber to the wrinkles. For the wrinkles on the right side, warm the color with some Cadmium Red Medium. Drybrush in some Titanium White for highlights.

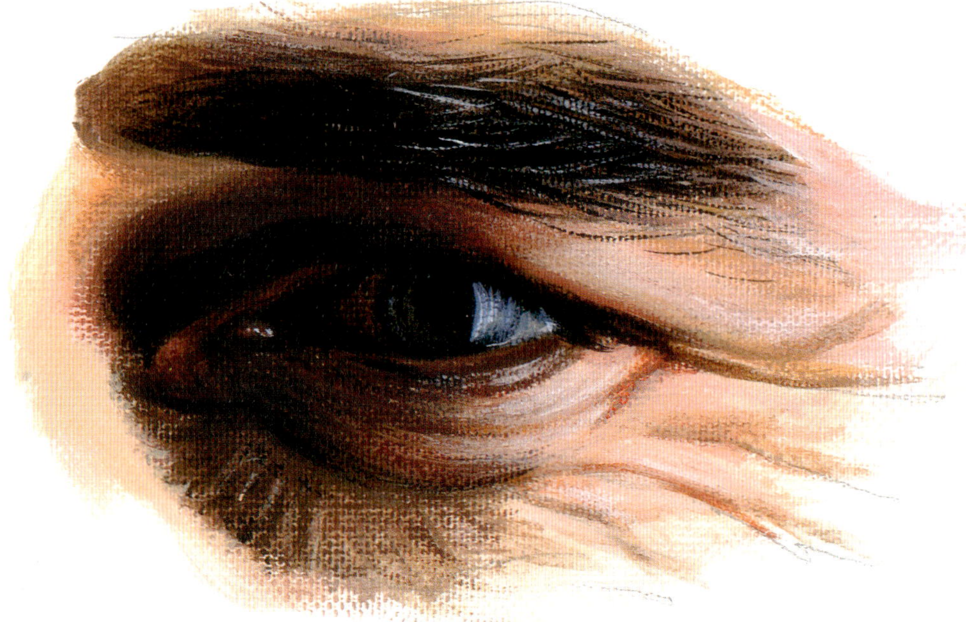

Ellipses

A circle is only a circle when seen from the front. The following examples show what happens when the eye is looking in a different direction.

All the eyes shown here are looking from side to side. This makes the iris and pupil seem less round and more narrow. They are condensed into vertical ellipses.

As with a circle, an ellipse can be drawn with a template as well. The shape should always be freehanded first, and then cleaned up with the template for accuracy.

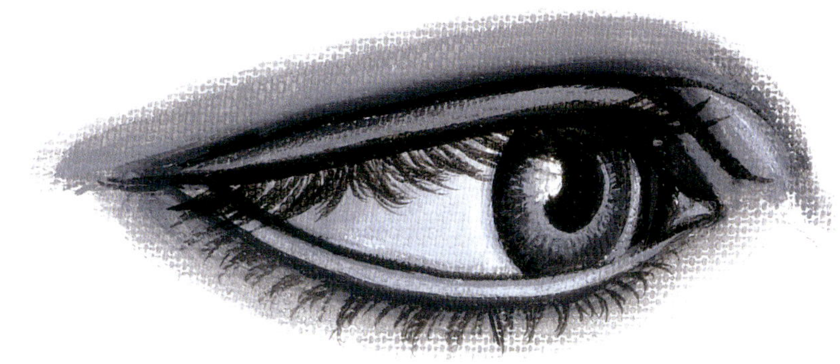

This eye is looking from side to side. It changes the iris and pupil into vertical ellipses.

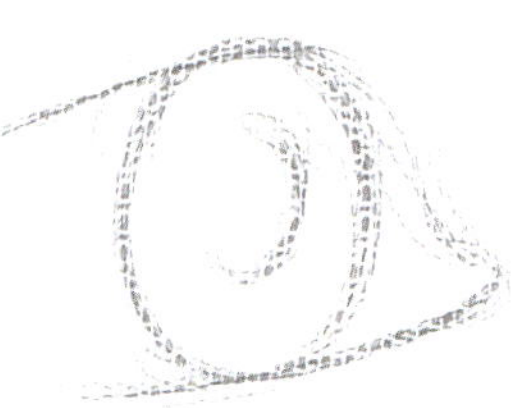

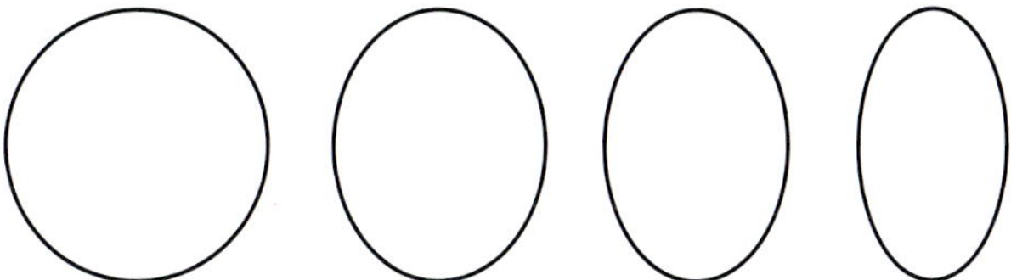

Vertical Ellipses
This is what happens to a circle when viewed from a vertical angle.

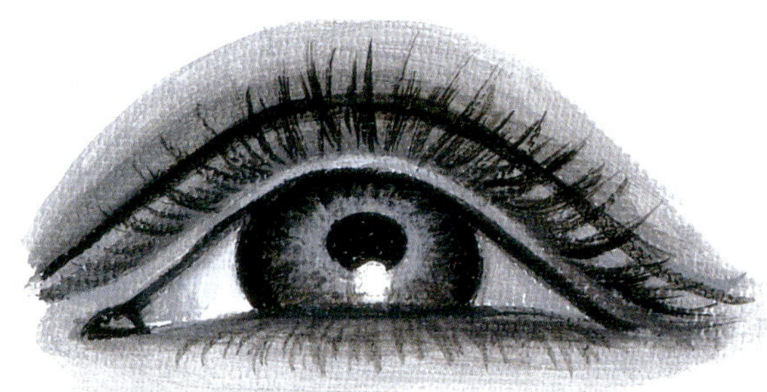

This changes the circle of the pupil and the iris into horizontal ellipses. The circle appears flattened and wider from side to side.

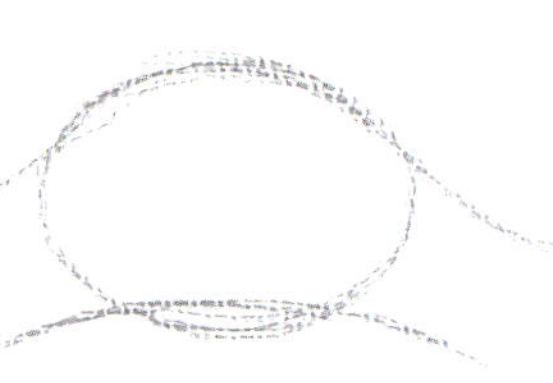

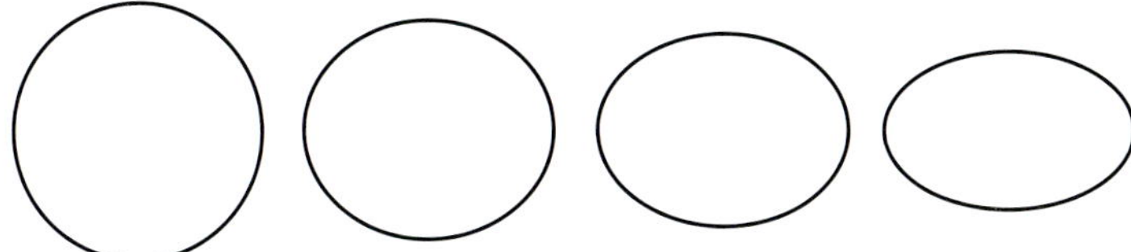

Horizontal Ellipses
This is what happens to a circle when viewed from a horizontal angle.

Profile

PIGMENTS
Alizarin Crimson, Burnt Umber, Cadmium Red Medium, Cadmium Yellow Medium, Ivory Black, Titanium White

BRUSHES
Nos. 1 and 2 round
No. 6 filbert
No. 3/0 liner

It's time to draw the eye at a different vantage point, showing the connection between the eye and the nose.

Viewing the eye from this perspective changes everything we have learned about eye anatomy. From this angle, you can still see both the iris and the pupil; however, they appear very elongated, not round at all. It is a circle in perspective.

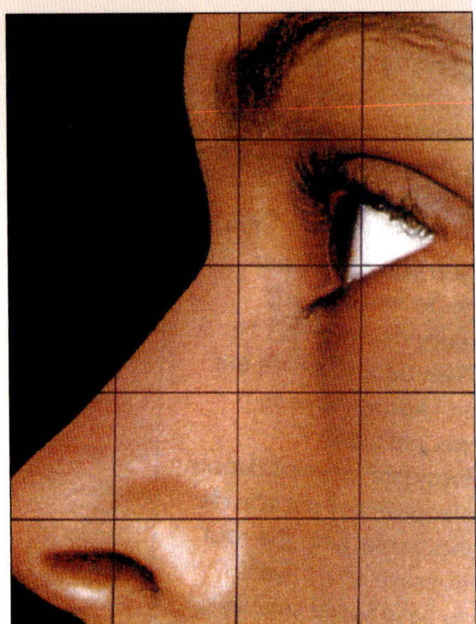

Reference Photo
Use the grid method to create the shape of this nose and eye on your canvas paper. Allow the boxes to guide you with the placement of the nose and eye. When you are happy with your line drawing and its accuracy, carefully remove the grid lines with your eraser.

Light Complexion Warm
Follow the instructions on page 23 to mix light, medium and dark versions of this peach color.

Add Burnt Umber and Alizarin Crimson to the mixture to create the shadows.

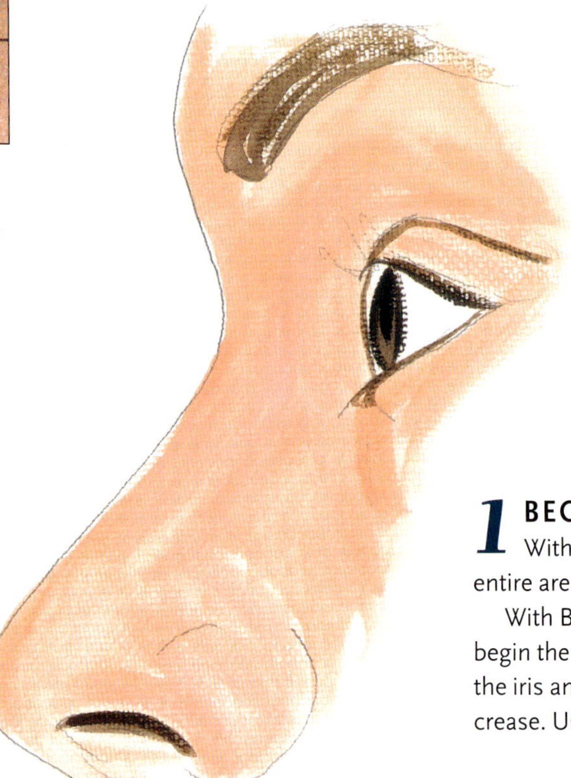

1 BEGIN WITH THE BASE

With the light peach color, basecoat the entire area using the no. 6 filbert.

With Burnt Umber and the no. 1 round, begin the eyebrow and the nostril. Fill in the iris and create the lash lines and eyelid crease. Use Ivory Black to fill in the pupil.

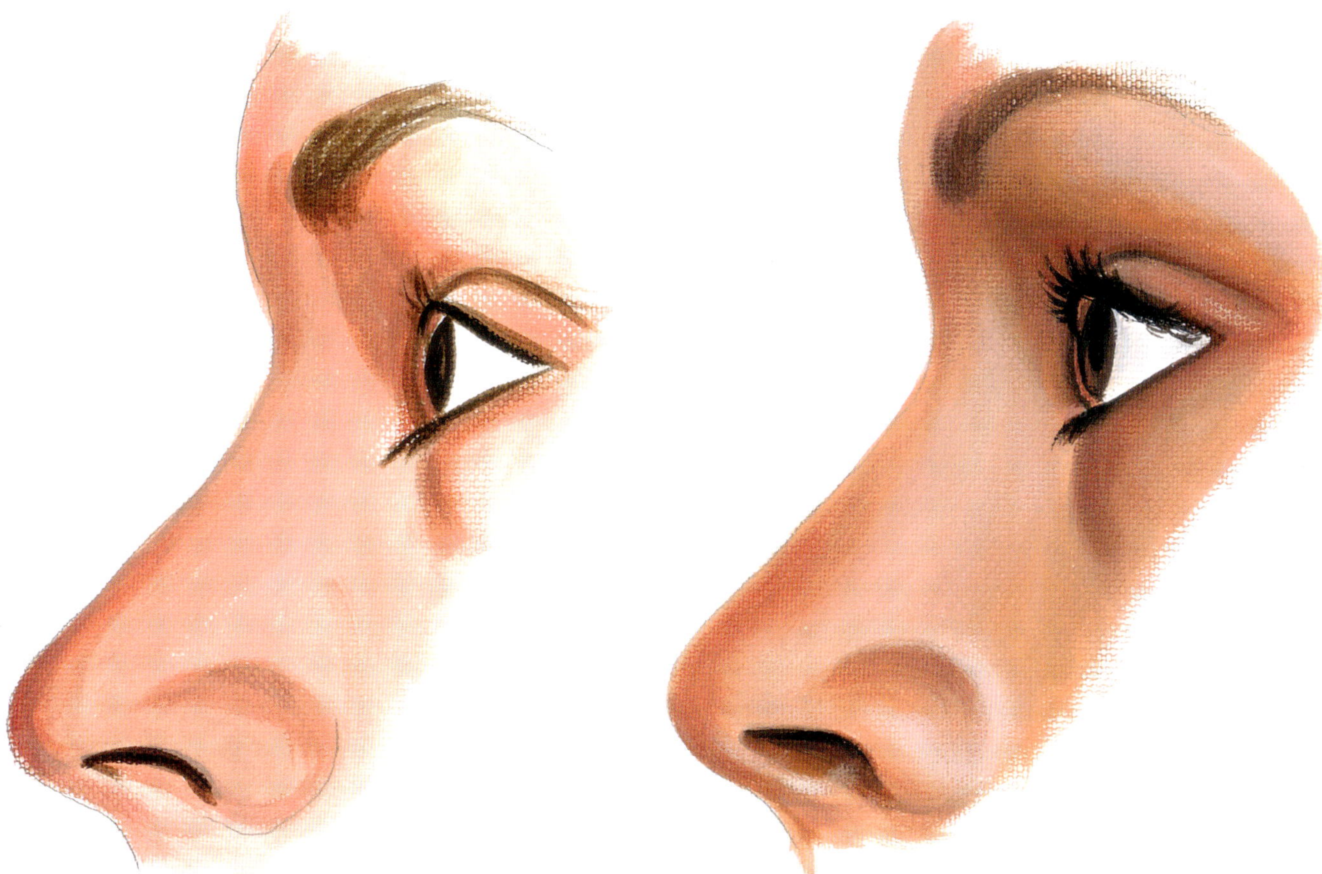

2 THE AWKWARD STAGE

Add some Burnt Umber and Alizarin Crimson to the light peach mixture and apply it down the bridge of the nose, the edge of the nostril, and between the brow and the eye using the no. 2 round.

At this angle, you can see the inside of the eyelid in front of the pupil. Create this reddish color with Cadmium Red Medium and a touch of Titanium White. Apply it with the no. 3/0 liner.

3 FINISH

Using the no. 2 round and a thicker application of paint, continue drybrushing the mixtures together. Add some of the shadow color inside the nostril area. Add Titanium White to the areas of highlight and to the sclera area. Add a touch of Burnt Umber to the white for the light shadow in the sclera.

With the no. 3/0 liner and Ivory Black, add the eyelashes with quick, curved strokes.

The Set

PIGMENTS
Ivory Black, Titanium White

BRUSHES
Nos. 1 round
No. 6 flat or filbert
No. 3/0 liner

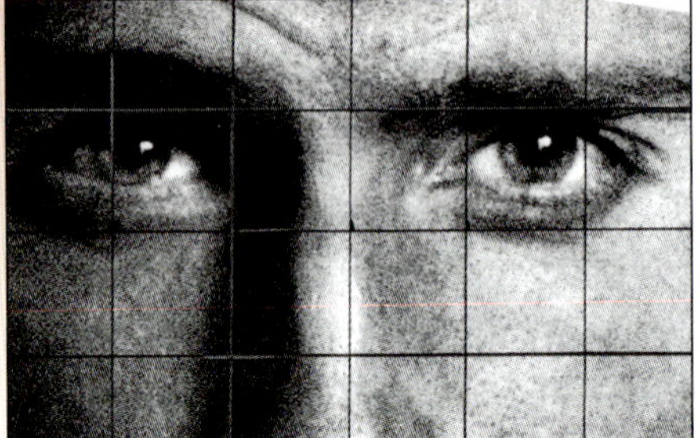

Reference Photo
Use the grid method to create these eyes on your canvas paper. When you are happy with your line drawing and its accuracy, carefully remove the grid lines with an eraser.

With a template, clean up the edges of the iris and pupil. Use the same hole in your template for both eyes. It is very important when rendering two eyes together that the irises and pupils are exactly the same size in each eye.

Now that you have practiced painting the eye, it is important to learn how to put two eyes together. It is difficult to paint portraits without first practicing the key elements of doing this.

Let's begin with two eyes directly from the front and paint them in a monochromatic black and white.

Gray Scale
Match your tones to this gray scale.

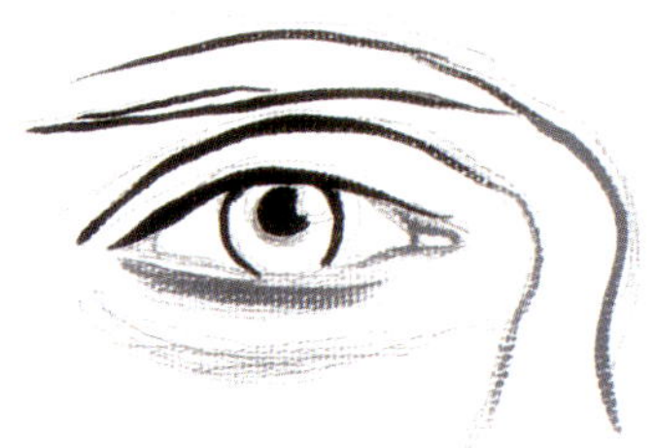

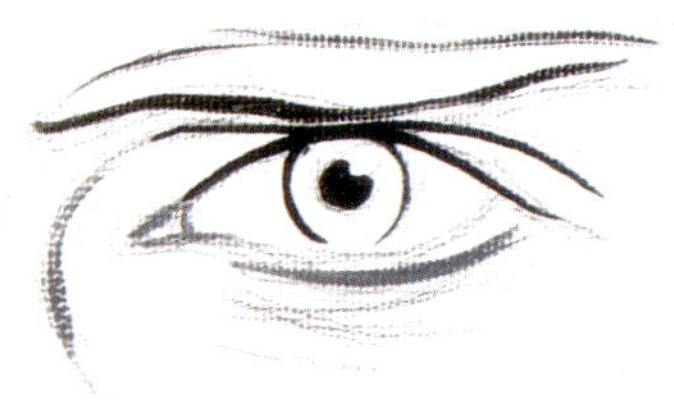

1 BEGIN WITH OUTLINES

With the no. 1 round, fill in the pupils, allowing a small area for the catchlights. The catchlights should be half in the pupil and half in the iris, and should be in the same spot in each eye.

Switch to the no. 3/0 liner and outline the iris, the lash line and the eyebrow. Add some white to the black to make a medium gray and outline the bridge of the nose. Paint in the line that represents the lower lid thickness. Refer to the gray scale.

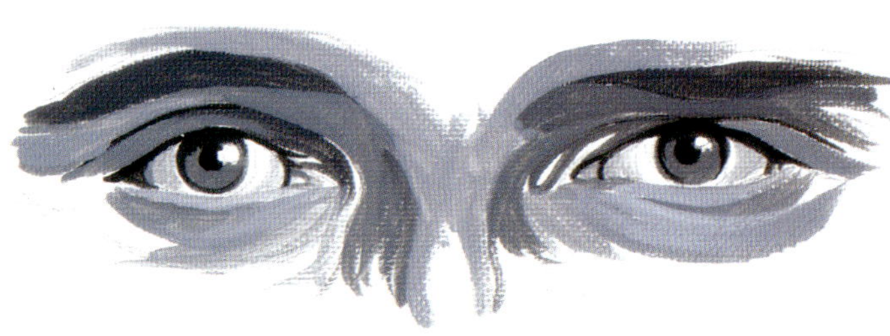

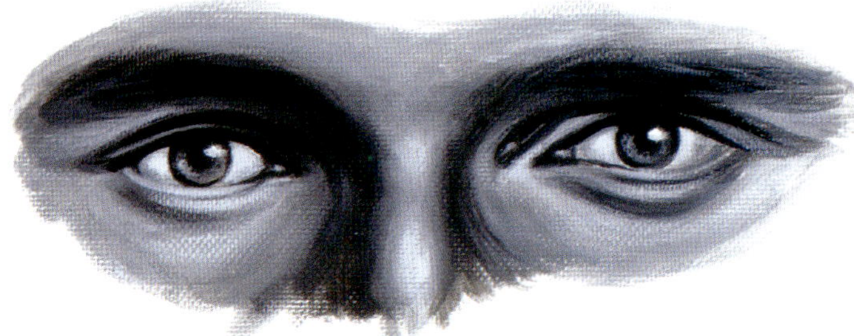

2 THE AWKWARD STAGE

With the no. 6 flat or filbert and medium gray, fill in the skin tone. Fill in the irises with the same mixture. Add more black to darken the medium gray mixture and fill in the eyebrows.

Add white to the sclera and shadow them with some light gray to make the eyes look rounded.

3 FINISH

Continue adding layers. Use light, medium and dark gray to drybrush the colors together. Use white for the highlight areas.

Add the hairs of the eyebrow with the no. 3/0 liner, layering black and medium gray with quick strokes.

Develop the details of the irises by adding some highlights around the pupils. Add white to the catchlights.

3/4-View

PIGMENTS
Ivory Black, Titanium White

BRUSHES
No. 1 round
No. 6 flat or filbert
No. 3/0 liner

The ¾-view is the most difficult because it involves a slight turn. Your brain will want you to draw these eyes straight on. You must resist the urge to make them symmetrical. You only see one side of the nose, and it blocks the view of the eye on the right. The pupils and irises are slight vertical ellipses. If you make them perfect circles, it will make the eyes look as if they are looking at you too much. Freehand the shapes, then use an ellipse template to clean up the edges.

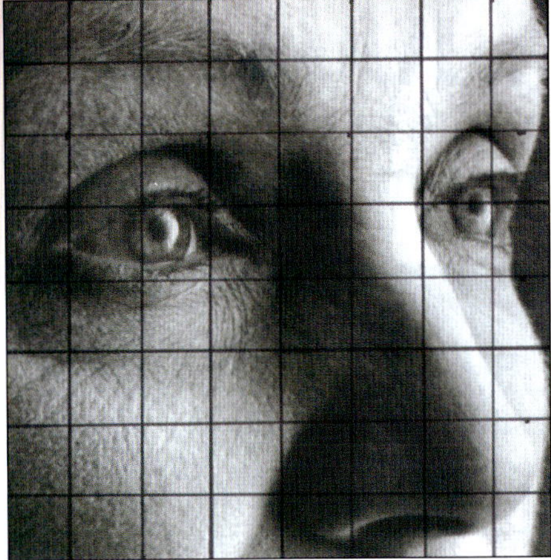

Reference Photo
Make your line drawing look like this before removing the grid lines with an eraser. Use a template to make the circles of the irises and pupils crisp.

Gray Scale
Match your tones to this gray scale.

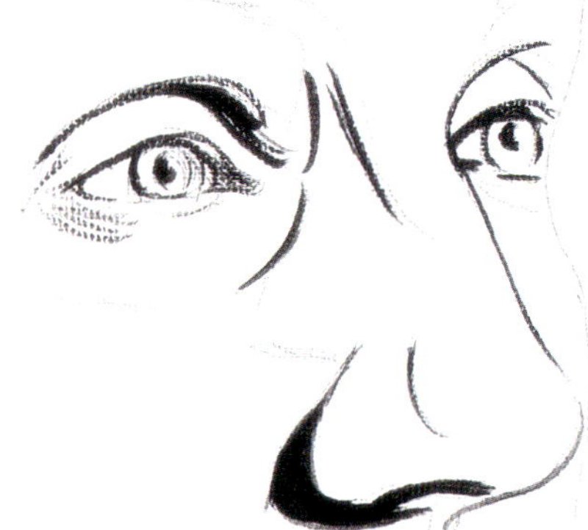

1 BEGIN WITH OUTLINE

With the no. 1 round, outline the features with black. Fill in the pupils, allowing a small area for the catchlights.

With black and medium gray, outline the major shapes using the no. 3/0 liner.

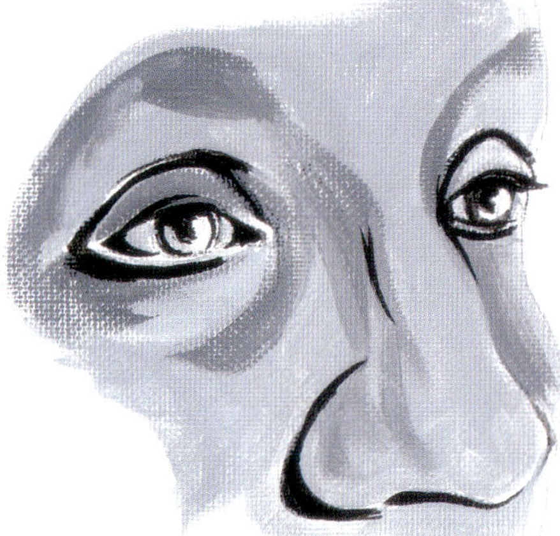

2 THE AWKWARD STAGE

With the no. 6 flat or filbert and medium gray, fill in the skin tone. Fill in the irises with the same color. Add more black to darken the medium gray mixture, and fill in the eyebrows.

Add white to the sclera and shadow them with some light gray.

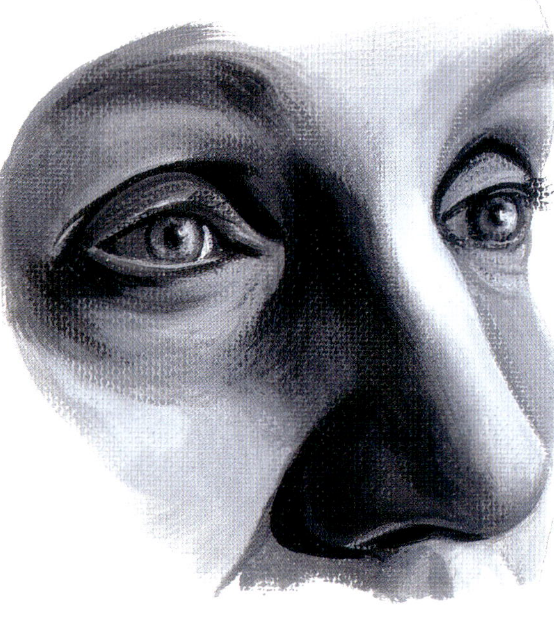

3 FINISH

Continue adding layers. Use light, medium and dark grays to drybrush the values together. Use white for the highlight areas.

Add the hairs of the eyebrow with the no. 3/0 liner, layering black and medium gray with quick strokes.

Develop the details of the irises by adding some highlights around the pupils. Add white to the catchlights.

The Set, In Color

PIGMENTS
Alizarin Crimson, Burnt Umber, Cadmium Red Medium, Cadmium Yellow Medium, Ivory Black, Titanium White

BRUSHES
Nos. 1 and 2 round
No. 6 flat or filbert
No. 3/0 liner

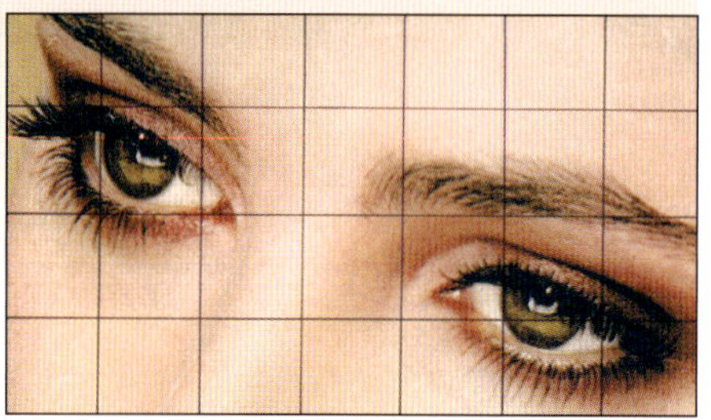

Reference Photo
Because the eyes are looking up, the irises still look circular. Use the grid method to create an accurate line drawing on your canvas paper. Use a template to make the circles of the irises and pupils crisp.

Let's practice painting two eyes together in full color. These eyes are a challenge because of the perspective. You might assume that they are vertical ellipses because of the ¾-turn. However, they are also looking up, which counteracts the effect. Because of that, they are actually circular. It is important to make these types of observations and assessments before you begin to paint.

Light Complexion Warm
Follow the instructions on page 23 to mix light, medium and dark versions of this peach color.

Add Burnt Umber and Alizarin Crimson to the mix to create the shadows.

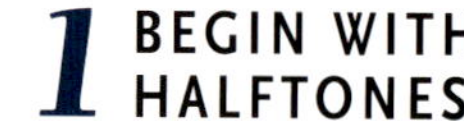

1 BEGIN WITH HALFTONES

With the no. 1 round, outline the iris, pupil, lash lines and lid crease with black. Fill in the pupil with black (half in the pupil and half in the iris), leaving a small area for the catchlight.

With the light complexion color mixture, fill in the skin tone with the no. 6 flat or filbert.

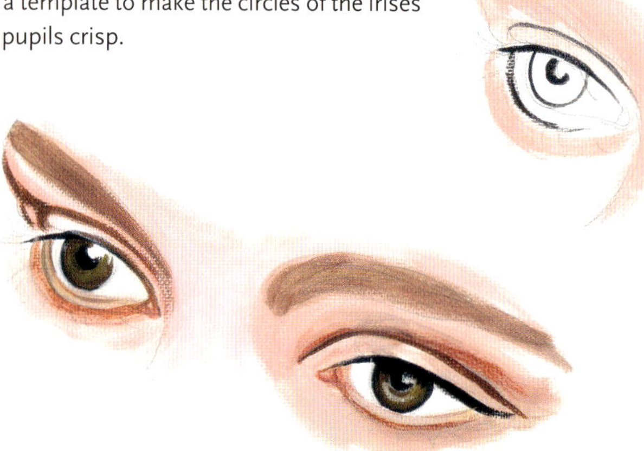

2 THE AWKWARD STAGE

Use the no. 1 round for this step. Mix an olive green with Cadmium Yellow Medium and a touch of black. Apply it to the iris area. Add an outline of Burnt Umber around the iris as well. Fill in the sclera with white that has a hint of Cadmium Red Medium added to it.

Mix a small amount of Alizarin Crimson with some Burnt Umber to create a shadow color and add the lid crease, corner membrane and lower lid thickness. Lighten this mixture with a dab of white and fill in the eyebrow area.

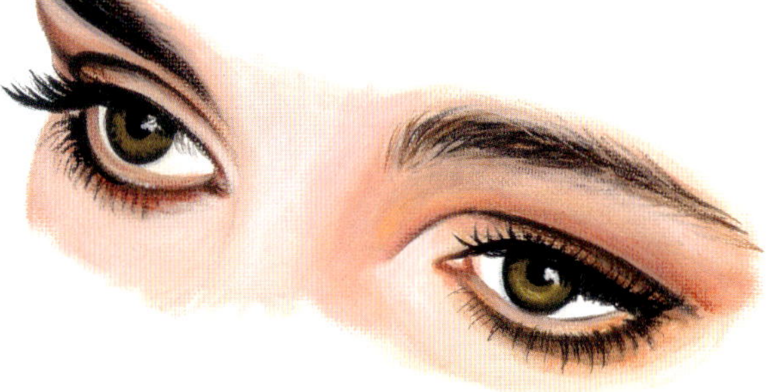

3 FINISH

Use the no. 2 round and a thicker application of paint to build up the skin color. Drybrush the highlights into the bridge of the nose and around the eyes.

With the no. 3/0 liner, add the eyebrows and the eyelashes. These are very prominent, so pay particular attention to the direction of the hair's growth.

Closed

PIGMENTS

Alizarin Crimson, Burnt Umber, Cadmium Red Medium, Cadmium Yellow Medium, Prussian Blue, Titanium White

BRUSHES

Nos. 1 and 2 round
No. 6 flat or filbert
No. 3/0 liner

When drawing facial features, it is always important to have a basic understanding of the anatomy. This photo clearly illustrates how big the eyeball is underneath the lids. The eyeball is like a large sphere. What we see under the lids is a very small fraction of the overall surface.

Light Complexion Warm

Follow the instructions on page 23 to mix light, medium and dark versions of this peach color.

Add Burnt Umber and Alizarin Crimson to the mixture to create the shadows.

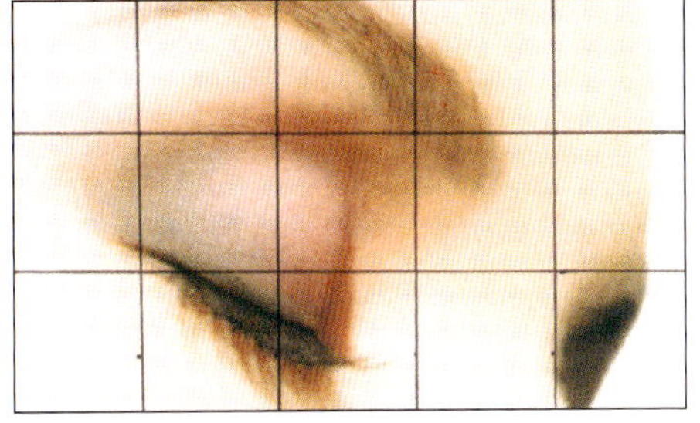

Reference Photo

This closed eye shows the large spherical shape of the eyeball underneath the eyelid.

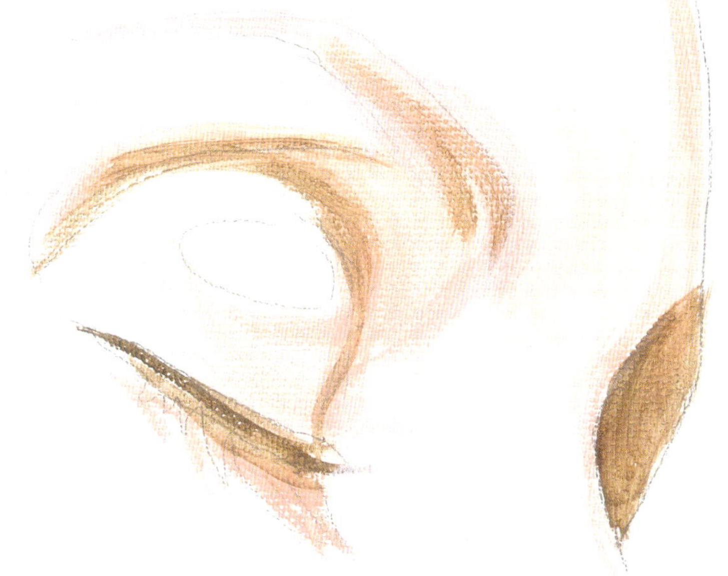

1 OUTLINE AND TONE

This painting is made up of smooth, curved surfaces. Basecoat the overall skin tone with the light complexion warm color using the no. 6 flat or filbert.

With diluted Burnt Umber and the no. 1 round, fill in the lash area. Fill in the shape representing the eye on the right behind the nose. Add Alizarin Crimson and Burnt Umber to the skin tone color to get a cool shadow color and use it to create the lid crease area and the shadow under the eyelashes.

2 THE AWKWARD STAGE

With thicker paint, build up the skin tone. Develop the eyebrow area, and make the cast shadow of the eye more prominent with the shadow colors. Use the no. 6 filbert to drybrush the colors together. Add the eyebrow on the right side with black and the no. 3/0 liner.

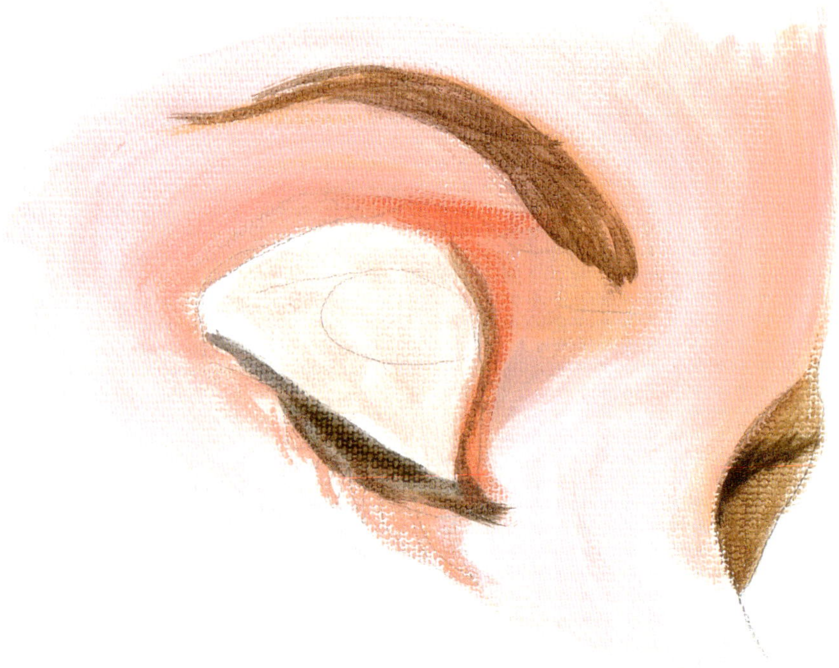

3 FINISH

This is a real sphere exercise, with all five elements of shading clearly delineated in the shape of the eyelid. The reflected light along the right edge makes the bulge of the eye very evident.

Continue building the skin tones, blending them together smoothly. Add a touch of Prussian Blue for the color of the eye shadow on the left side.

Add the eyelashes with the no. 3/0 liner. Use Burnt Umber for the first layer and then add black to the ends and to the lash line. The lashes appear lighter in the middle.

Add the eyebrow hairs with very quick strokes using both diluted Burnt Umber and the cool shadow color. Highlight some of them with the medium peach mixture to keep them looking soft.

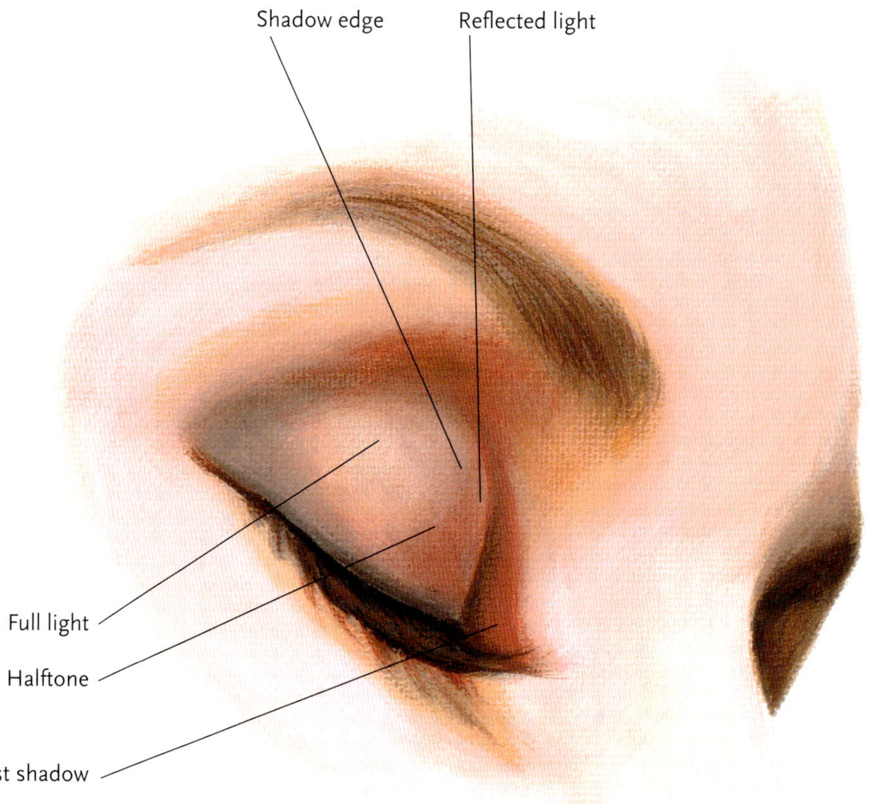

Looking to the Side

PIGMENTS
Alizarin Crimson, Burnt Umber, Cadmium Red Medium, Cadmium Yellow Medium, Ivory Black, Titanium White

BRUSHES
Nos. 1 and 2 round
No. 6 flat or filbert
No. 3/0 liner

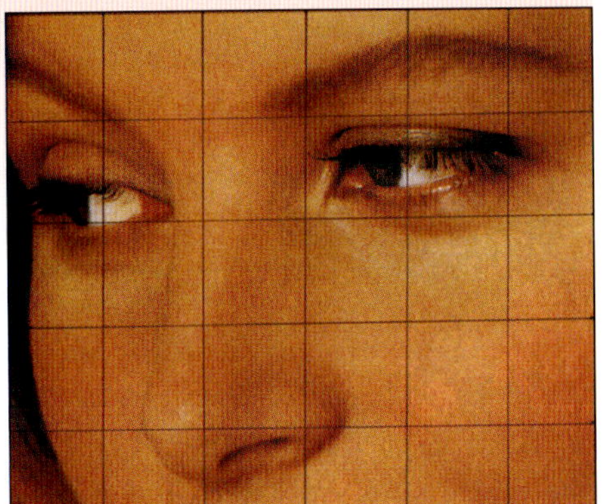

Reference Photo
Use the grid method to create these eyes on your canvas paper. Resist the urge to correct the angle of these features and straighten them up.

The skin tone in this photo is much richer than the others, and the eyes are really turned, making the irises vertical ellipses. You see more of the sclera than the iris and eye color.

Light Complexion Warm
Follow the instructions on page 23 to make light, medium and dark versions of this peach color.

Add Burnt Umber and Alizarin Crimson to the mixture to create the shadows.

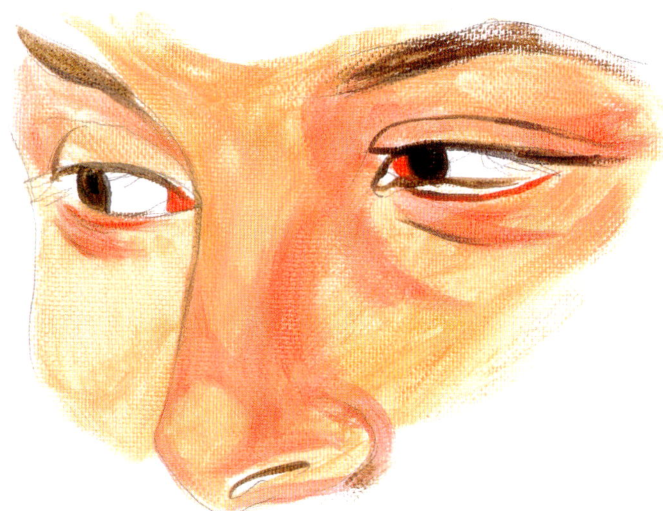

1 OUTLINE AND SKIN TONE

With the light complexion color, basecoat the entire skin area using the no. 6 flat or filbert. Add some Cadmium Red Medium to that color and apply the darker area around the eyes, in the corner membrane, and down the bridge of the nose using the no. 2 round.

With black and the no. 3/0 liner, outline the iris and fill in the pupil. With Burnt Umber, add the color to the iris, eyebrows and inside the nostril. Outline the lash line and lower lid thicknesses.

2 THE AWKWARD STAGE

Build up the skin tones with thicker applications of paint, drybrushing all the colors together with the no. 6 flat or filbert. Add black using the no. 1 round to deepen the color of the lash line.

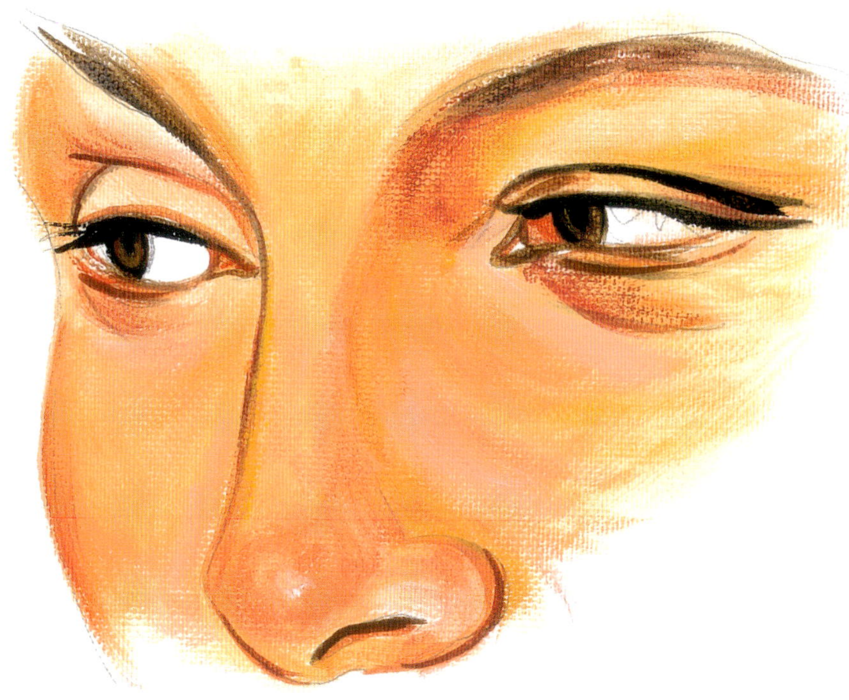

3 FINISH

Continue building the skin tones as in the previous step until the canvas is completely covered and the tones are continual and smooth. Add the eyebrows and eyelashes with the no. 3/0 liner and Ivory Black.

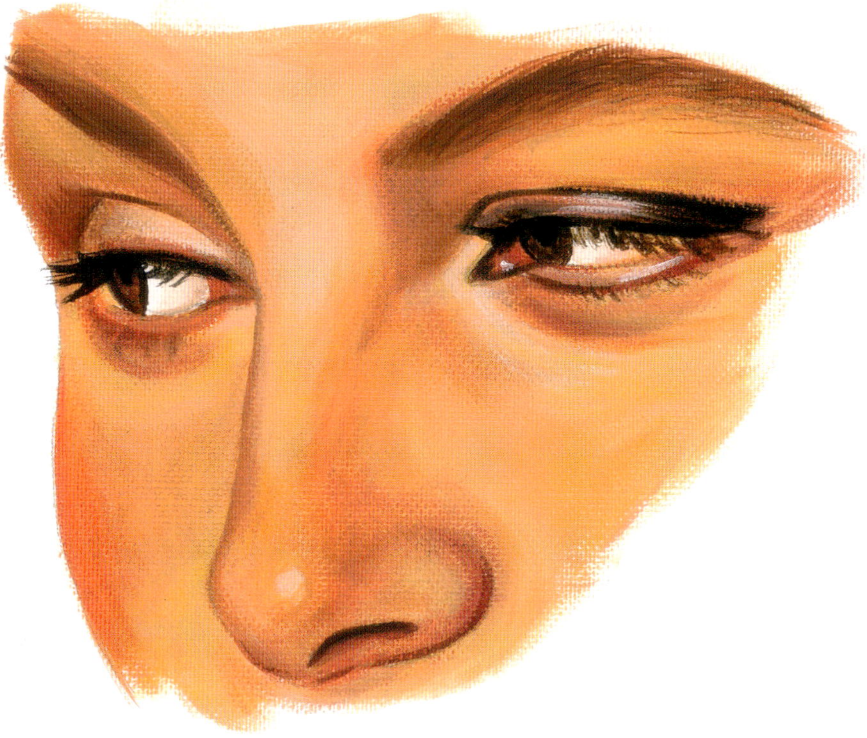

Looking Up

PIGMENTS
Alizarin Crimson, Burnt Umber, Cadmium Red Medium, Cadmium Yellow Medium, Titanium White

BRUSHES
No. 1 round
No. 6 flat or filbert
No. 3/0 liner

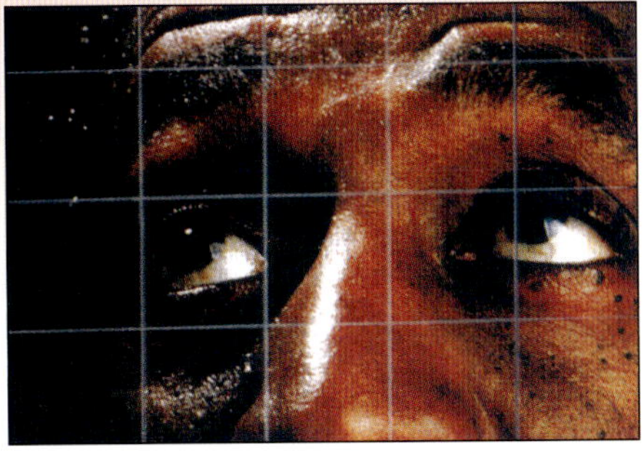

Reference Photo
The upward gaze makes horizontal ellipses. Use the grid method to draw them on your canvas paper. Freehand the shapes of the irises and pupils first, and then make them crisp with an ellipse template.

These eyes are looking up, making them horizontal ellipses. Look at the amount of sclera that shows below the irises. The white of the eye only shows like this when the eyes are looking up.

The darkness of the skin here makes the eyes jump out at you, creating bright highlights for extreme contrasts.

Dark Complexion Warm
Follow the instructions on page 23 to make light, medium and dark versions of this skin tone. This skin is full of rich brown tones that are warmed up with the Cadmium Red Medium.

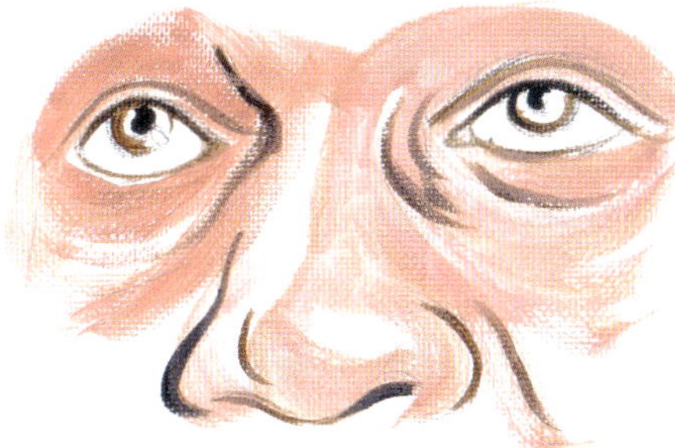

1 OUTLINE AND SKIN TONE

Dilute the light version of the dark complexion warm and base in the skin tone with the no. 6 filbert or flat. This skin tone is on the cooler side, so mix in a lot of the Alizarin Crimson.

With Burnt Umber and the no. 1 round outline the iris. Fill in the pupil with black using the no. 3/0 liner. Use Burnt Umber to outline the edges of the nose and around the eyes.

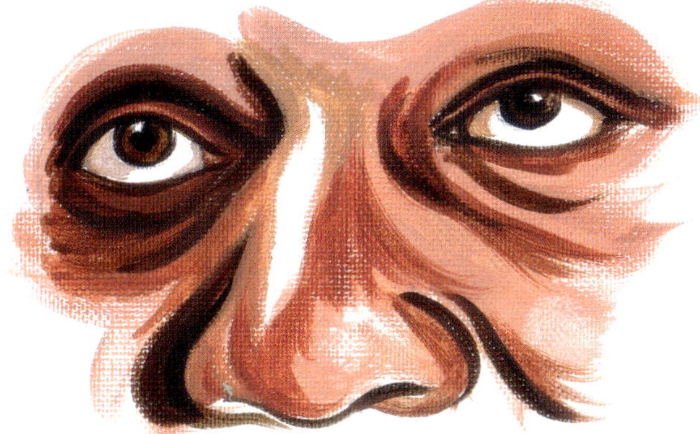

2 THE AWKWARD STAGE

Add Burnt Umber to get a shadow mixture and create the shadow edges of the eyes and nose. This looks very rough right now because of all the deep contrasts. Don't worry if it looks choppy and unblended. The patterns of tone are what are important at this point.

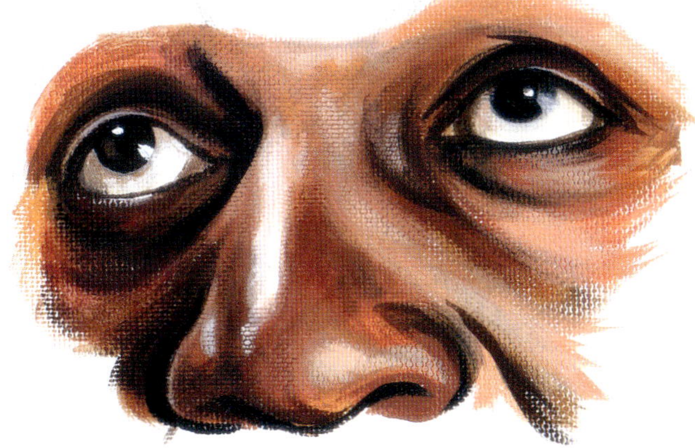

3 FINISH

This is where the blending comes in. With a thicker application of paint and the no. 6 flat or filbert, drybrush to layer and soften the colors together.

Other Characteristics

The key to making eyes look realistic is to capture them as shapes. Look for the five elements of shading. Look at the white highlight areas. Look at black areas of glasses as just shapes too. They go together just like a puzzle to create the overall form. Everything is about capturing what you actually see, not what you know it "should" look like.

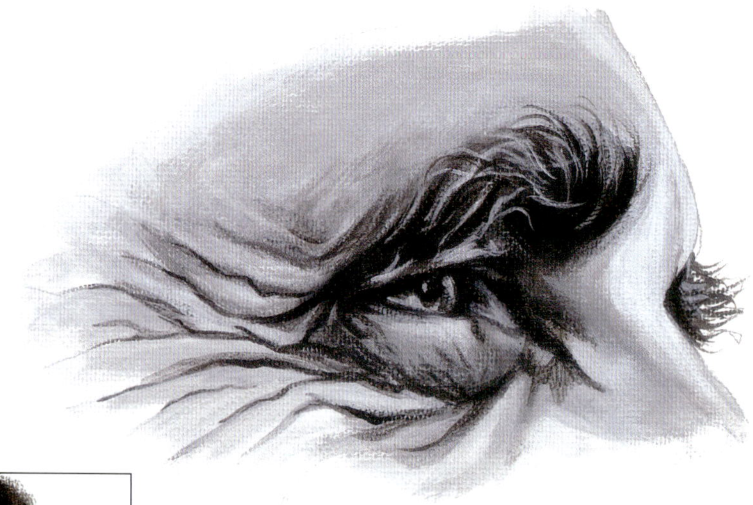

Paint in Layers
Finding photos of interesting features will give you lots of good practice. The wrinkles and bushy eyebrow hairs here are all done with the no. 3/0 liner and applied in layers. Place the dark areas first and then place the light details.

Glass Shadows Affect the Face
Glasses affect the look of the shadows and highlights, distorting part of the eye anatomy. Look for where light and dark patterns are transferred onto the face. Paint only what you see.

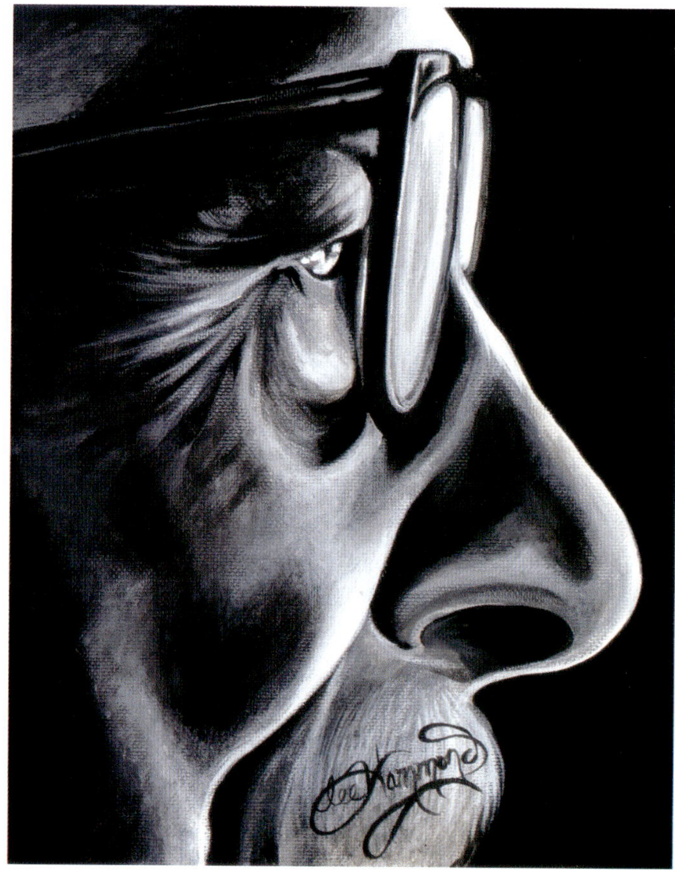

Look for Light and Dark Patterns in Glasses
Create a grid to practice drawing all the patterns you see in these glasses. Then try your hand at painting them.

Profile With Glasses

PIGMENTS
Burnt Umber, Cadmium Red Medium, Cadmium Yellow Medium, Ivory Black, Prussian Blue, Titanium White

BRUSHES
Nos. 1 and 2 round
No. 4 filbert

This is a good project for learning how to paint eyeglasses. Rather than painting the entire portrait, I chose to focus on the eyeglasses. While they may seem somewhat difficult, you will see by the step-by-step approach that they can be simply created with abstract shapes and areas of color.

Light Complexion Warm
Follow the instructions on page 23 to make light, medium and dark versions of this skin tone.

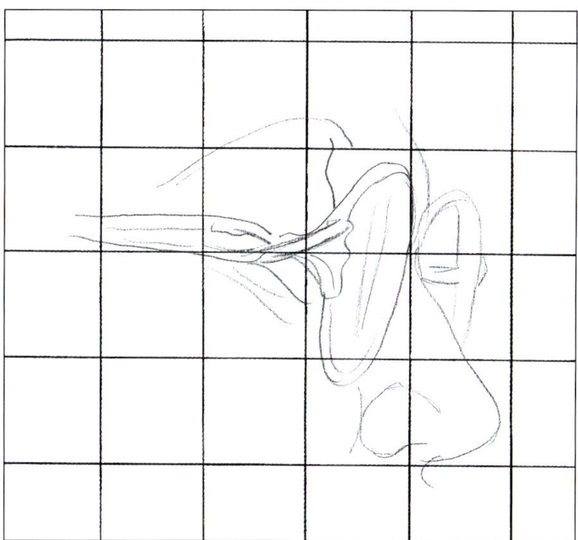

Line Drawing
Draw a grid on your canvas paper and copy the shapes you see in each box. Watch for the shapes within each box, and resist the urge to draw what you "remember" glasses to look like. See them purely as puzzle piece shapes!

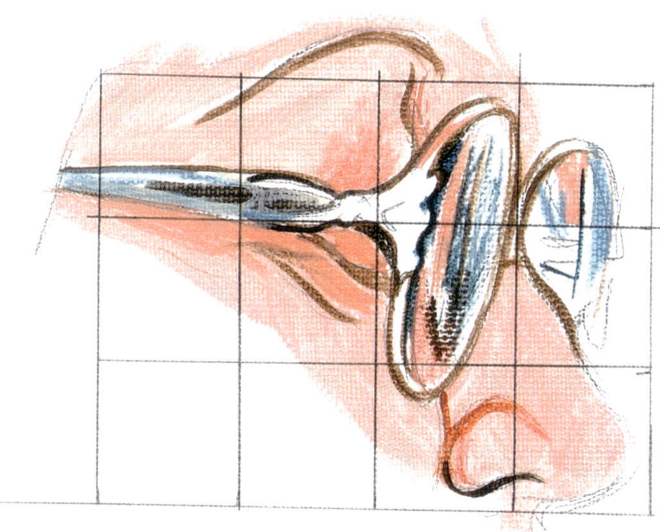

1 FIRST LAYERS

Remove the grid lines from your canvas when you are sure of the accuracy. I left them in this illustration to help you see the abstract painted shapes in the glasses.

Use the no. 4 filbert to basecoat the skin with the light complexion warm middle tone. Switch to the no. 2 round and apply this mixture in the glass area, too. Use the no. 1 round to outline the shapes of the frames and the lenses with diluted Burnt Umber. Use the diluted Burnt Umber and the no. 1 round to add her eyebrow and the lines around her eye and nose as well.

With a mixture of Prussian Blue and Titanium White, apply some light blue to the frames using the no. 1 round. Add this light blue color inside the lens area, too. These shapes are mere streaks. Don't try to be overly exact. They represent reflections of color and are very abstract around the eyes.

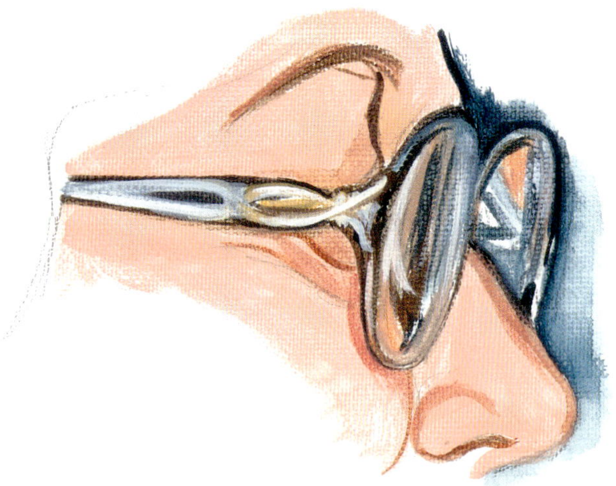

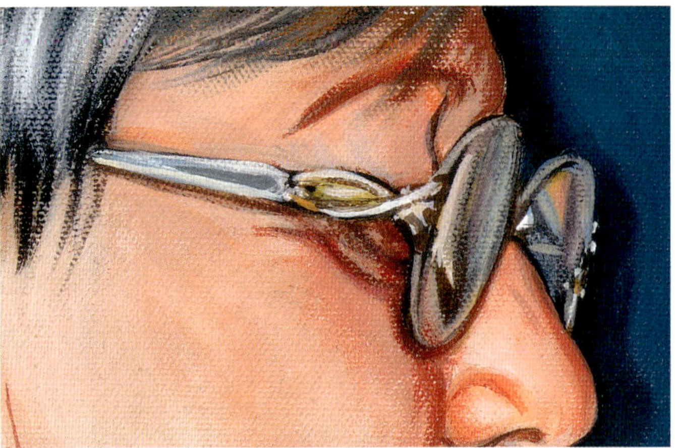

2 THE AWKWARD STAGE

Continue adding small nuances of color with the no. 1 round. The glasses reflect all the surrounding colors of the skin and background. The colors overlap in puzzle-like shapes. This is the way to create the illusion of shine in both the frames and the glass. It is all about contrasts.

Work in the gold color of the frames using Titanium White, a touch of Cadmium Yellow Medium, and a bit of Burnt Umber. Create the darkest areas of the glasses with pure black. Create the lightest highlights with pure white.

Begin the background with a diluted mixture of Prussian Blue and Ivory Black. Add this mixture into the patterns reflecting in the glass lenses. Use the background color to help create the light edges of the glasses on the right.

Begin the shadow underneath the glasses with the darker version of the skin tone mixture.

3 FINISH

This is where the blending comes in. With a thicker application of paint, drybrush to layer and soften the colors together. Go back and forth adding light and dark colors until your glasses look as realistic as mine. Keep darkening the shadow on the skin that is created by the glasses. This is very important, and should not be overlooked. It is this shadow that makes the glasses appear to be resting on the face

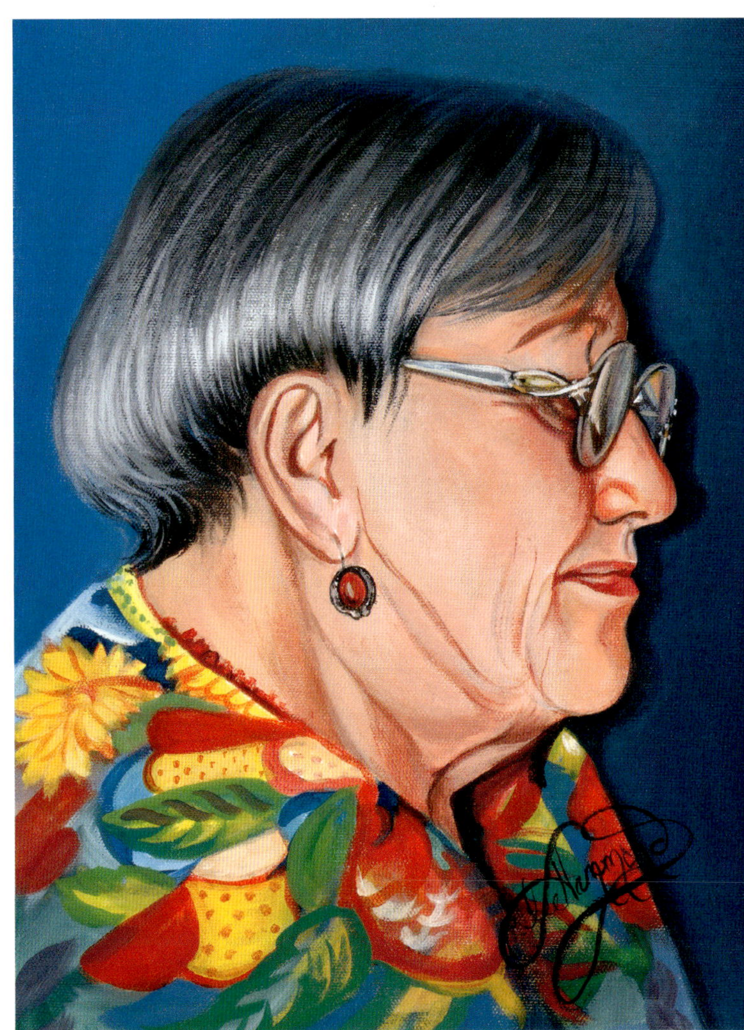

Glass Shadows Affect the Face

Glasses affect the look of the shadows and highlights, distorting part of the eye anatomy. Look for where light and dark patterns are transferred onto the face.

A profile can be a great way to capture personality. My friend Trudy is one of the most interesting people I know. I took this picture during one of our trips together, and it captures her as she was working on her artwork, lost in thought. Even though you cannot see her eyes, you can feel her essence.

The Ear

By now you've learned how important shapes are when drawing or painting. Look at anything you want to capture as interlocking puzzle pieces.

The ear is one of the facial features that will test that theory and your ability to implement it. My students are constantly telling me how difficult it is for them to accurately depict an ear. They find the shapes very difficult to capture.

Everyone's ears are unique. However, each one has the same fundamental structure, which you should commit to memory.

Keys to Painting Ears

The ear is multi-surfaced and multi-dimensional. There is an inner ear and an outer ear.

- The outer ear overlaps the inner, creating a ridge that reflects light and casts a shadow.
- The "cup" of the ear has raised cartilage areas that resemble a curved Y-shape.
- Every raised area of the ears' surface will reflect light, so the contrasts can be extreme.
- Ears sit at a slight angle. Do not make them straight up and down.

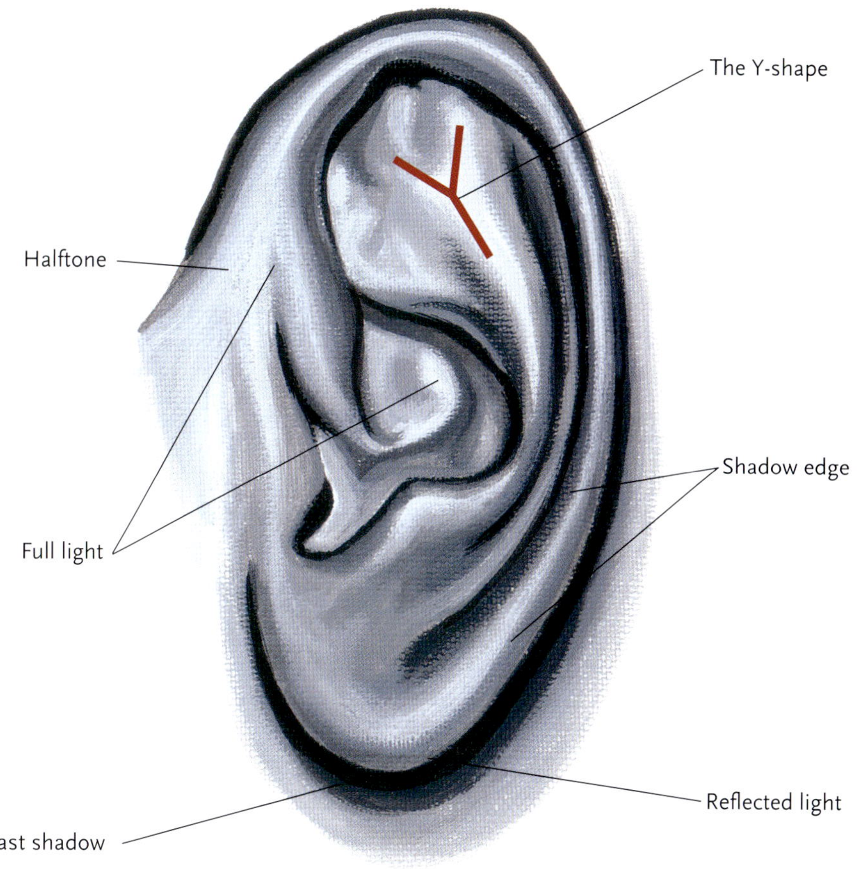

Ear Parts to Remember
The ear is made up of multiple shapes within shapes. It is multidimensional with many overlapping surfaces. Though all ears are unique, they all share these basics.

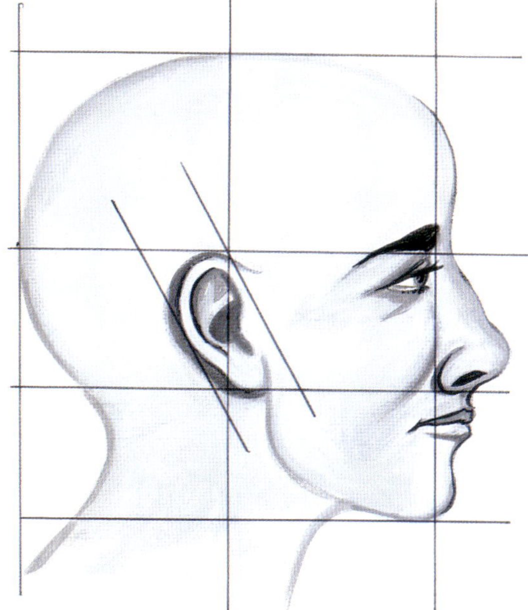

Ear Placement
Look at how the ear relates to the other facial features. The diagram lines show how the ear lines up with the eyes and the nose.

Monochromatic

PIGMENTS
Ivory Black, Titanium White

BRUSHES
Nos. 1 and 2 round

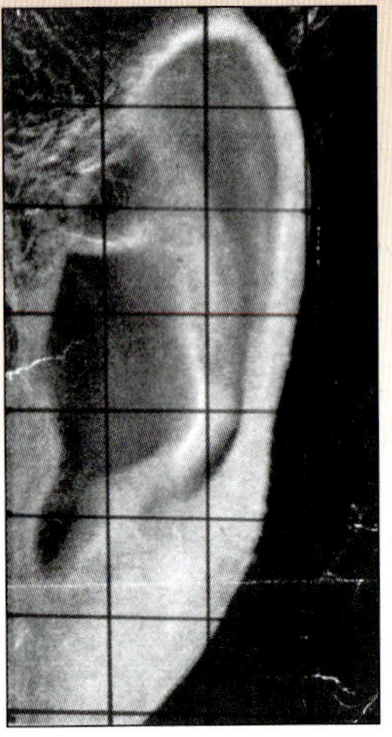

Reference Photo
The ear is made up of interlocking shapes. Use the grid method to capture this ear on your canvas paper.

As we have for the other features, let's begin with a black-and-white study. Look for all the surfaces and overlapping shapes when creating the line drawing.

Gray Scale
Match your tones to this gray scale.

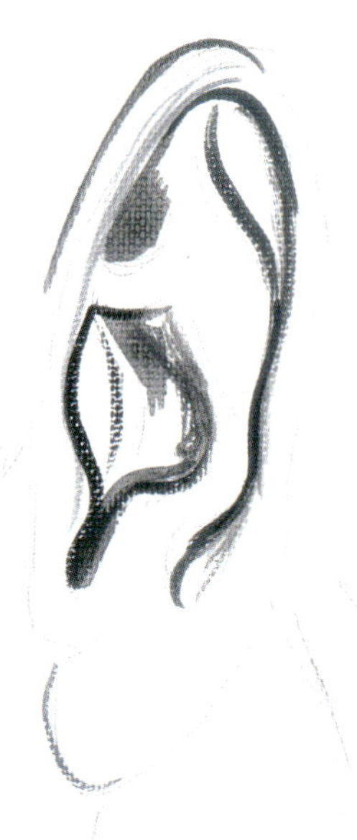

1 OUTLINE THE SHAPES
With the no. 1 round and black, outline the basic shapes of the ear to separate the surfaces.

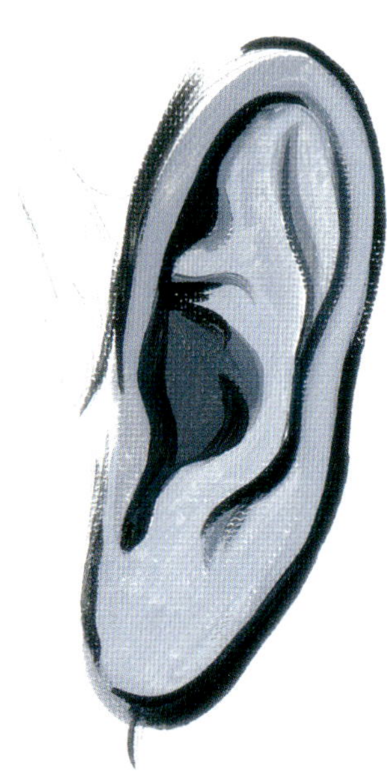

2 THE AWKWARD STAGE
Mix a medium gray and fill in the entire ear with the no. 2 round. Fill in the cup with dark gray. Add a black cast shadow behind the ear to start the illusion of the ear rising away from the head.

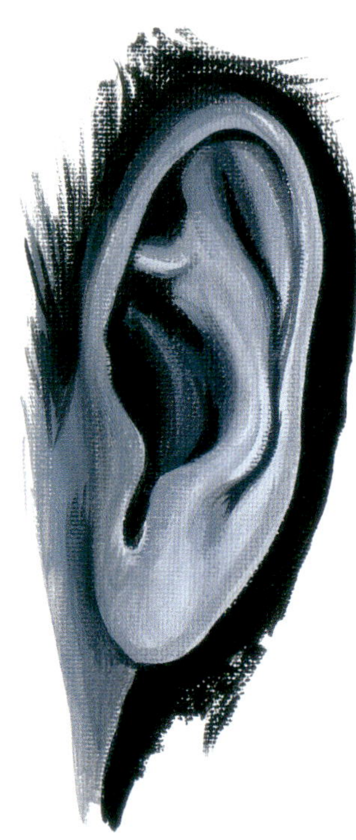

3 FINISH
The final stage is all about adding the five elements of shading to create the illusion of form. Apply shadow edges inside all the rims and edges you see to show the reflected light.

Add light, medium and dark tones to create the form, drybrushing to blend them together. The black background helps the light edges of the ear look more pronounced. Create the illusion of hair with a few loose brushstrokes. Add bright areas of highlight last with pure white.

Full Color

PIGMENTS

Alizarin Crimson, Burnt Umber, Cadmium Red Medium, Cadmium Yellow Medium, Titanium White

BRUSHES

Nos. 1 and 2 round
No. 3/0 liner

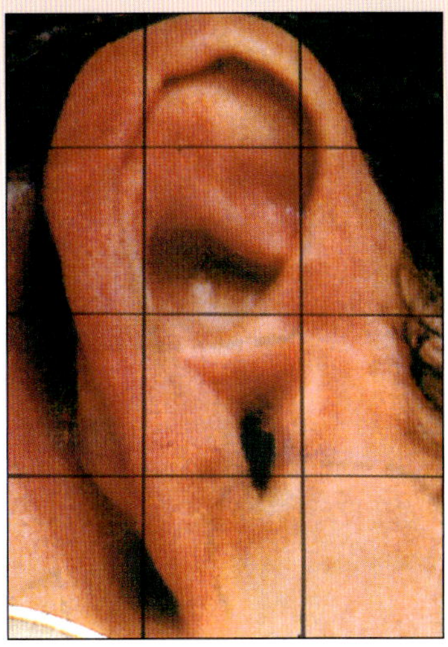

Reference Photo
Use the grid method to capture this ear on your canvas paper. Remember to look for interlocking shapes.

Now for some color...

Light Complexion Warm
Follow the instructions on page 23 to make light, medium and dark versions of this peach color.

Add Burnt Umber and Alizarin Crimson to the mixture to create the shadows.

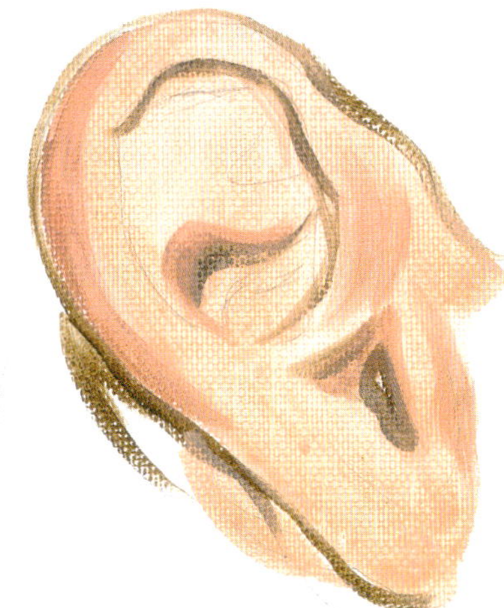

1 HALFTONES AND OUTLINES

With a diluted application of the medium peach mixture, basecoat the entire ear with the no. 2 round, allowing the pencil lines to come through. Add Alizarin Crimson and Burnt Umber to create cool shadow colors and outline the inner shapes of the ear using the no. 1 round.

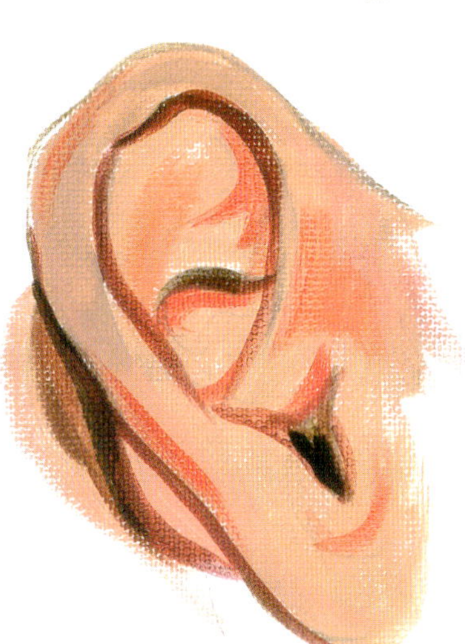

2 THE AWKWARD STAGE

Build the tones with thicker applications. The values are darker toward the inside and lighter toward the middle. Mix Burnt Umber with black and create a dark shadow behind the ear.

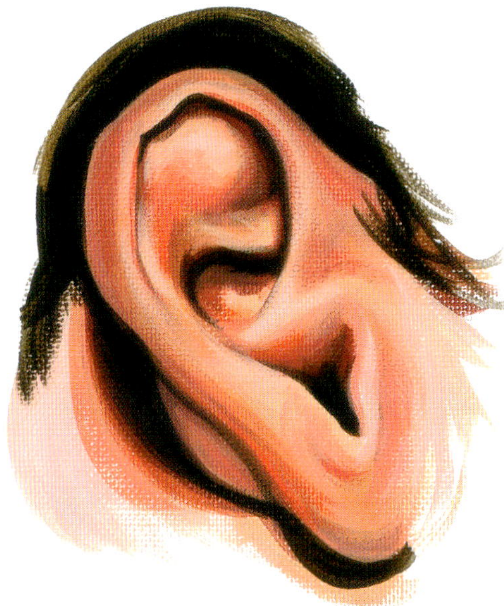

3 FINISH

Continue layering and blending the colors of the ear with the light complexion skin tones. Look for the areas of light and dark.

Use white and the no. 3/0 liner to add the fine highlights to the edges and the protruding areas.

From the Back

PIGMENTS
Alizarin Crimson, Burnt Umber, Cadmium Red Medium, Cadmium Yellow Medium, Ivory Black, Titanium White

BRUSHES
Nos. 1 and 2 round
No. 3/0 liner

The lighting here makes the highlight areas on the front of the ear very intense and creates a beautiful cast shadow. Notice how the shape of the ear is replicated in the shape of the shadow.

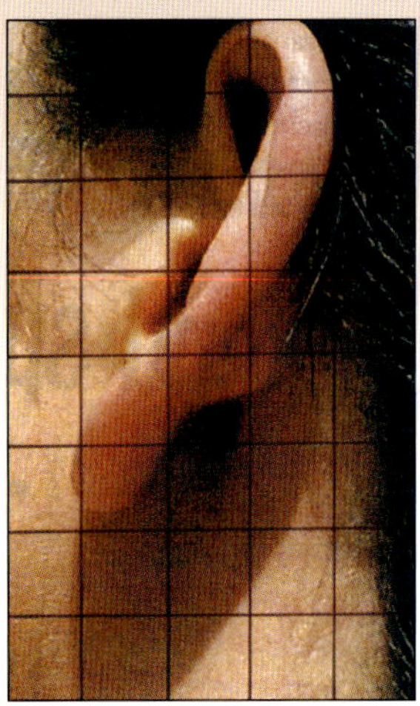

Reference Photo
Use the grid method to capture this ear on your canvas paper.

Light Complexion Warm
Follow the instructions on page 23 to mix light, medium and dark versions of this peach color.

Add Burnt Umber and Alizarin Crimson to the mixture to create the shadows.

This ear has a lot more light areas, so lighten the values accordingly by using more white.

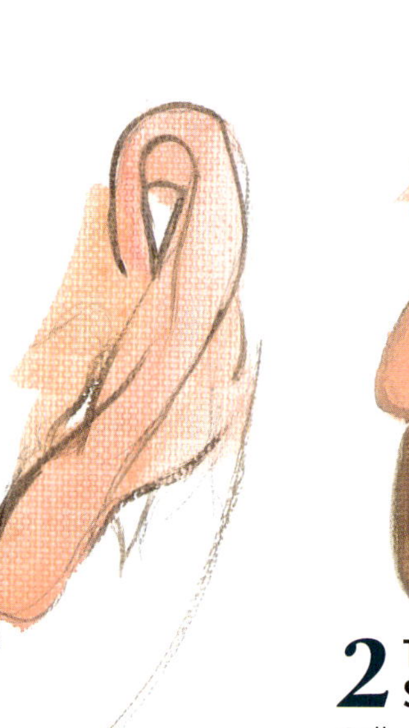

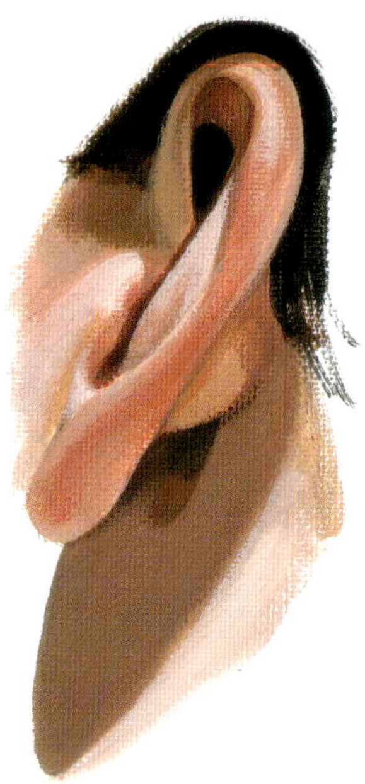

1 HALFTONES AND OUTLINE

With a diluted application of the medium peach mixture, base in the entire ear with the no. 2 round allowing the pencil lines to show. Add Alizarin Crimson and Burnt Umber to the mixture to get the cool shadow colors. With the no. 1 round, outline the inner shapes of the ear with the cool colors.

2 THE AWKWARD STAGE

Still using the no. 2 round, build the values with a thicker application of paint, making them lighter on the front of the ear. With a diluted mixture of Burnt Umber, Alizarin Crimson and a touch of white, apply the cast shadow of the ear.

3 FINISH

Continue layering and blending the colors of the ear with the light complexion skin tones. Look for the areas of light and dark. Add the illusion of hair behind the ear with Burnt Umber and black.

Use white and the no. 3/0 liner to add the fine highlights to the edges and protruding areas. Add highlights to the edges, rims and areas that protrude.

From the Front

PIGMENTS
Alizarin Crimson, Burnt Umber, Ivory Black, Titanium White

BRUSHES
No. 1 round
No. 3 filbert

Most portraits are viewed from the front, so this is the view you will most likely paint. Here, you will not use any of the standard skin tone mixtures from page 23. Just mix as you go for this variation.

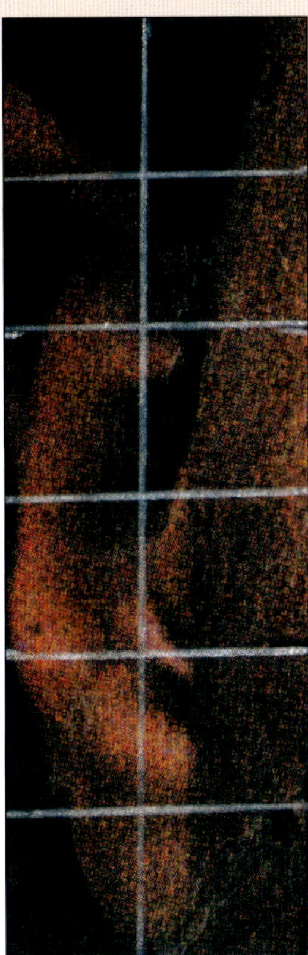

Reference Photo

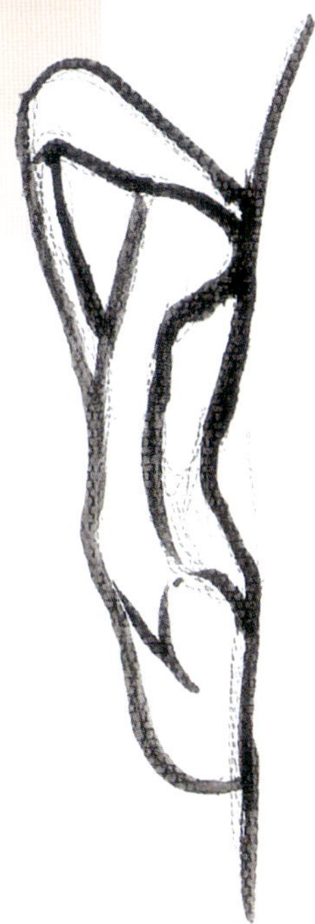

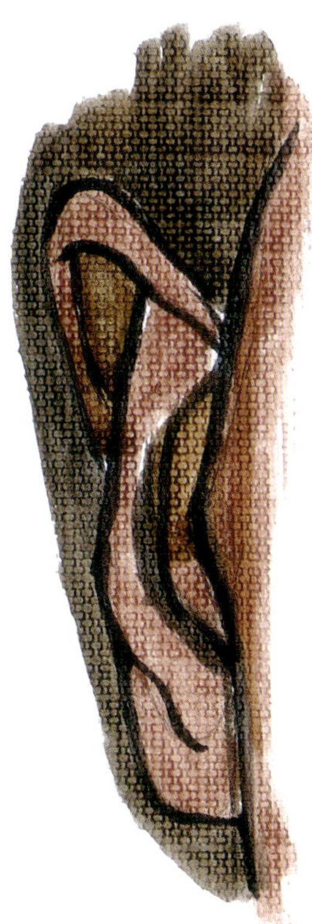

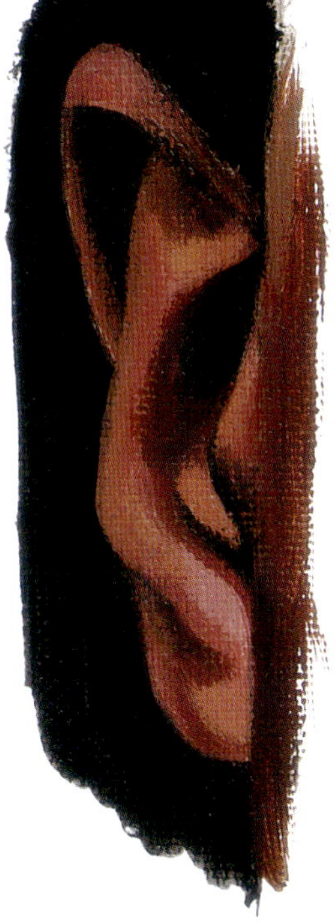

1 OUTLINE

With the no. 1 round, outline the edges and shapes of the ear with black.

2 THE AWKWARD STAGE

Mix a diluted Burnt Umber with a touch of Alizarin Crimson. Wash in the skin tone using the no. 3 filbert. Wash in the background and hair area with pure Burnt Umber using the no. 3 filbert as well.

3 FINISH

Using the no. 3 filbert and the skin tone colors from the previous step, cover the canvas as you create the shadows by adding more Burnt Umber to the skin tone mixture. Shadows occur anywhere areas recede, such as the inside of the ear and on the shadow edge of the earlobe.

Switch to the no. 1 round and add a touch of white to the skin tone mix for the highlights on the edges of the ear and any areas that protrude.

Completely fill in the background and hair with Burnt Umber. Using a circular motion and the no. 3 filbert, add a touch of black.

Painting Hair

Before you pull the entire face together into a portrait, it is important to know how to paint hair. No matter how well you paint the face, if the hair is not executed in a realistic way, the painting will look unfinished.

With all paintings, it is very important to have the face finished first. You need to have the color of the skin underneath the hair. If the skin color does not show through, the hair will look like an afterthought.

It takes many, many, many layers to make hair look real. Like everything else about art, it will require practice and patience!

Follow the step-by-step exercises to learn how to draw a variety of different hairstyles. While there are too many hairstyles to show everything possible, these will give you the foundation you need to create just about anything.

Hair Color

Even with a million styles and shades, the pigments that make up hair are relatively simple. Any of the samples on page 89 can be altered by adding or subtracting pigment. You can make a blonde lighter by adding more yellow or darker with more Burnt Umber. Study your subjects well, and really look at their individual hair colors. Chances are their hair is made up of multiple shades.

The more color something has in it, the more realistic it will appear. Do not be afraid of experimenting! The beauty of acrylic is if you don't like it, cover it up!

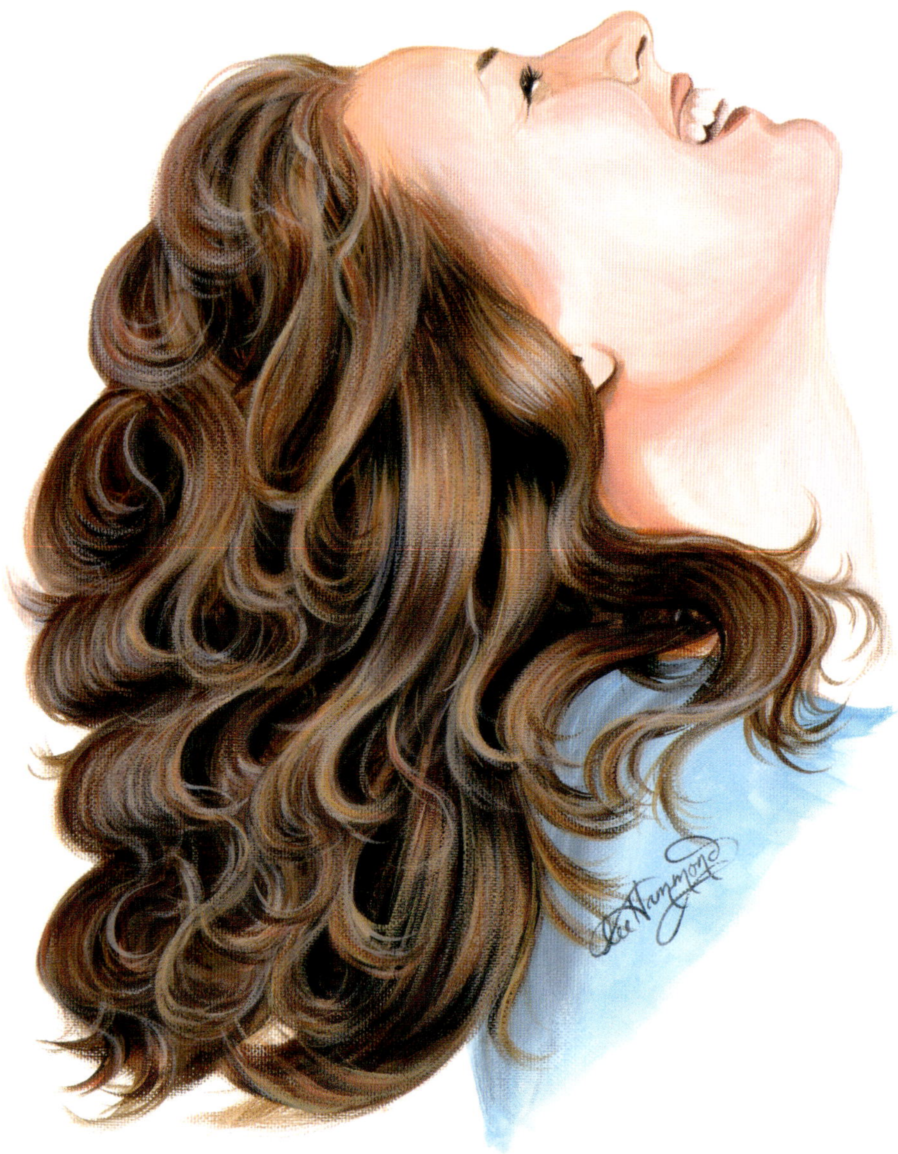

Depend on Brushstrokes and Layers for Realistic Hair
The hair is built up in many layers. Brushstrokes replicate the hair direction and give the illusion of hair strands. The more layers that you apply, the fuller the hair will appear. You can see how the waves of the hair here have been painted in layers. The brushstrokes follow the hair direction and give the illusion of hair strands.

Keys to Painting Hair

- Light hits areas that protrude.
- Hair is very shiny and reflective, so highlights are bright.
- Shadows occur where hair curves.
- Create curves with brushstrokes. I use the no. 2 filbert for undertones, then the no. 3/0 liner for strand details.

Blonde Mixtures

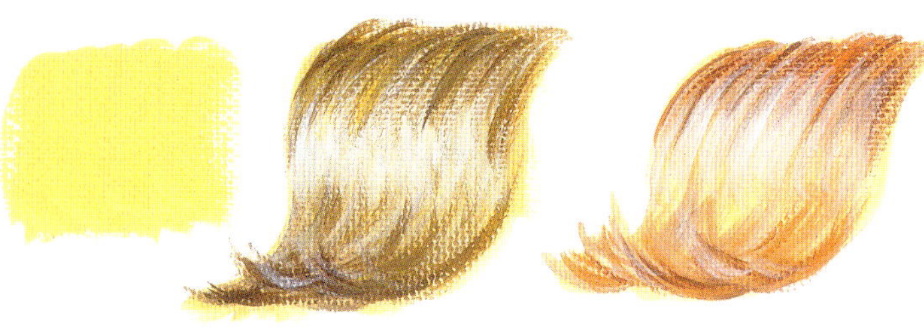

Yellow Undertone = Titanium White + Touch of Cadmium Yellow Medium
I use this mixture for most blonde, light brown and red hair. I basecoat with this for blonde hair colors.

Yellow Undertone + Burnt Umber
Hair colors will change according to how much light and shadow is on them. Use more Burnt Umber in darker areas. Use white for highlights.

Yellow Undertone + Cadmium Red Medium
This makes red hair. To deepen it, add a little Burnt Umber. Again, this color can be lightened or darkened by adding or subtracting color.

Brown Hair Mixtures

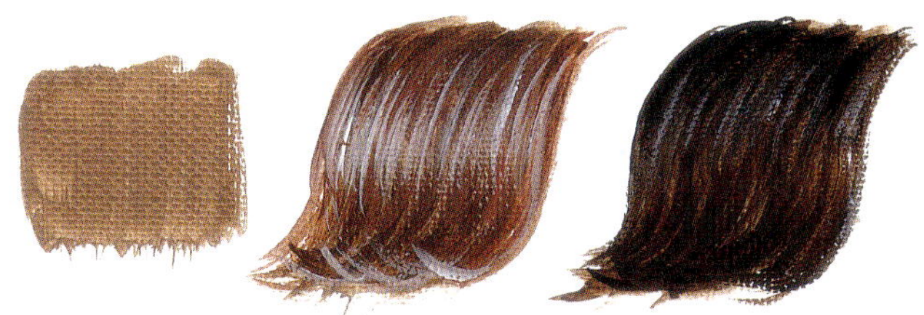

Brown Undertone = Titanium White + Touch of Burnt Umber
I use this for brunette hair.

Brown Undertone + Touch of Cadmium Red Medium
This creates warm brown hair. The dark areas are mostly pure Burnt Umber.

Brown Undertone + Touch of Ivory Black
This makes deep brown hair. For both examples, use white for the highlight areas.

Gray Hair Mixtures

Gray Undertone = Titanium White + Touch of Ivory Black
This is the undertone for gray hair.

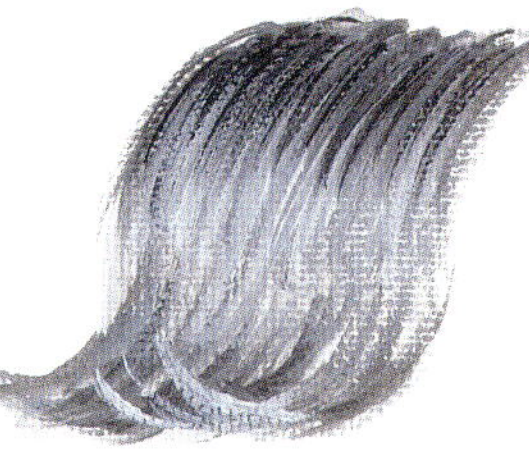

Even Amounts of Black and White
This gives the look of steel gray hair.

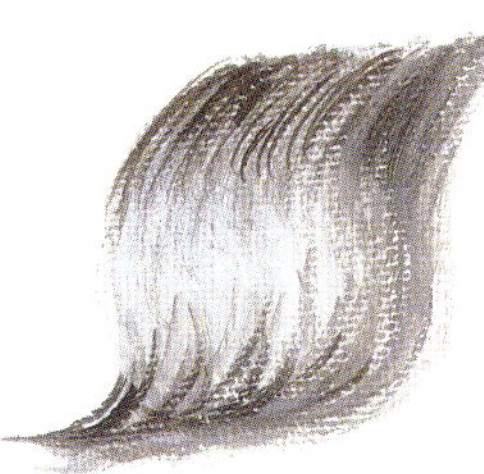

Gray Undertone + Touch of Burnt Umber
This makes a brownish cast for salt and pepper hair.

Gray Undertone + Touch of Prussian Blue
The blue cools the gray for bluish-gray hair.

Black Hair Mixtures

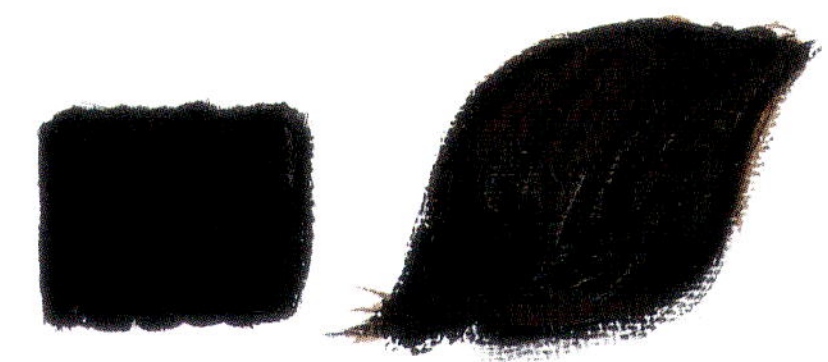

Black Undertone = Ivory Black
The following examples show a warm black and a cool black.

Ivory Black + Touch of Burnt Umber
A warm black is a shade that has a touch of brown in it.

Ivory Black + Touch of Prussian Blue and Titanium White
When outdoors, very dark hair will reflect some blue from the sky, making a cool black.

Short and Straight

PIGMENTS
Burnt Umber, Cadmium Yellow Medium, Titanium White

BRUSHES
No. 3 filbert
No. 3/0 liner

Straight hair that curves often shows up in children's styles. This style illustrates a very important feature, which I refer to as the *band of light*. The highlights that encompass the shape of the head depicts the head's roundness. The dark areas are where the hair curls under or bends as it comes out of the part.

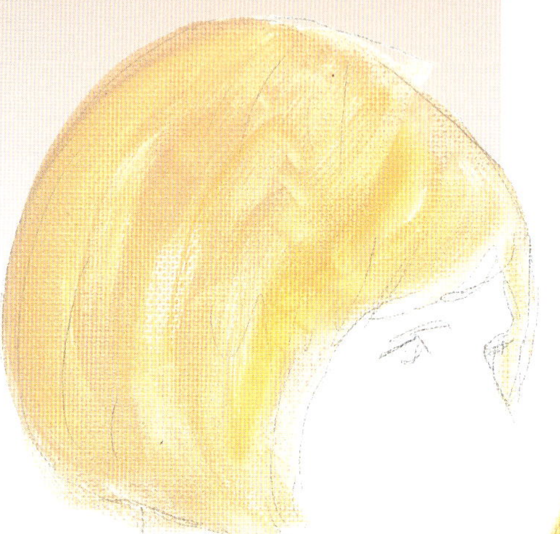

1 UNDERTONES
Basecoat the hair in with a light mixture of Titanium White tinted with a touch of Cadmium Yellow Medium and Burnt Umber using the no. 3 filbert. Curve your brushstrokes with the shape of the hair.

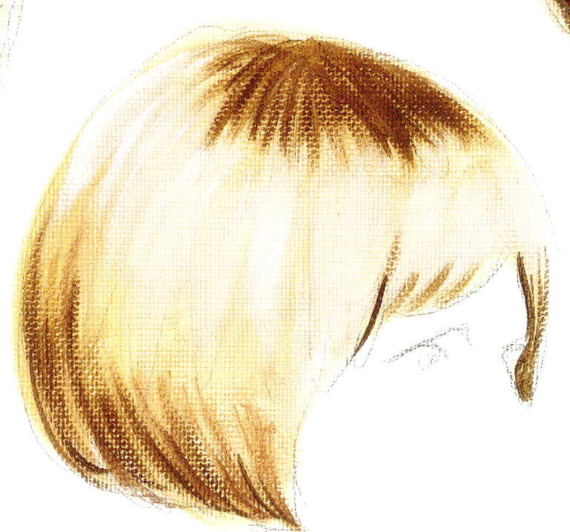

2 THE AWKWARD STAGE
To establish the band of light, add a bit more Burnt Umber to the yellow mixture to create the dark areas. With the no. 3/0 liner, use quick strokes to add the dark mix to the top of the head where the part is. Develop the tone following the hair direction, stopping midway.

Now, stroke upward from the tips of the hair to develop the curve. Leave the midsection light.

Add Titanium White to the band of light using the same brush and stroke.

3 FINISH
Keep using the no. 3/0 liner as you keep applying layers of light and dark until the two work together. Layer them together; do not allow them to stop abruptly. It must look smooth and continual. The more layers you add, the fuller the hair will appear.

Short and Gray

PIGMENTS
Burnt Umber, Ivory Black, Titanium White

BRUSHES
No. 3 filbert
No. 3/0 liner

This is a typical short hairstyle. Even though it does not encompass the head like the style before, it still curves and has a band of light.

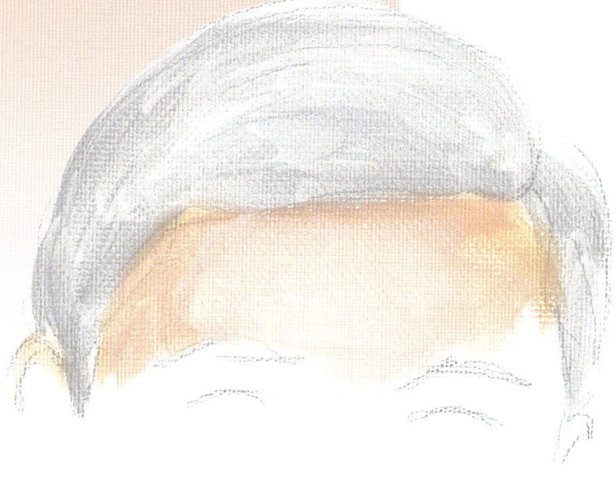

1 UNDERTONE
Basecoat the shape of the hair with the gray undertone using the no. 3 filbert. Even though this is a light application, make sure your strokes still represent the direction of the hair.

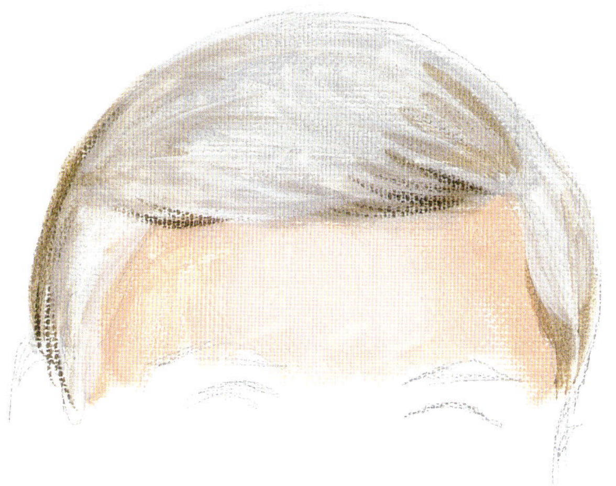

2 THE AWKWARD STAGE
This gray hair has the salt and pepper look. Add a touch of Burnt Umber to the mixture, and apply it to the darker areas using the no. 3/0 liner and quick strokes.

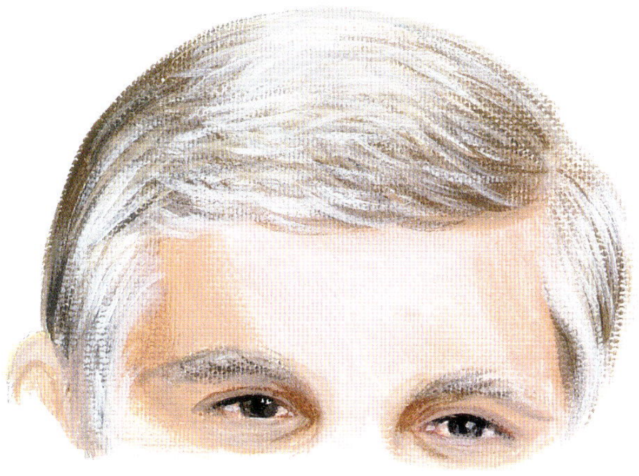

3 FINISH
Still using the no. 3/0 liner, add layers of dark gray (gray undertone plus Burnt Umber) and Titanium White for highlights until the band of light is developed and the shape of the hair seems rounded and full. The brushstrokes must represent the length of the hair.

Wavy and Layered

PIGMENTS
Burnt Umber, Cadmium Red Medium, Cadmium Yellow Medium, Titanium White

BRUSHES
No. 3 filbert
No. 3/0 liner

This hair is a bit more complicated due to the layered cut and the natural wave. See how it curves over the ear? Let your brushstrokes create this look.

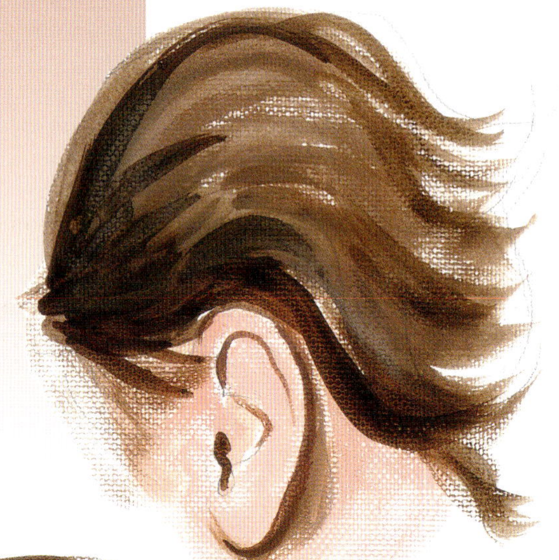

1 UNDERTONE
Add a touch of Burnt Umber to diluted Titanium White with the no. 3 filbert and diluted Burnt Umber to fill in the hair area with curved brushstrokes. Use less paint toward the back where the light hits.

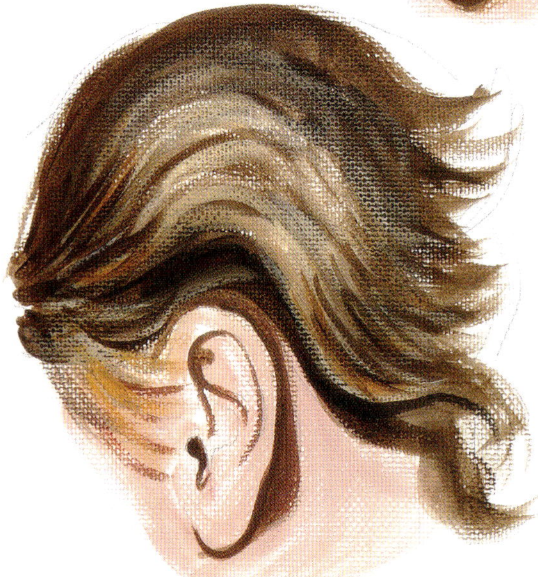

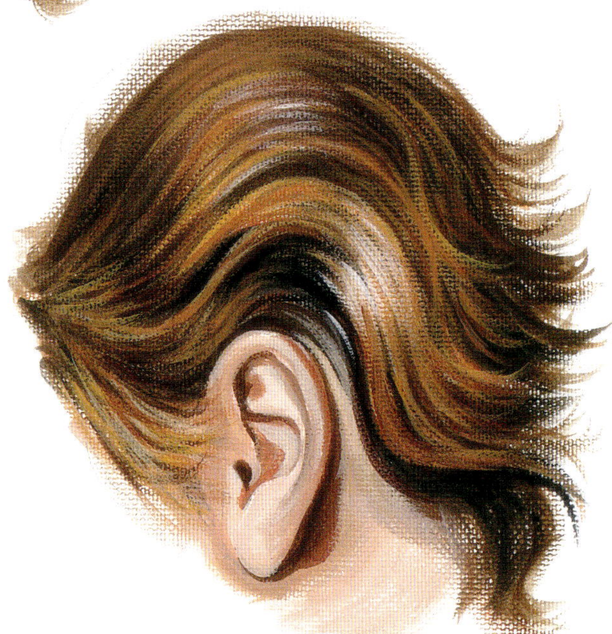

2 THE AWKWARD STAGE
Switch to the no. 3/0 liner and add a little Cadmium Red Medium to the Burnt Umber for a reddish tint. Use curved brushstrokes. Begin the band of light in the curve by adding a touch of Cadmium Yellow Medium and Burnt Umber to Titanium White for a dull white.

3 FINISH
Still using the no. 3/0 liner, add layers with quick strokes. Add more of the red and a little Cadmium Yellow Medium to the brown to make the hair look reflective and shiny. Overlap the ends to make it appear more wispy and layered.

More Layers

PIGMENTS
Burnt Umber, Cadmium Red Medium, Cadmium Yellow Medium, Titanium White

BRUSHES
No. 3 filbert
No. 3/0 liner

This hair is very similar in color to the previous exercise. Use quick brushstrokes to get this extremely layered look.

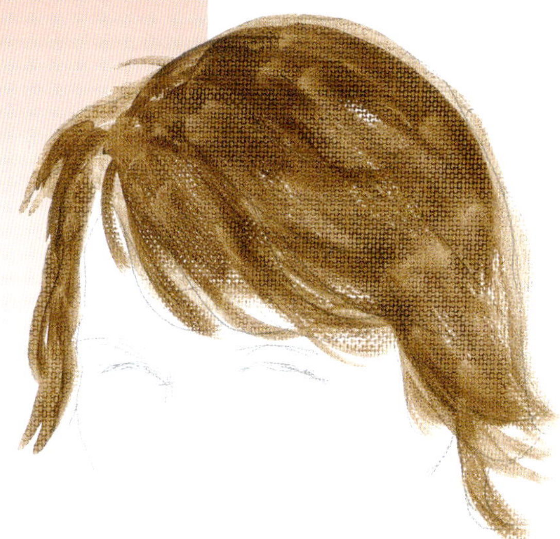

1 UNDERTONE
Basecoat the overall hair shape with diluted Titanium White with a touch of Burnt Umber using the no. 3 filbert. Make sure your brushstrokes go in the direction of the layers to create the foundation.

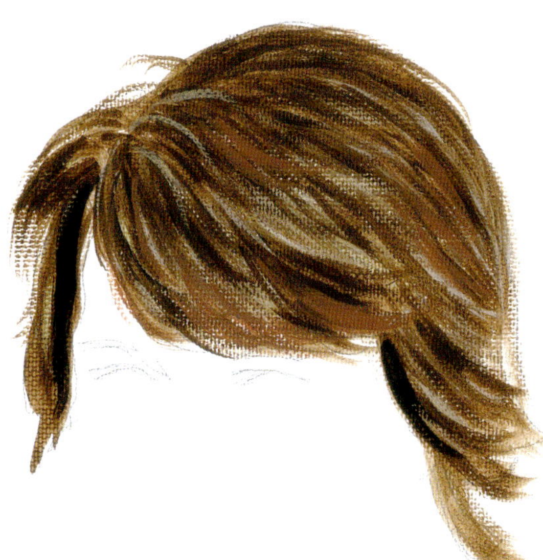

2 THE AWKWARD STAGE
With the no. 3/0 liner, add lights and darks. Add some Cadmium Red Medium to the brown mixture for a warm, reddish cast. Alternate light and dark using quick strokes to build the look of many layers.

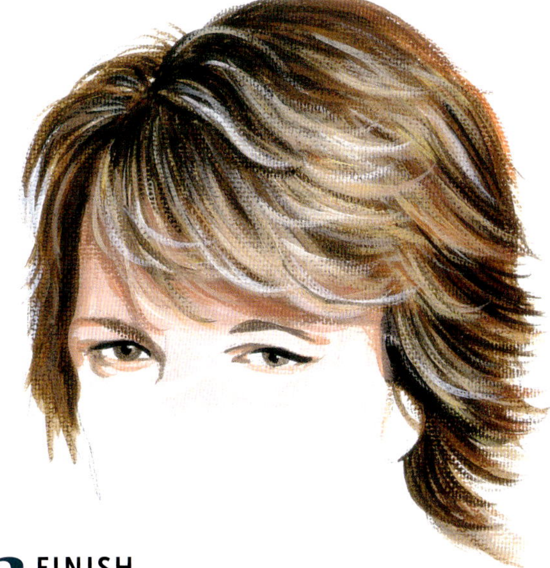

3 FINISH
The band of light is visible on the right side. Mix Titanium White with a small touch of Cadmium Yellow Medium for the highlights. Use the no. 3/0 liner to add some Cadmium Red Medium to the light mixture for the red tones. The strokes must be quick at the tips to make the hair strands taper at the ends and appear wispy. You do not want harsh, thick strokes!

Long and Wavy

PIGMENTS
Burnt Umber, Cadmium Red Medium, Cadmium Yellow Medium, Titanium White

BRUSHES
No. 3 filbert
No. 3/0 liner

Long, wavy hair is approached a little differently. You want to begin depicting the many waves before laying in any undertone.

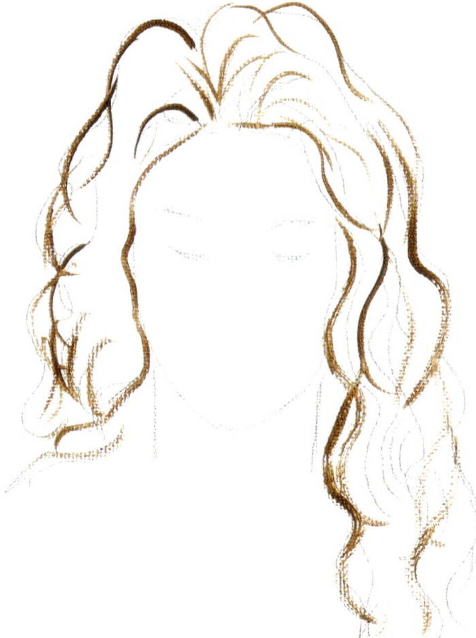

1 ADD THE WAVES
Use the no. 3/0 liner with diluted Burnt Umber to add the curves and direction of the hair. Use curved brushstrokes to represent the waves.

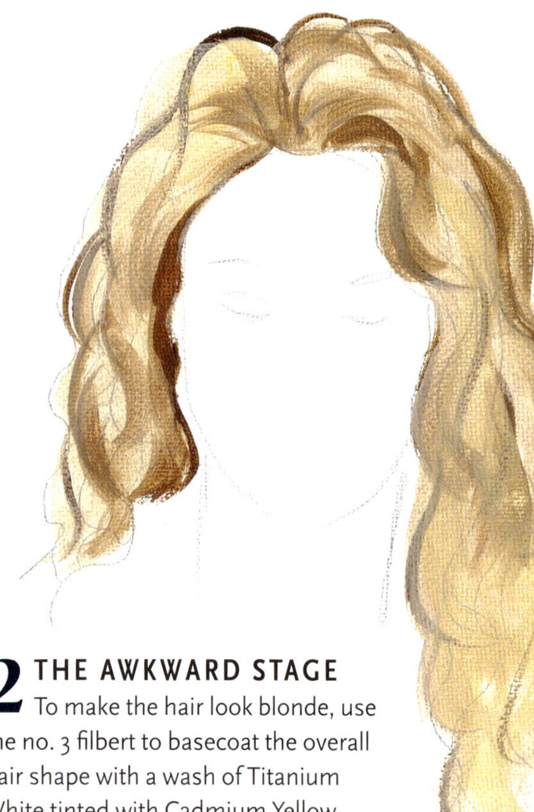

2 THE AWKWARD STAGE
To make the hair look blonde, use the no. 3 filbert to basecoat the overall hair shape with a wash of Titanium White tinted with Cadmium Yellow Medium.

3 FINISH
Apply many layers alternating among the different blonde color mixtures (page 89) to make the hair look full and thick. Use the no. 3/0 liner, mimicking the waviness of the hair. Add Burnt Umber underneath to make it look shadowed around the neck and behind the ear.

To give the hair the frosted look, mix a little Burnt Umber into Titanium White.

Coarse and Dark

PIGMENTS
Alizarin Crimson, Burnt Umber, Ivory Black, Prussian Blue, Titanium White

BRUSHES
No. 3 filbert
No. 2 round

To create this type of hair, you'll use the scrubbing and dabbing techniques (page 28). The results are amazingly realistic.

It is very important to establish the skin tone on the forehead and to allow it to show underneath the hair. Once the face is finished, you can base in the dark hair color.

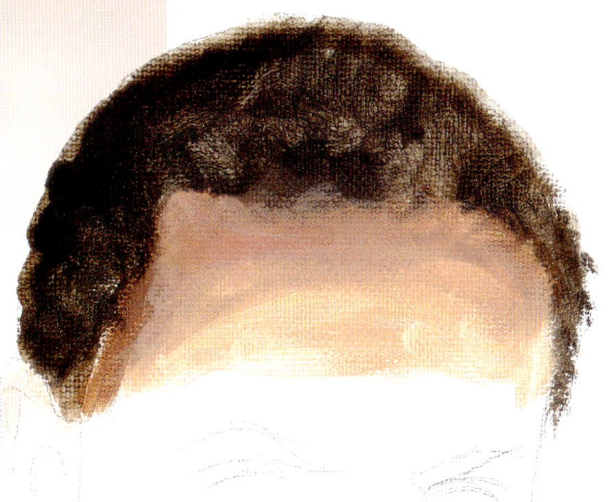

1 UNDERTONE
Use the dark complexion cool skin tone mixture (page 23) and the no. 3 filbert to apply the color to the forehead. Bring the color well up into the hairline and scalp area, for it will show through.

After scrubbing Burnt Umber into the hair area with circular strokes, repeat the process with some diluted black.

With the no. 3 filbert and diluted Burnt Umber, scrub in the entire hair area with small, circular strokes. Use the brush a little on the side.

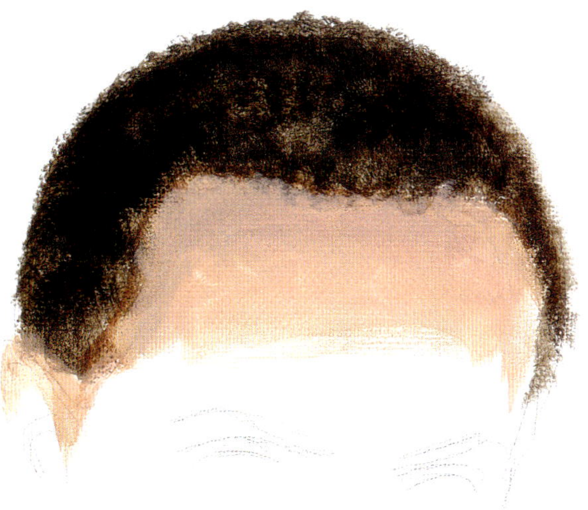

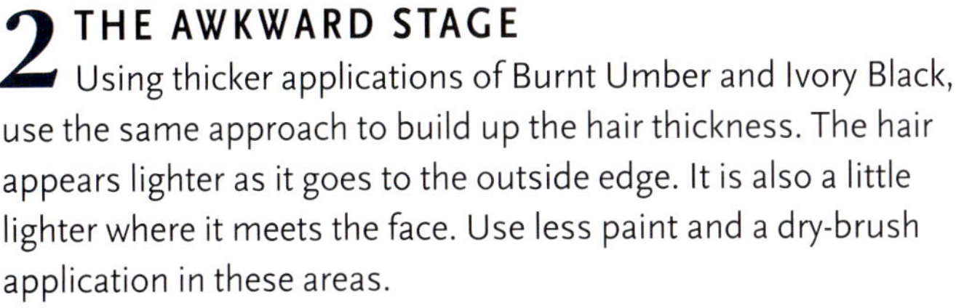

2 THE AWKWARD STAGE
Using thicker applications of Burnt Umber and Ivory Black, use the same approach to build up the hair thickness. The hair appears lighter as it goes to the outside edge. It is also a little lighter where it meets the face. Use less paint and a dry-brush application in these areas.

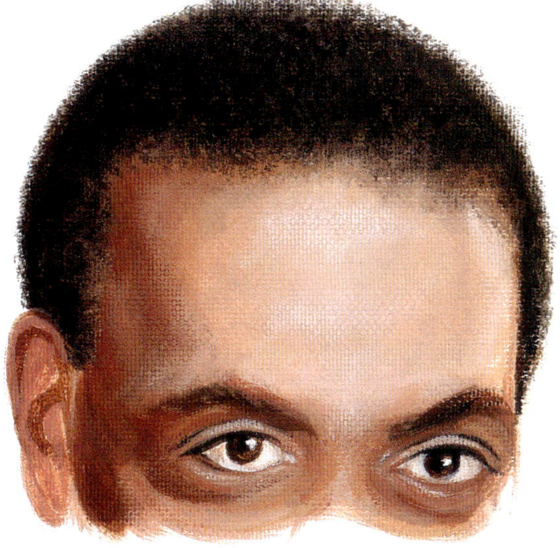

3 FINISH
To make the hair appear full and fluffy, use less paint and dab the hair with a dry-brush approach. This type of hair is not as reflective, so there won't be an obvious band of light. But it still has subtle areas of light and dark. Dab some of the skin tone into the area where the hair meets the face. Lighten the Burnt Umber with a tiny bit of Titanium White and dab this into the top of the head using the no. 2 round.

This is one of my favorite portraits. It is of my friend Mark, who is a successful country singer. The sideways glance and large smile tells us he's looking at something out of our view that is bringing him joy. Artwork should make you think and evoke a mood.

I used the background to replicate his personality, one that is lively and dynamic. The streaking brushstrokes liven up the painting. A traditional smooth background would have been contrary to the pose, and would not have nearly the same impact.

MARK KNIGHT
16" x 12" (41cm x 30cm)
Created from an image by Jarrett Gaza, photographer

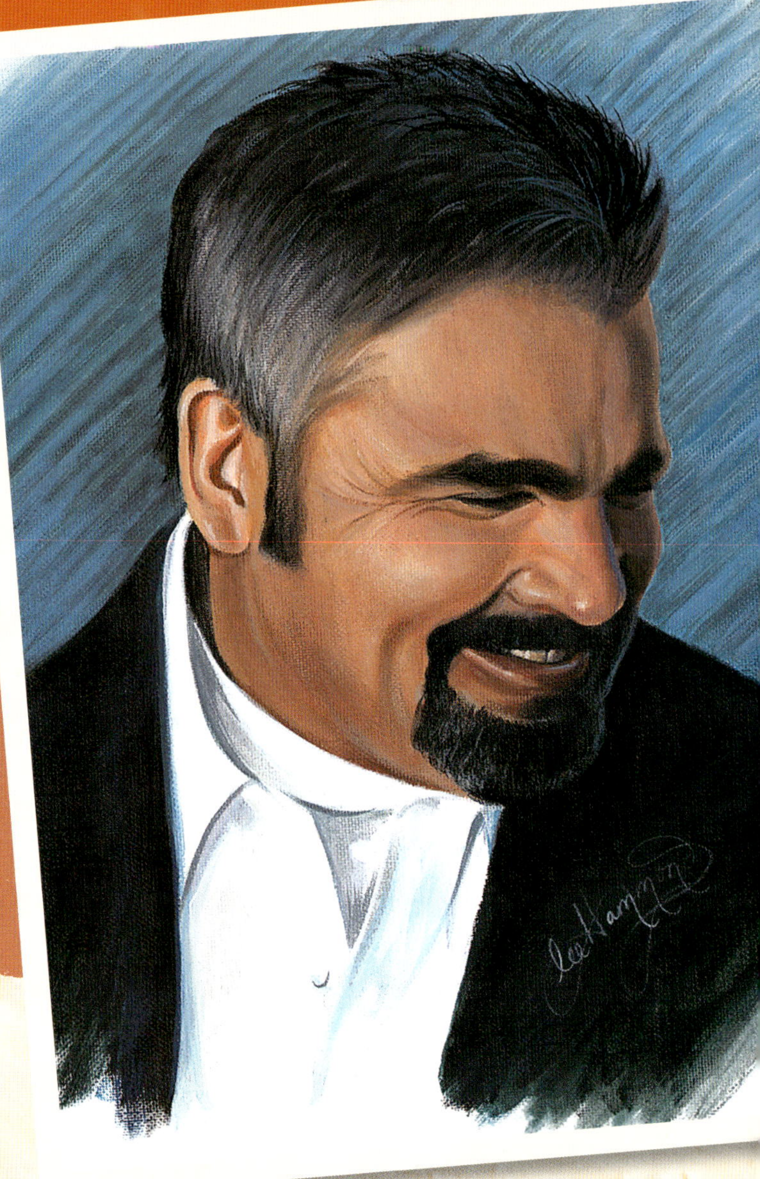

PART 3

PAINTING THE FULL PORTRAIT

The previous chapters have taught you all the basics for good portrait painting. If any of the material still seems difficult, go back and practice before beginning these full portrait exercises. It requires practice and more practice. You might also consider reviewing my book, *How to Draw Lifelike Portraits From Photographs* (North Light 1995).

Once you feel comfortable, you can forge ahead! Take the line drawings you created in Part One and follow along. Have fun!

Backview

PIGMENTS
Alizarin Crimson, Burnt Umber, Titanium White

BRUSHES
No. 1 round
No. 3 filbert
No. 2 flat
No. 3/0 liner

Use the line drawing you created on page 38 to complete this painting. It is a fairly easy project that requires little color and very few facial features due to the pose.

Practice creating this value scale using the three colors before you begin.

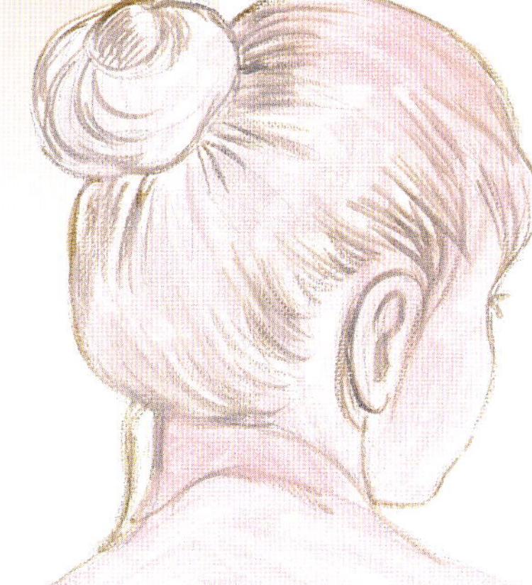

1 UNDERTONE AND OUTLINE

First outline the entire form with diluted Burnt Umber and the no. 3/0 liner.

Using the no. 3 filbert, basecoat the entire form with a very light pink color made by mixing a small touch of Alizarin Crimson into Titanium White.

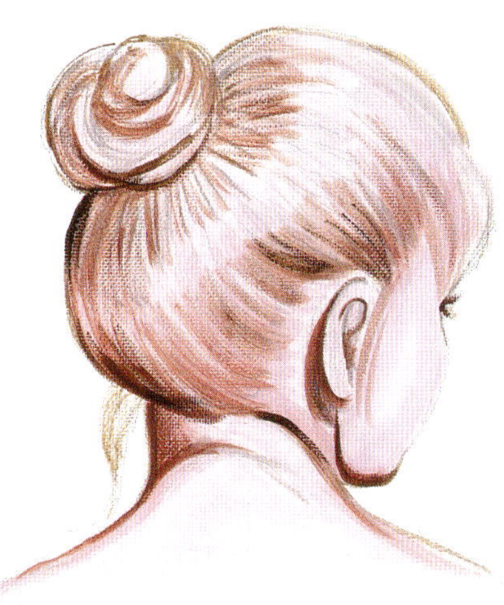

2 THE AWKWARD STAGE

Add more Alizarin Crimson and a touch of Burnt Umber to the pink mixture to create a shadow color. Use this and the no. 1 round to develop the shadows on the chin, behind and in the ear, and on the back of the neck. Use the no. 3/0 liner for smaller areas like along the edge of the chin and inside the ear.

With the same mixture, develop the direction of the hair, including the band of light on both the head and the bun.

3 FINISH

Mix a brighter pink (Titanium White with more Alizarin Crimson than before) to make the skin tones seem warmer. Add this on the outside edges of the shadows to give the skin tone a warm glow and make the shadow areas seem less harsh.

Use a no. 2 flat to drybrush some white highlights into the face and shoulder areas to gently fade the white into the pink.

Detail the hair with the no. 3/0 liner and quick strokes that follow the hair direction. Use pure Burnt Umber for the dark areas and pure white for the bright highlights.

It will take many layers to create this hair, so do not quit too soon!

Shadow Study

PIGMENTS
Ivory Black, Prussian Blue, Titanium White

BRUSHES
Nos. 1 and 2 round
No. 3 filbert
No. 3/0 liner

This is a fun painting and it does not require a lot of time. It is good for instant gratification! Take the line drawing from page 39, and follow along.

Practice creating this value scale using the pigments above before you begin.

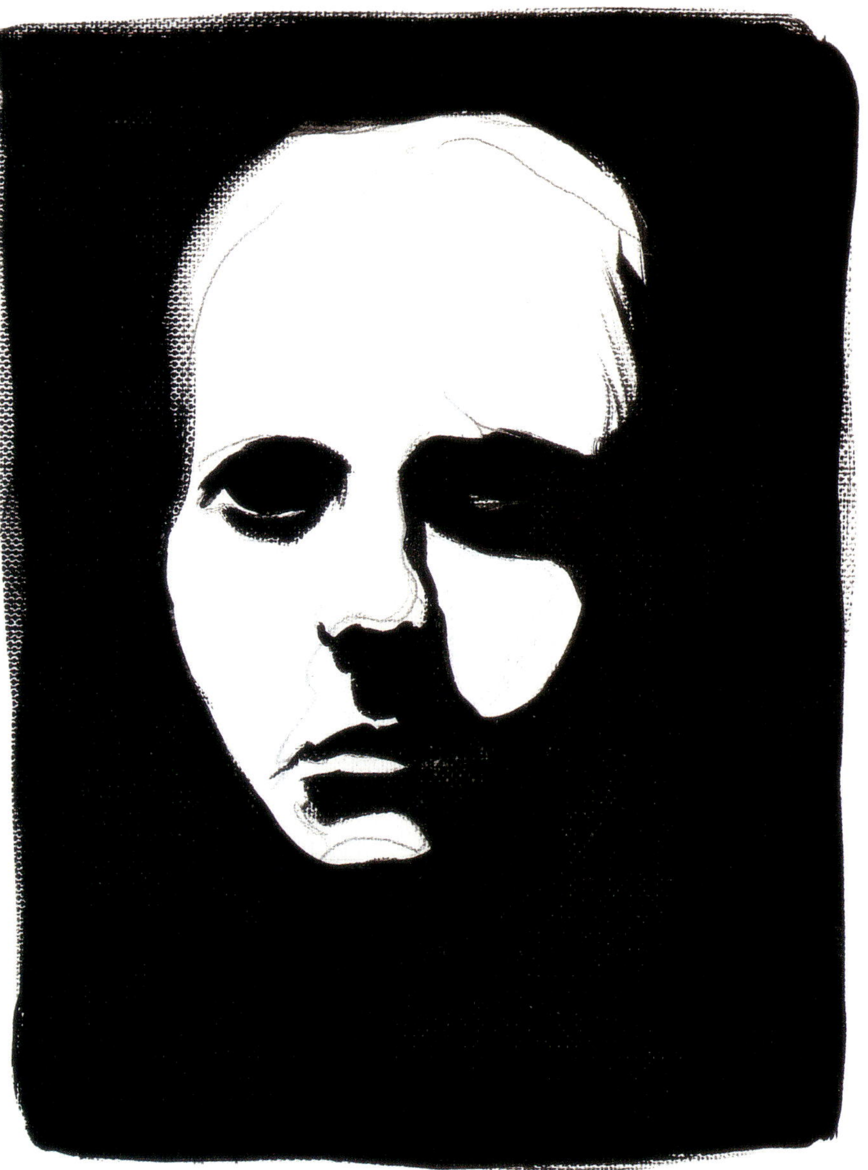

1 BEGIN WITH BACKGROUND AND DARK FACIAL FEATURES

With Ivory Black and the no. 3 filbert, fill in the entire background with black, leaving the face. Switch to a small no. 1 round and fill in the features of the face as shown. It looks very abstract at this stage. Resist the temptation to put in more detail than you need.

2 THE AWKWARD STAGE

Fill in the entire face area with Titanium White using the no. 3 filbert.

Add a touch of Ivory Black along with a touch of Prussian Blue to Titanium White to create a middle tone of cool blue-gray for the halftone area of the face. Refer to the value scale on page 98 for guidance. This is the color that transitions the bright white and pure black together. Allow the color to remain more gray than blue. Prussian Blue is very strong, so if it is too blue, add more black and white to tone it down. Apply this mixture with the no. 2 round around the edges of the features as shown.

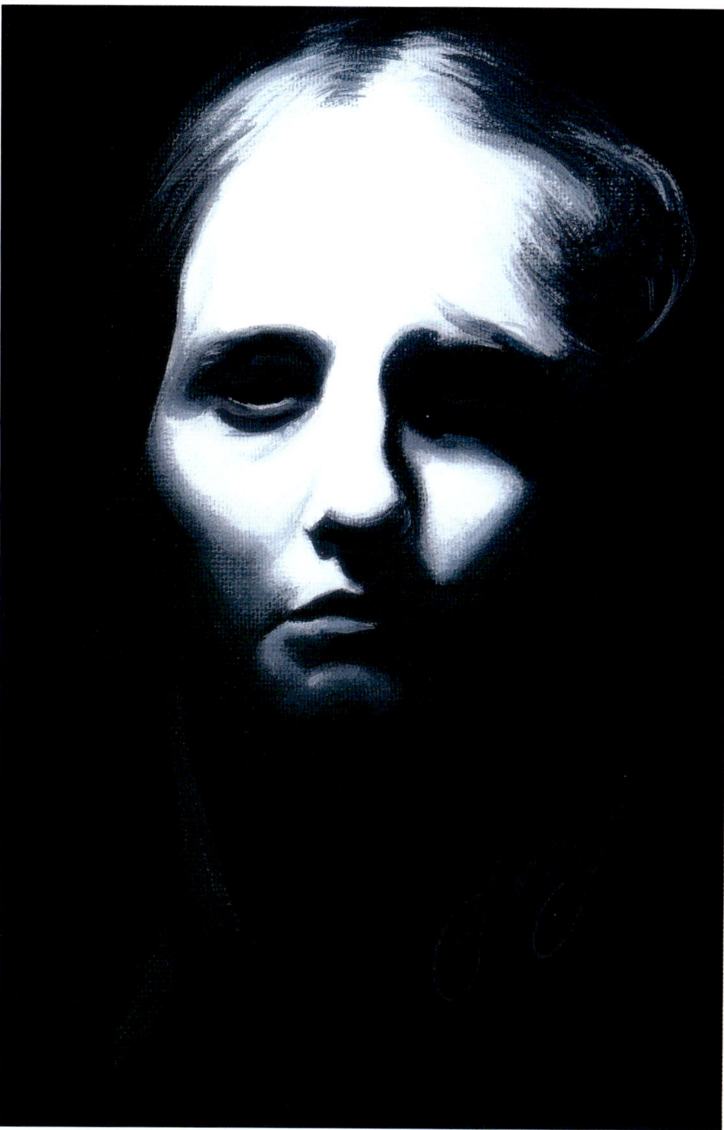

3 FINISH

To finish, you want to soften the tones together. Add a touch of white to the middle blue-gray color that you mixed for step 2 to make it a couple of tints lighter. Add it along the inside edge of the features with the small no. 2 round. Drybrush to gently blend this color into the white. If it still appears choppy, use pure white and drybrush it back into the color. Sometimes you will need to go back and forth to get the colors to transition well. Be patient!

Use the no. 3/0 liner to develop the illusion of hair strands coming out from the part. Alternate pulling strokes with pure white, a light blue-gray mixture and dark blue-gray mixture. The darker color should fade into the black.

Elderly Man

PIGMENTS
Ivory Black, Titanium White

BRUSHES
No. 2 round
No. 3 filbert
No. 3/0 liner

Now it's time to capture the entire face. Get the line drawing of the elderly man that you did on page 40. Be certain that your line drawing is accurate before you begin to paint. Make corrections or capture things you may have missed before you begin.

Gray Scale
Match your tones to this gray scale.

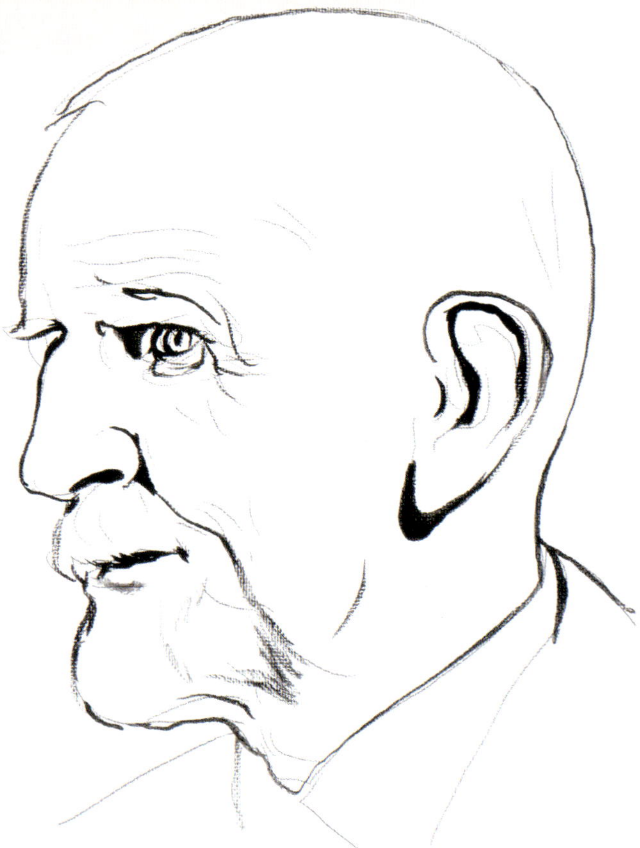

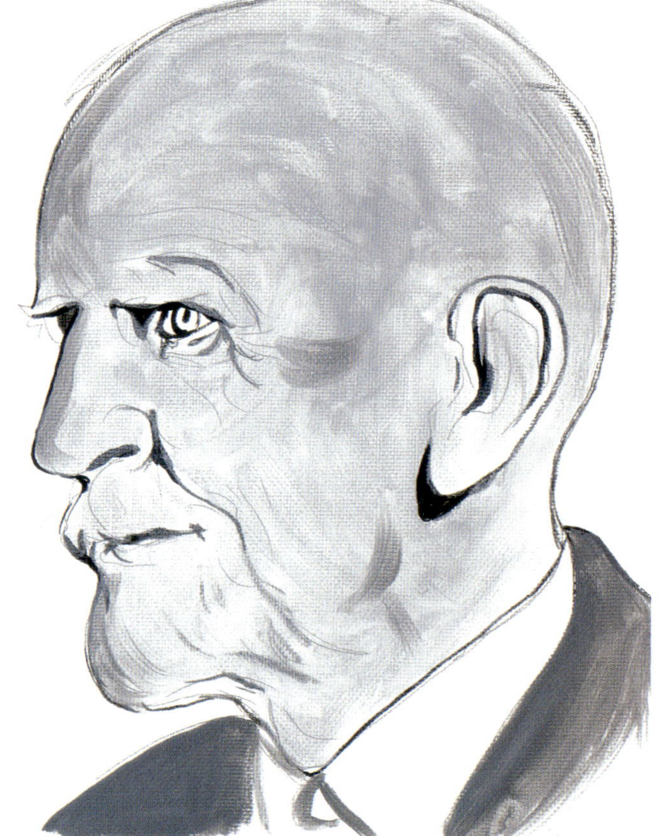

1 OUTLINE AND DARK TONES

With the no. 3/0 liner and Ivory Black, outline the subject and details. Draw with the paint, using as much accuracy as possible. This pose makes the features appear distorted, so pay attention to detail and shape. For instance, the iris in the eye is a vertical ellipse.

2 LAY THE FOUNDATION

Create a medium gray by mixing black into white. Use the no. 3 filbert and a diluted application of paint to fill in the entire face and hair area. This is the foundation of your portrait. Fill in the shoulders of the jacket.

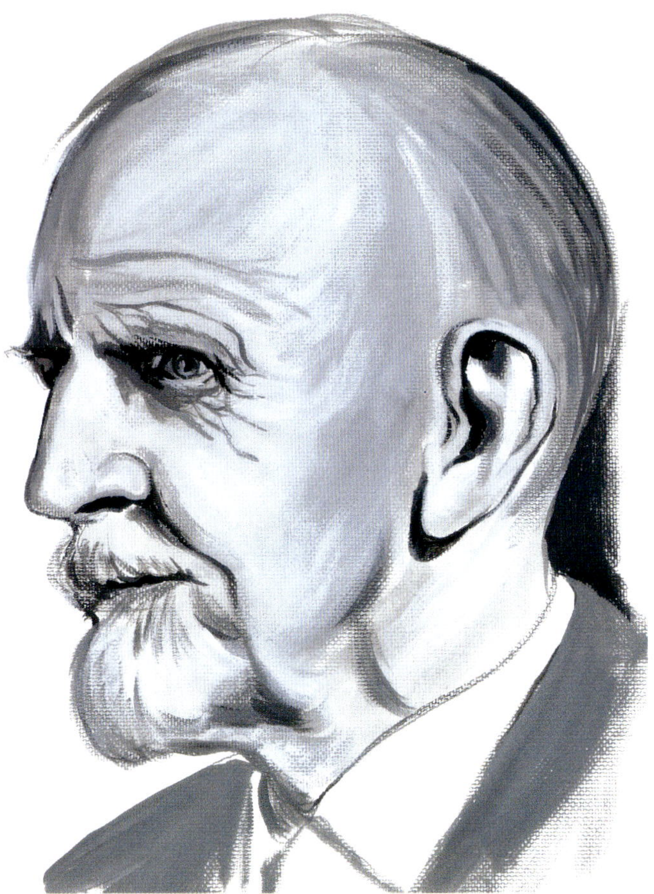

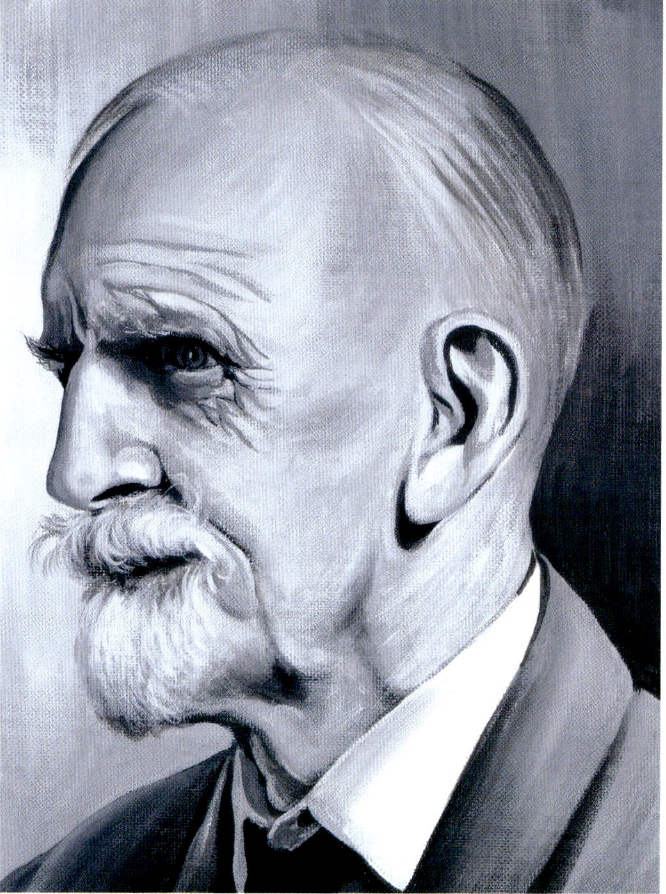

3 THE AWKWARD STAGE

This is somewhat of a rough-in stage where the tones and details are slowly evolving. Use thicker applications of medium and light gray to drybrush in the shadows and highlights of the face using the no. 3 filbert. Use the no. 3/0 liner and some medium gray to draw in the lines and creases around the eyes and forehead.

Use various tones of gray for the background. Darker backgrounds will enhance the light areas of a portrait, so place dark gray behind the light edge of the neck. Lighter backgrounds will enhance darker areas of the portrait, so place the light gray behind that.

Using the no. 3/0 liner, add the shadow areas and the color of the eye. Remember, this is a vertical ellipse.

4 FINISH

Use the no. 2 round as you take your time and slowly add the tonal changes using various shades of gray. Refer to the gray scale for comparison. Drybrush to soften each tone, creating a gradual blended appearance.

Continue building up and drybrushing together the tones of the face to get gradual transitions. Complete the background using the dark over light and light over dark technique that you began in step 3 before moving on. Allow your brushstrokes to show for an artistic look.

After you've finished the background, you can finish the moustache. Use various shades of gray to layer quick strokes of hairs with the no. 3/0 liner. Allow the small hairs to overlap into the background.

Complete the jacket, using the same light against dark technique and allowing your brushstrokes to show.

Baby

PIGMENTS

Alizarin Crimson, Burnt Umber, Cadmium Red Medium, Cadmium Yellow Medium, Ivory Black, Prussian Blue, Titanium White

BRUSHES

Nos. 1 and 2 round
No. 3 filbert
No. 3/0 liner

Now it is time to dive into a full-color situation. Even though thc color mixtures may be a bit more difficult, the approach and procedure will remain the same. Take the line drawing of the baby from page 41, and follow along.

Even though this baby has a dark complexion, the youthfulness of the skin keeps it light.

Light Complexion Cool
Follow the instructions on page 23 to mix light, medium and dark versions of this skin tone. Add more white to lighten the values further.

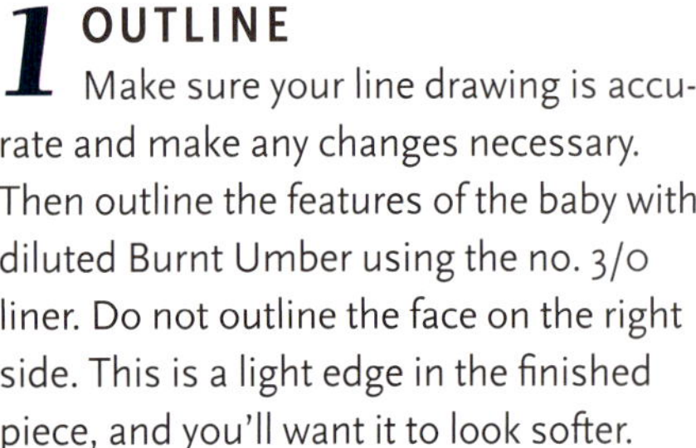

1 OUTLINE

Make sure your line drawing is accurate and make any changes necessary. Then outline the features of the baby with diluted Burnt Umber using the no. 3/0 liner. Do not outline the face on the right side. This is a light edge in the finished piece, and you'll want it to look softer.

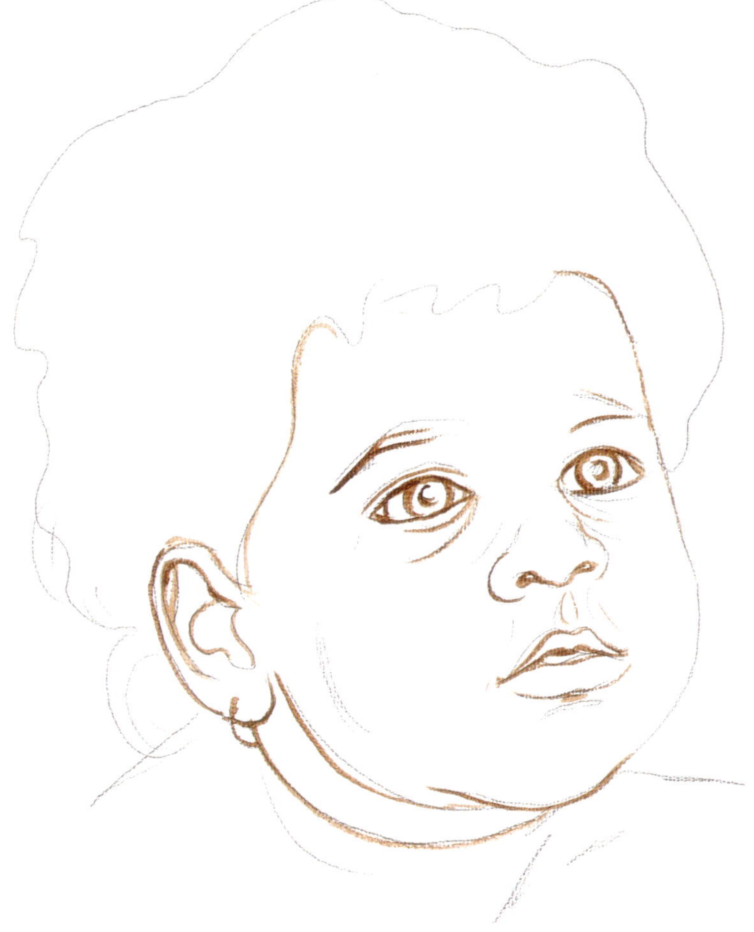

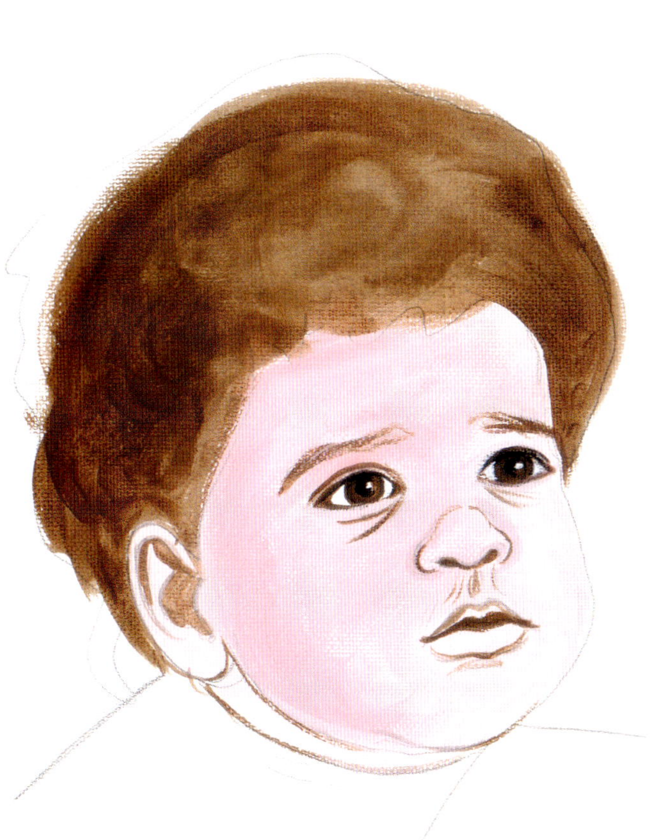

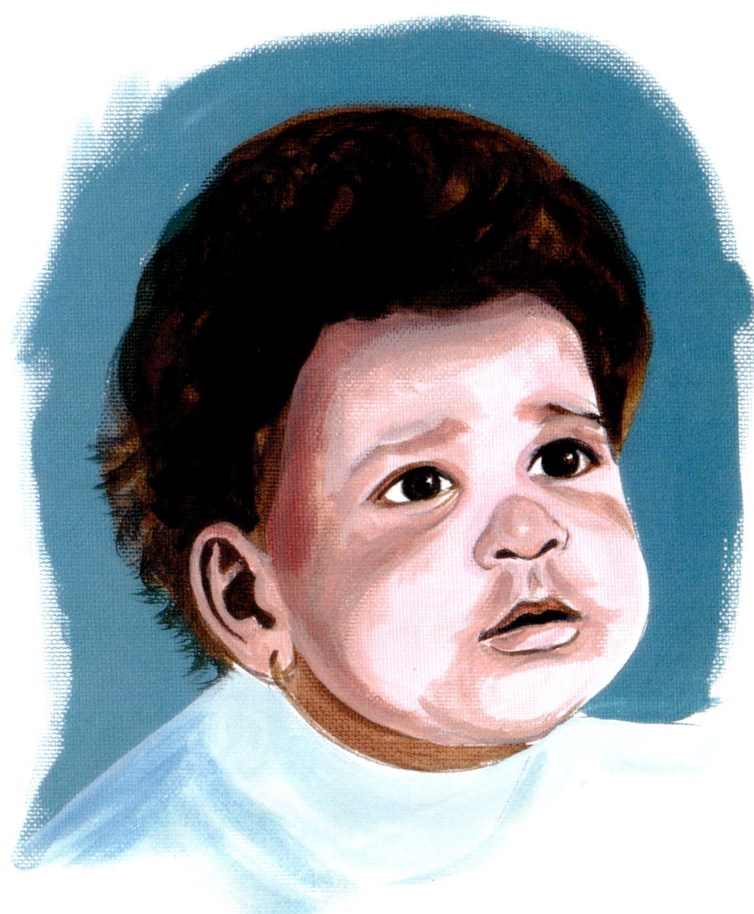

2 CREATE BASE TONES

Mix a touch of Alizarin Crimson into Titanium White to get a base tone pink. Fill in the entire face and neck area with this color using the no. 3 filbert.

With a diluted application of Burnt Umber, fill in the hair area using the no. 2 round. Don't worry about the curls right now. They go in after the background color has been applied.

Use the no. 3/0 liner to fill in the iris of the eye with Burnt Umber and the pupil with black. Leave the small areas for the catchlight. Fill in the inside of the ear with diluted Burnt Umber.

3 THE AWKWARD STAGE

This is where things look pretty choppy. You are building the five elements of shading for roundness. This baby's face strongly resembles the sphere. Add the contours with the cool shadow colors made by mixing Burnt Umber, Alizarin Crimson and Titanium White using the no. 2 round. Apply this to the neck and the contours of the face.

Mix an aquamarine color using Titanium White, Prussian Blue, and a small amount of Cadmium Yellow Medium and lay in the background using the same brush. Basecoat the shirt with a lighter version of that background color. This makes it look like a light-colored shirt reflecting the surroundings.

Using the no. 1 round with Burnt Umber and Ivory Black, create the fullness of the hair and curls. Use pure Burnt Umber for the lighter areas, and add black to the paint for the shadow areas.

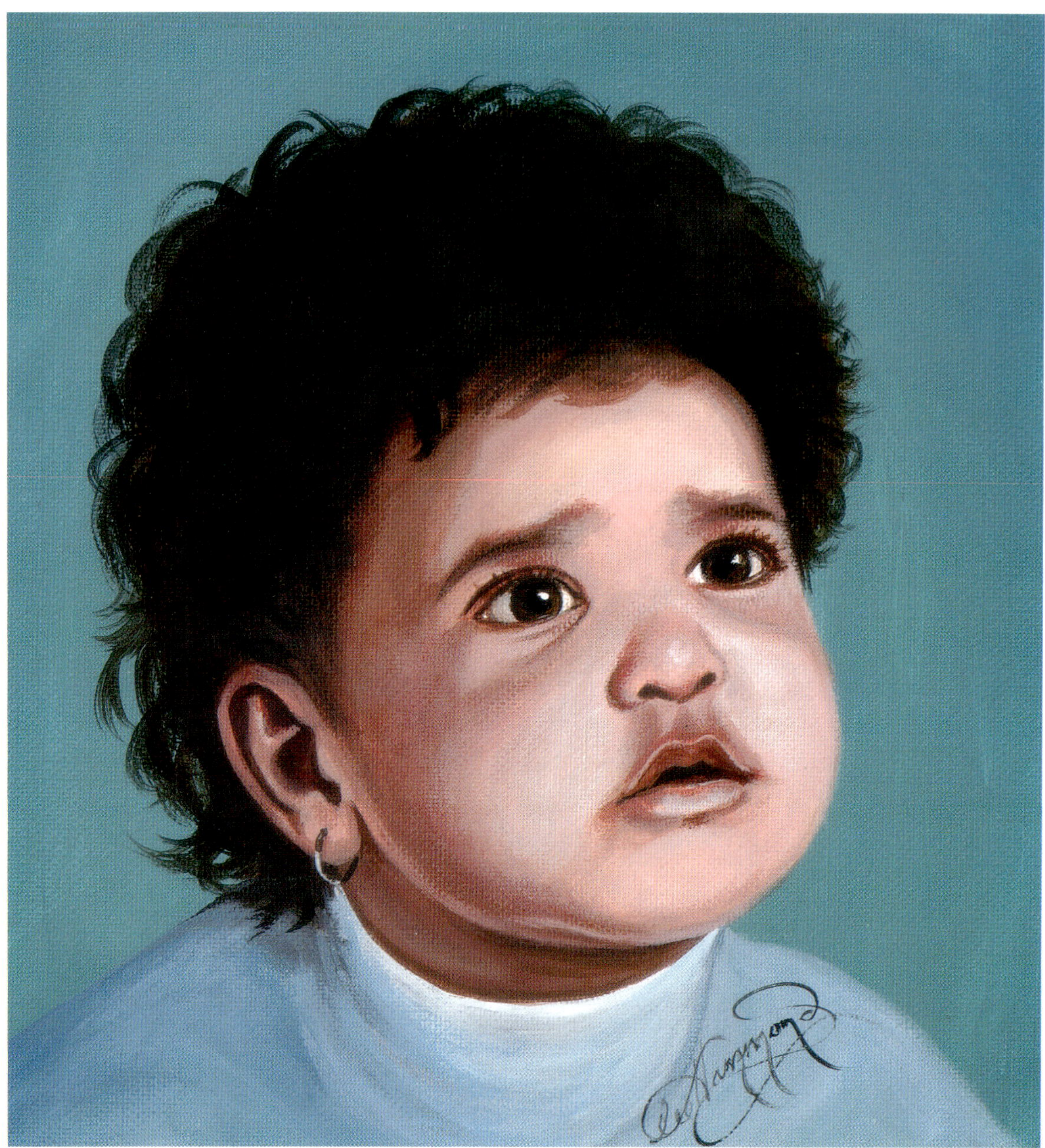

4 FINISH

Continue adding and blending the colors for a soft look. This skin has a lot of Alizarin Crimson in it, which makes a beautiful pink. The shadow areas are made with Titanium White, Alizarin Crimson, and a touch of Burnt Umber. Drybrush the colors together until the face looks smooth and spherical. Add white to Alizarin Crimson to create a reflected light mixture; use this along with pure Titanium White and the no. 1 round to add highlights to the front of the face and the tip of the nose. Be sure the reflected light is very obvious along the jawline.

Deepen the color of the hair by adding some Ivory Black to Burnt Umber. Even though the hair is very dark with not many highlights, it is still important to apply the color with the hair direction. Bring the curls out into the background.

Toddler

PIGMENTS
Alizarin Crimson, Burnt Umber, Cadmium Red Medium, Ivory Black, Prussian Blue, Titanium White

BRUSHES
Nos. 1 and 2 round
No. 1 flat
No. 3 filbert
No. 3/0 liner

Now you'll create another portrait of a youngster, but this one has a much deeper complexion. His face has more brown tones, rather than pink hues.

Use the line drawing you created on page 42 to paint this little guy. When you are sure of your accuracy, follow along.

Brown Complexion Warm
Mix Titanium White, Burnt Umber, and a touch of Cadmium Red Medium, per the directions on page 23.

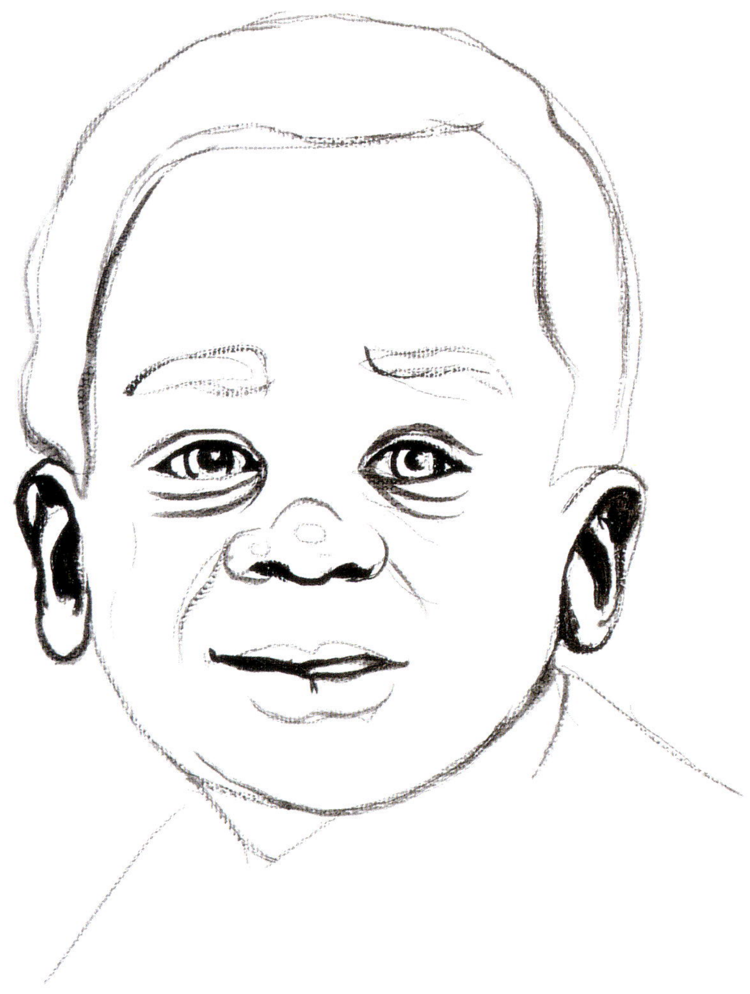

1 OUTLINE

With the no. 3/0 liner and Ivory Black, outline the features and shapes of the little boy's face.

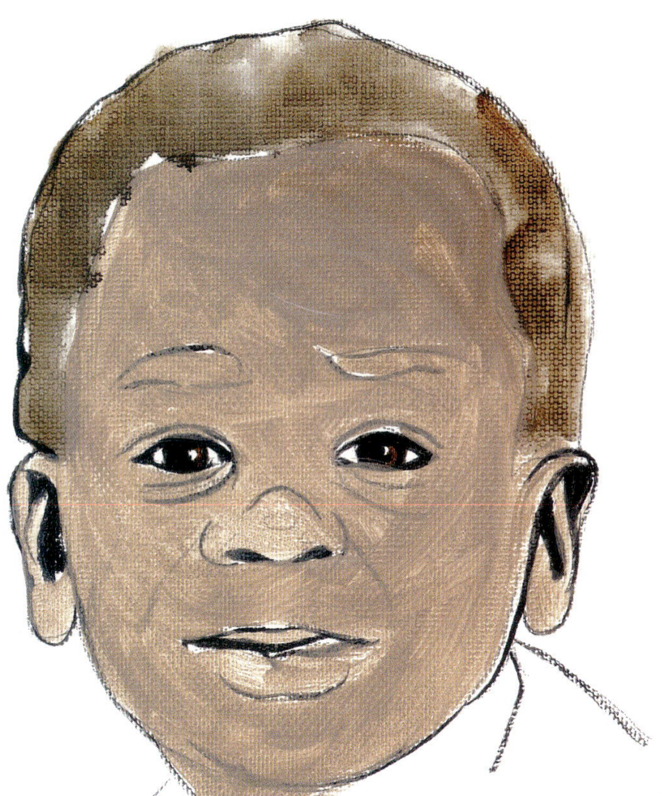

2 UNDERTONE

With a diluted mixture of Burnt Umber and a touch of Titanium White, basecoat the entire portrait using the no. 2 round. Make the area of the hair a little darker.

Fill in the iris with Burnt Umber and the no. 1 round. Fill the pupil with Ivory Black using the no. 3/0 liner. Leave a small dot in the eye for the catchlight, which is half in the iris and half in the pupil.

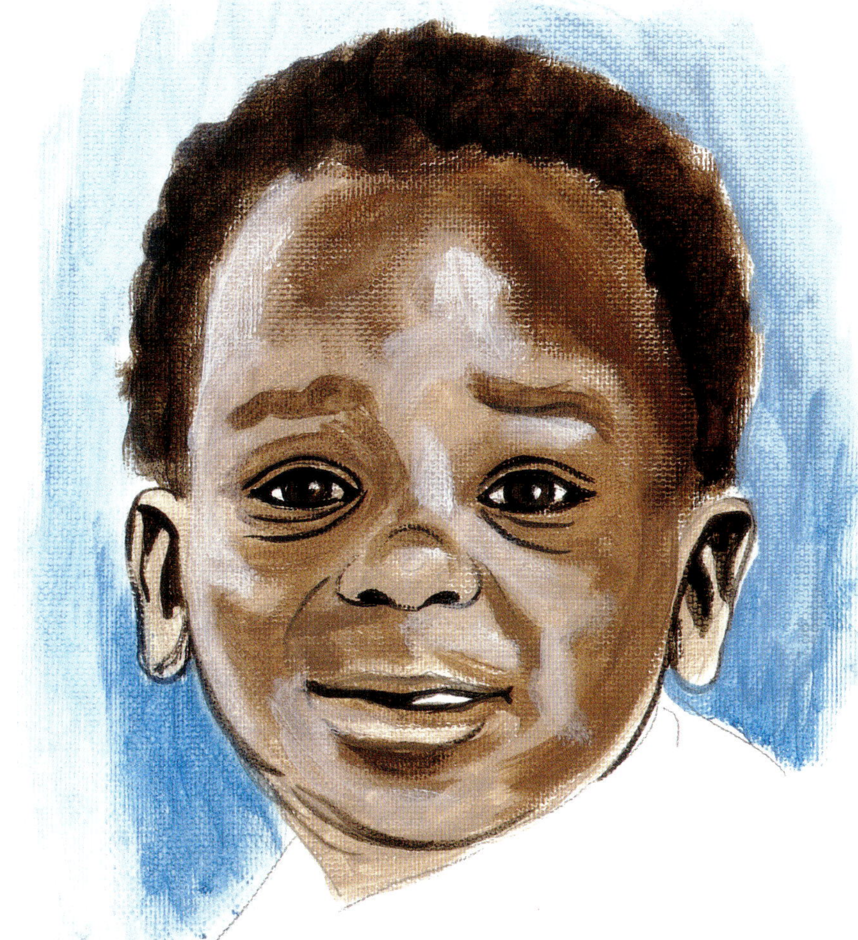

3 THE AWKWARD STAGE

Using a thicker application of Burnt Umber and Titanium White and the no. 3 filbert, develop the shadow and highlights of the face. Remember the five elements of shading. This stage of the painting creates the illusion of roundness and form. The application is still loose and choppy.

Begin the background by washing in a diluted application of Prussian Blue and the no. 3 filbert.

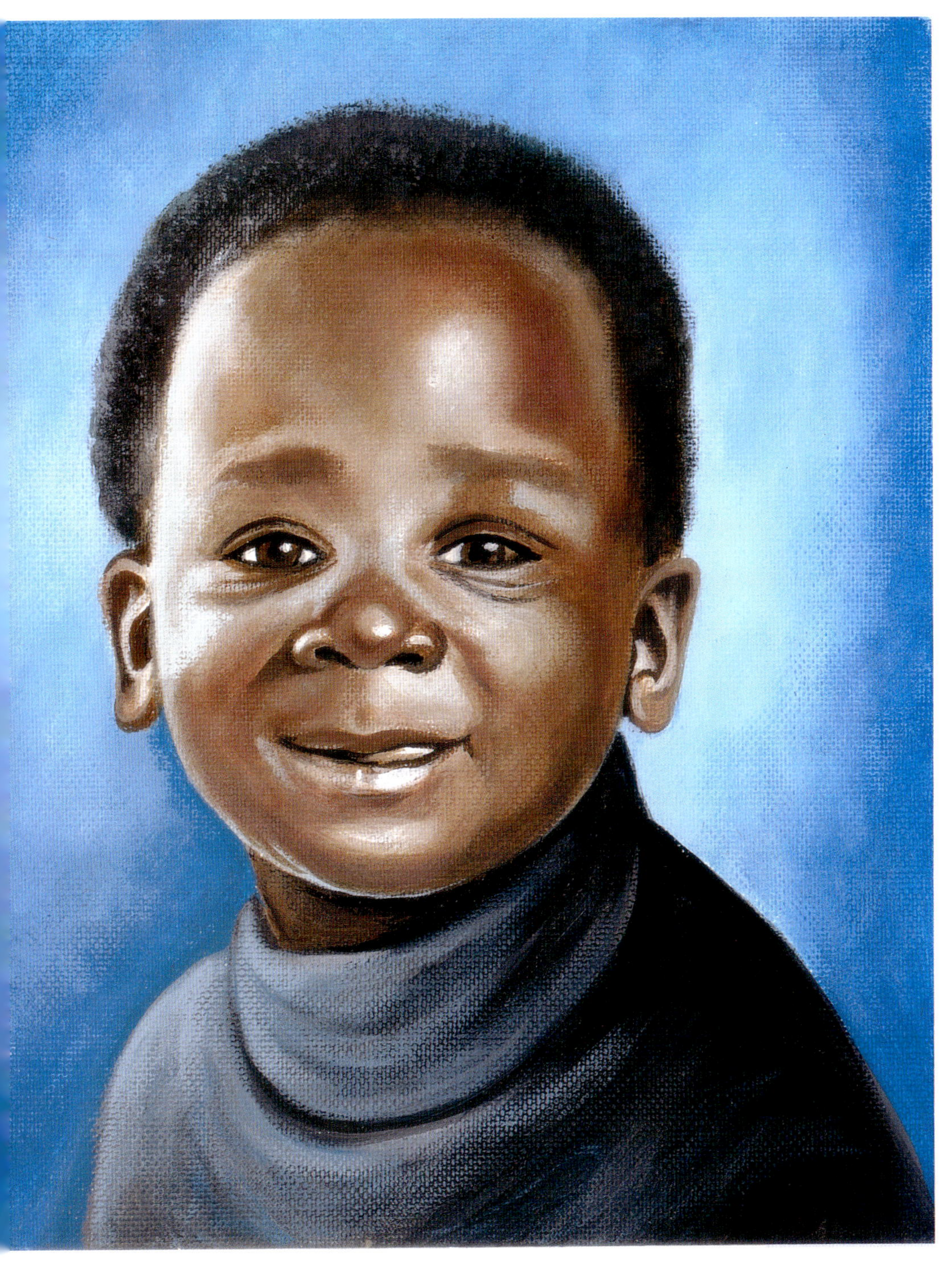

4 FINISH

Use the five elements of shading to complete his sphere-like features. The light source is on the left, so make everything darker on the right side. You'll want to use more white in the mixtures for his left side. Add more layers of paint and drybrush the colors together for a smooth look.

Use the no. 1 flat to paint in the shadow areas; add a touch of Alizarin Crimson to the brown complexion warm mix. This gives his dark skin a warm glow, and keeps it from looking monochromatic.

Make his hair fluffy using a no. 1 flat and a scrubbing motion for a dry-brush effect. Refer to the section on hair (pages 88–95) for a reference to the technique. Use just a little paint and a circular motion. Use Burnt Umber first, as a foundation. Add Ivory Black for volume. Repeat the process until it looks full and fluffy. Finally, dab some of the background color into it, as a reflecting color.

Leave his clothing as simple as possible. Using the light source as a guide, paint in a turtleneck using the no. 3 filbert and Prussian Blue mixed with Titanium White and Ivory Black. The right side is very dark, and the left side is very light.

Finish the background with the no. 3 filbert painting light over dark, dark over light.

3/4-View, Adult Female

PIGMENTS

Alizarin Crimson, Burnt Umber, Cadmium Red Medium, Cadmium Yellow Medium, Ivory Black, Prussian Blue, Titanium White

BRUSHES

Nos. 1 and 2 round
No. 3 filbert
No. 2 flat
No. 3/0 liner

This is my daughter LeAnne; we'll use her portrait for our study of an adult profile. Grab the line drawing you created on page 43, and follow along.

This is an example of a ¾-turn, along with an extreme lighting situation. The face on the right side fades into the darkness of the background. This is my favorite type of portrait.

Light Complexion Cool
Follow the instructions on page 23 to mix light, medium and dark versions of this tone. Add more white to lighten the values further.

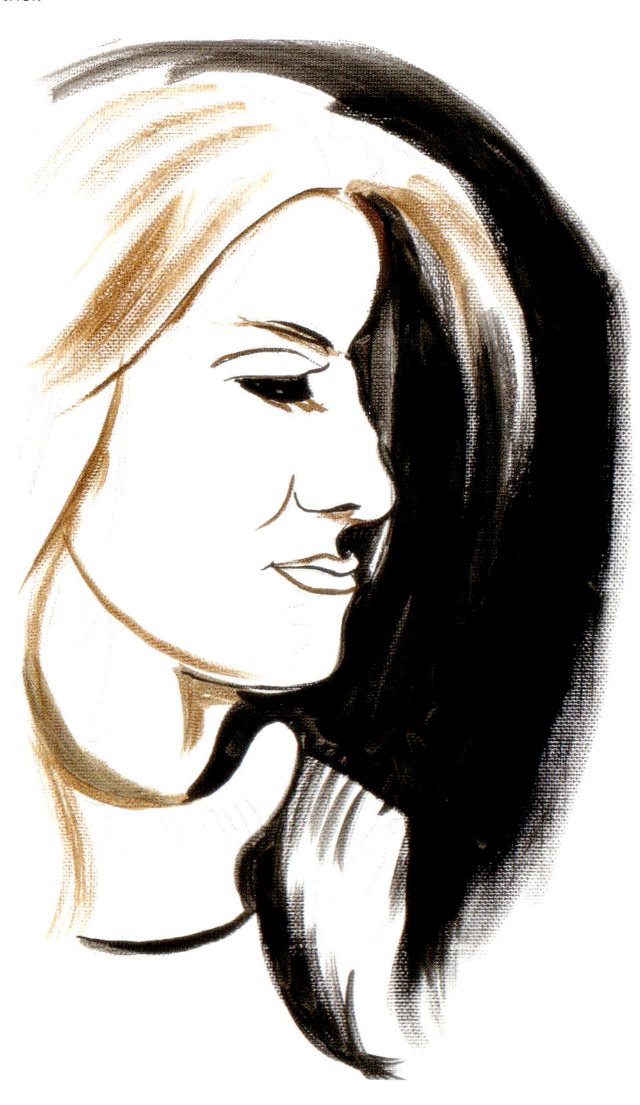

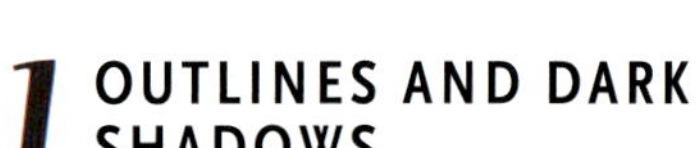

1 OUTLINES AND DARK SHADOWS

With the no. 2 round, detail the direction of the hair and the jawline with a diluted Burnt Umber. Use straight Ivory Black and the no. 3/0 liner to draw in the shapes of the lips, eyebrow and eyelash area.

Base in the background with Ivory Black and the no. 3 filbert. Allow the hair to get lost on the right side.

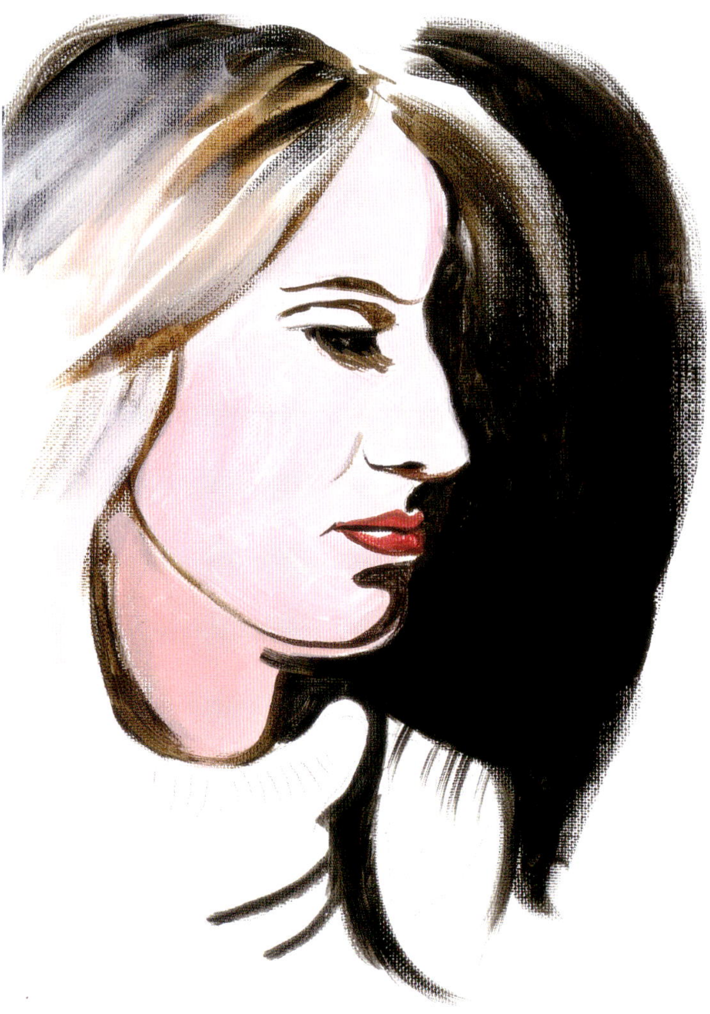

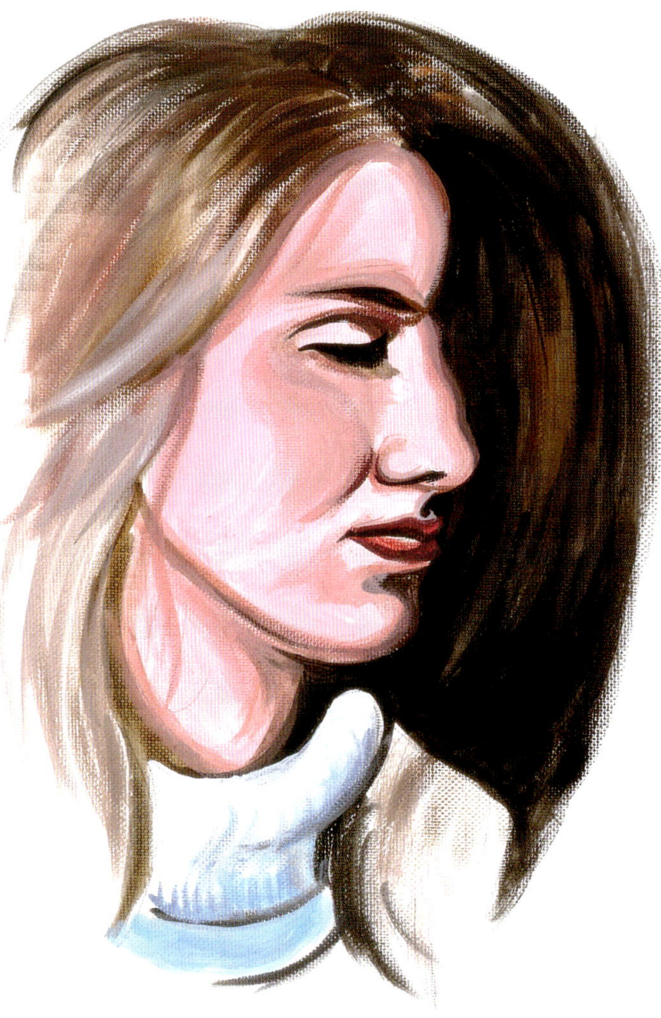

2 UNDERTONE

LeAnne's complexion is very pale. This painting is very cool in its coloration due to the very dark background. Mix a diluted application of her skin tone by adding a small amount of Alizarin Crimson into some Titanium White. Apply it to the face area with the no. 3 filbert. Her blonde hair reflects the color of her skin, so streak some of this color into her hair on the left as well.

With the no. 1 round, apply the lip color with Alizarin Crimson.

Begin her hair with Burnt Umber and the no. 2 round. Follow the direction that the hair is going with your brushstrokes. Carry some of the Burnt Umber into the dark side of the hair on the right. Allow it to fade into the black background.

Loosely wash in the rest of her hair with Ivory Black and Burnt Umber.

3 THE AWKWARD STAGE

Using the no. 2 flat and a diluted mixture of the cool complexion colors plus a little Burnt Umber, develop the contours and shadow areas of the face as shown. Look for the shadow areas in the cheek, forehead, neck, and down the bridge of the nose.

Prepare a diluted Prussian Blue and Titanium White mixture for the turtleneck. Using the no. 2 round, curve the brushstrokes, replicating the sweater's form.

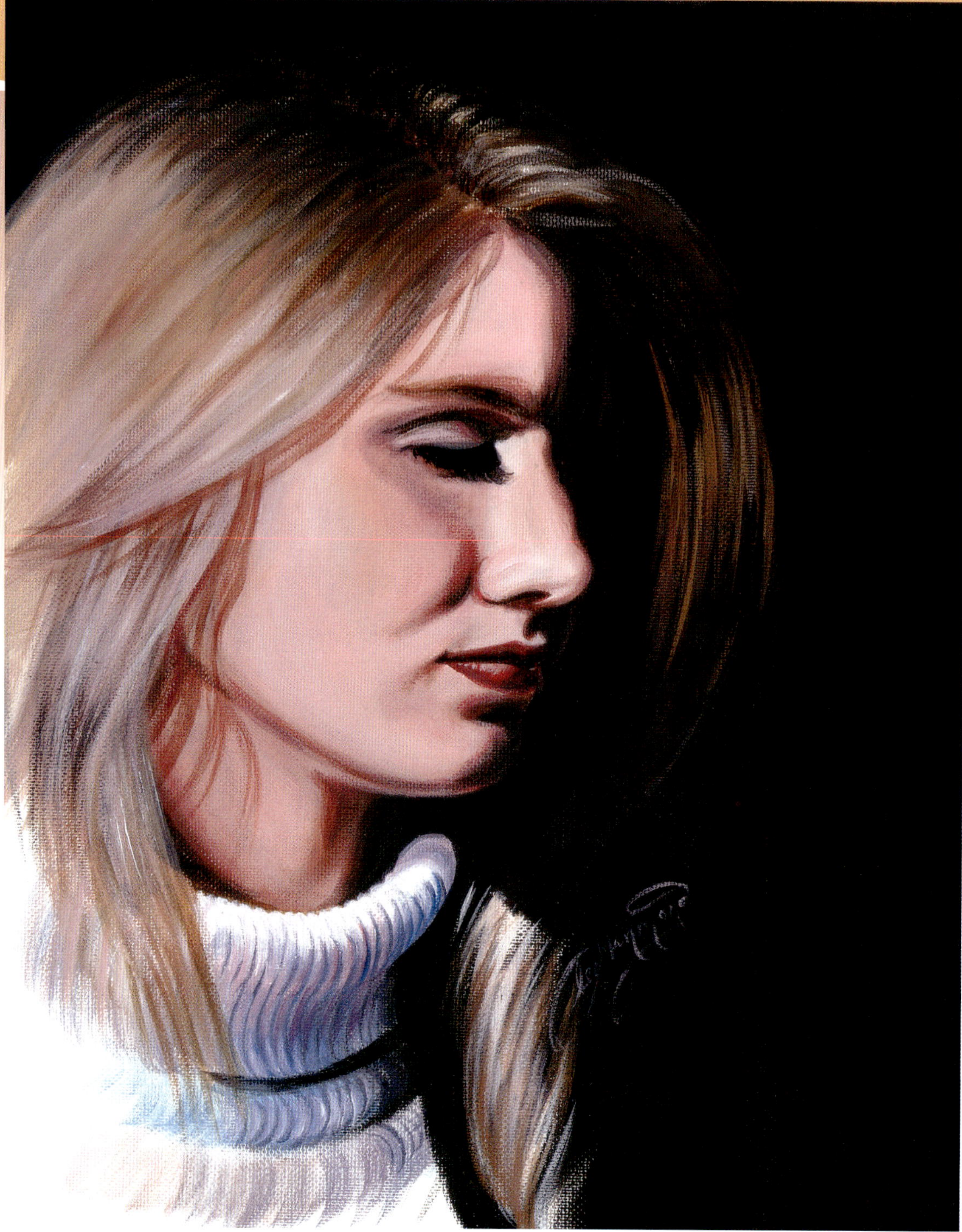

4 FINISH

Use the no. 1 round for this step. Soften all of the colors together by drybrushing in thicker applications of paint.

Build up the Prussian Blue/Titanium White mixture for the turtleneck, allowing your strokes to replicate the ribbing of the sweater. Mix a bit of Alizarin Crimson into Titanium White to get the pink reflective color to add to the blue tones of the sweater.

Add more layers of color to her hair, allowing them to streak together to replicate hair strands. Alternate using the dark brown tones (Burnt Umber), and the lighter tones (Burnt Umber, Titanium White, Cadmium Yellow Medium and Cadmium Red Medium). Add those mixtures to the right side, too.

Asian Skin Tone

PIGMENTS
Burnt Umber, Cadmium Red Medium, Cadmium Yellow Medium, Ivory Black, Prussian Blue, Titanium White

BRUSHES
Nos. 1 and 2 round
No. 4 filbert
No. 3/0 liner

I love the look of porcelain-like skin. This photo of my student's sister-in-law is a wonderful example of an extremely pale, smooth complexion. Her delicate Asian features were a joy to paint.

Light Complexion Warm
Create a very light version of this mixture beginning with Titanium White + touch of Cadmium Red Medium + touch of Cadmium Yellow Medium, per the instructions on page 23.

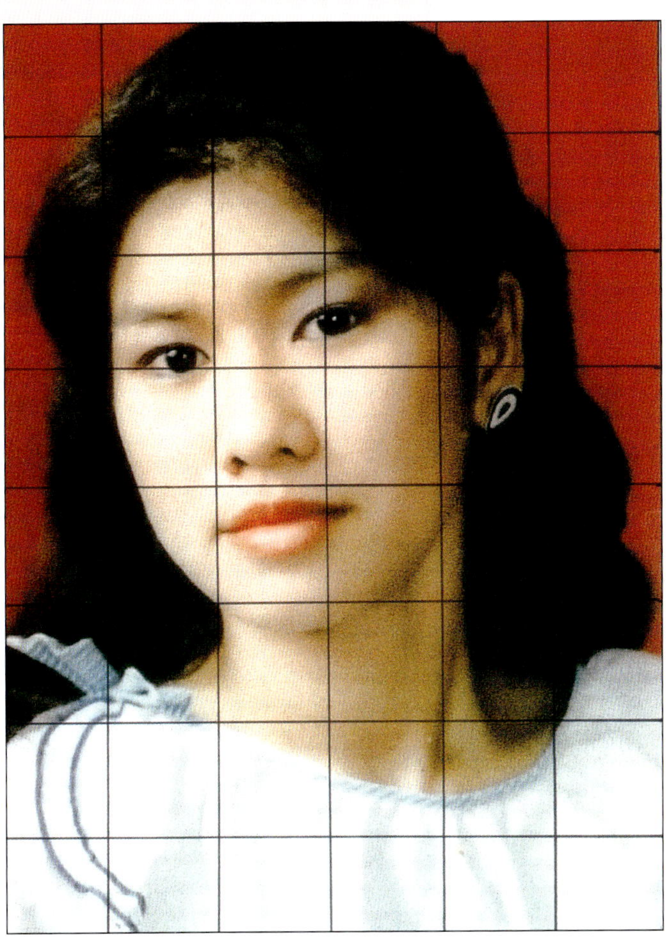

Reference Photo
This portrait of Jemma, my student's sister-in-law, makes good use of complementary colors. The red background is a perfect enhancement for the green outfit, both of which accentuate the colors of the skin.

Carefully study the shapes of the photograph and draw what you see inside each box.

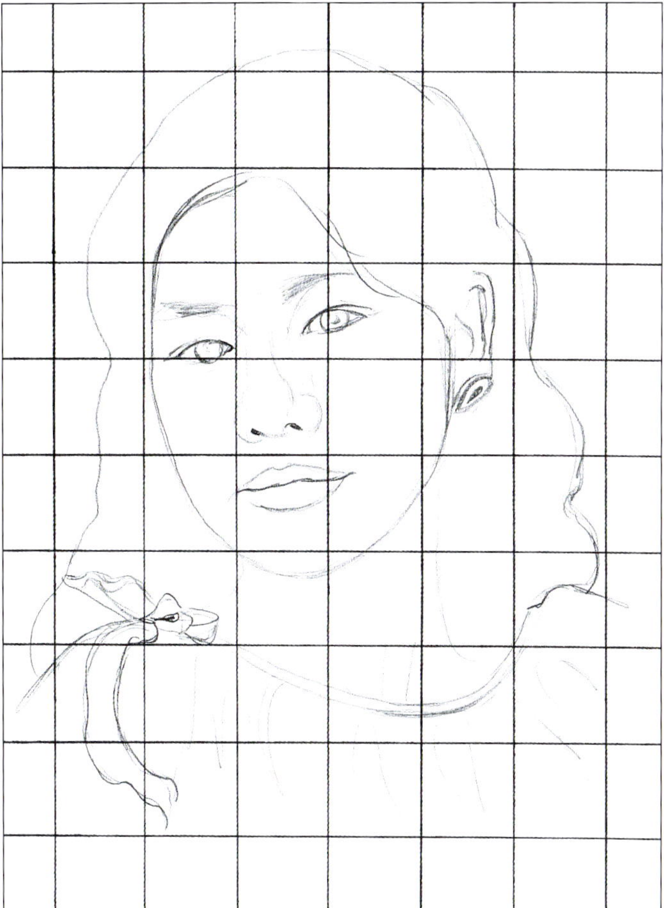

Line Drawing
Use the grid technique to create an accurate line drawing on your canvas paper. When you have the shapes accurately drawn, remove the grid lines with your eraser, leaving the image behind. Your line drawing should look like this on your canvas.

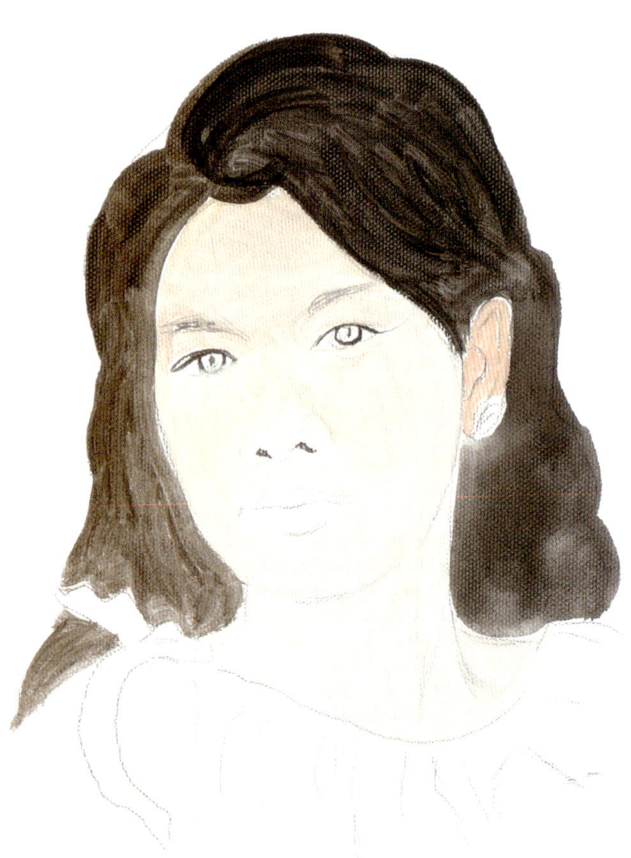

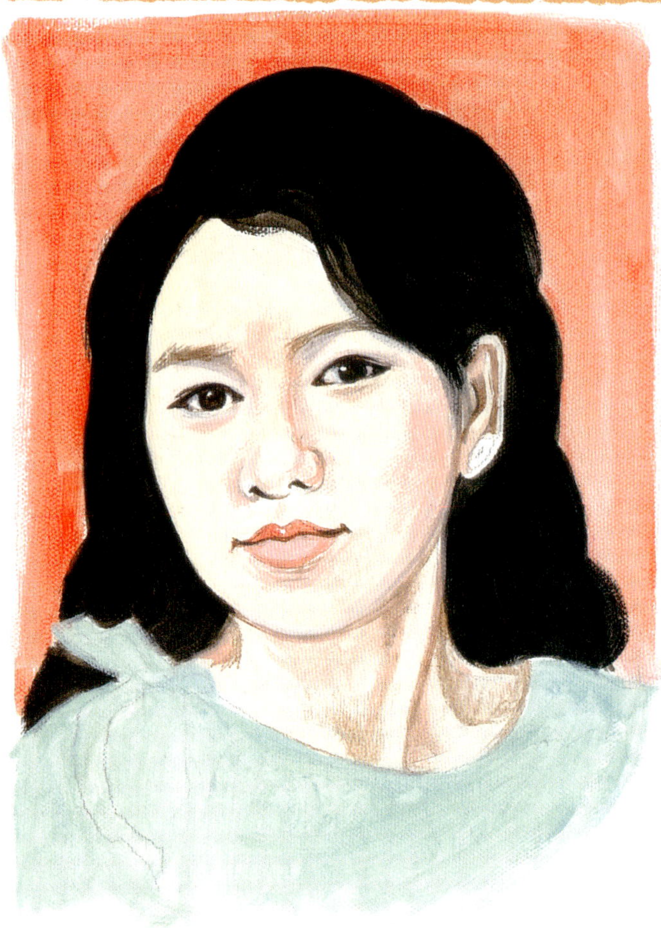

1 APPLY FIRST LAYERS

With the no. 1 round, paint in the lash line of the eyes and outside edges of the irises with diluted Ivory Black. This is done to make sure the direction of the gaze is accurate, which is very important. Fill in the nostril areas with the diluted black too, so you don't lose track of them when painting in the skin color.

Base in the entire face with a diluted application of your very light, light complexion warm mixture using the no. 4 filbert. Mix Burnt Umber with Ivory Black to get her hair color. Fill in the entire hair area with a diluted application of the hair mixture using the no. 4 filbert.

2 THE AWKWARD STAGE

Prepare a puddle of diluted Cadmium Red Medium for the background color. Use the no. 4 filbert to fill in the entire background area. Mix the pretty mint green color of her dress by adding a small amount of Prussian Blue into a puddle of Titanium White, then add a touch of Cadmium Yellow Medium. With the no. 4 filbert, fill in the entire area of her dress.

Use the no. 1 round to fill in her irises with Burnt Umber. Add pupils with Ivory Black. Make sure to center these in her irises and leave areas for the catchlight, half in the pupil and half in the iris. With the Burnt Umber, develop the shape of her eye. Use some diluted Burnt Umber to base in eyebrows, too.

Prepare a thicker puddle of her skin tone and apply it to her face again. Add more Cadmium Red Medium to that mixture to create a slightly deeper base. Apply it with the no. 2 round between the eyebrows, along the sides of the nose, and along the right side of the face. Add some Burnt Umber to this mixture and develop the shadow areas of her neck and fill in details of the ear.

Apply the background pigment to the upper lip and along the edge of the lower lip. Add some white to this mixture and fill in the bottom lip. Mix Burnt Umber with a touch of Alizarin Crimson and apply very thin lines between the lips and in the corner of the mouth using the no. 3/0 liner.

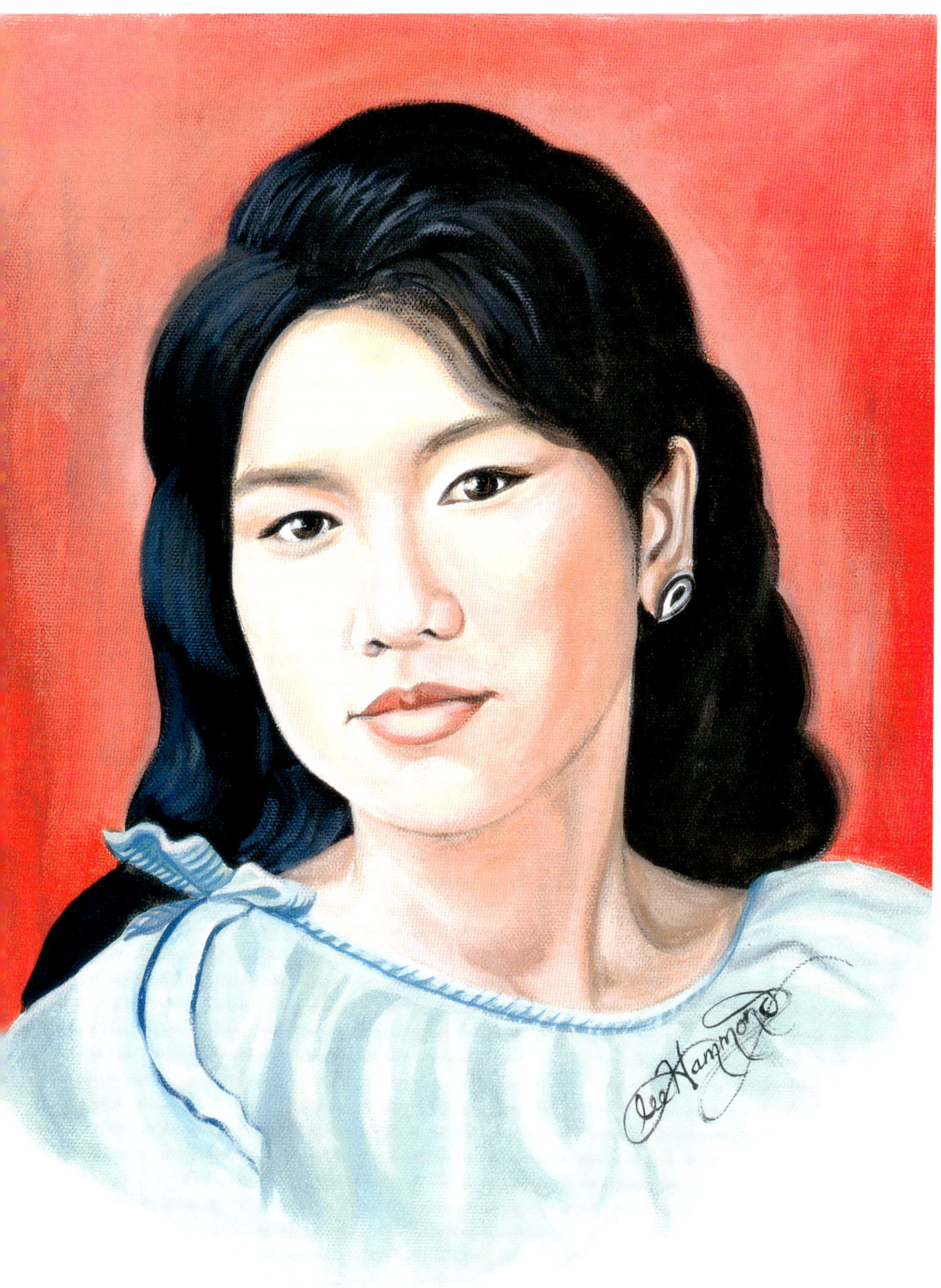

3 FINISH

This final step is all about adding small details for realism with thicker paint applications. Fill in the hair once more with a thicker application of the black/brown mixture. Give the hair dimension by adding highlights with the no. 2 round and a mixture of Burnt Umber with a touch of white. Make sure your brushstrokes go along with the direction of the hair and its curves. Once the brown highlights dry, add more highlights on top of those with a light mixture of Prussian Blue and white.

Add white highlights to the bridge of her nose and above her eyelids to create more dimension. Add fullness to the upper lip using small light and dark shapes. The little dark shapes will seem to recede and the little light ones will seem to come forward. This creates form, just as in the sphere. Use the no. 1 round to add small patches of light and dark versions of the light complexion warm mixture following this finished example. Build the shading gradually with small applications of paint. Don't quit until things appear smooth and the creation of form is completed. Go back and forth between adding shadows and highlights.

For the dress, create lighter and darker versions of the mint green you used in step 2. For the darker, add more Prussian Blue. For the lighter, add more white. Add the small pin stripes of the bow and neckline using the darker dress mixture and the no. 1 round. Notice how the stripes curve with the roundness of the fabric. Fill in the lights and darks of the rest of the dress using the no. 4 filbert.

To complete the painting, add the earring with black and white using the no. 1 round.

Adult Male

PIGMENTS

Burnt Umber, Cadmium Red Medium, Cadmium Yellow Medium, Ivory Black, Prussian Blue, Titanium White

BRUSHES

Nos. 1 and 2 round
No. 4 filbert

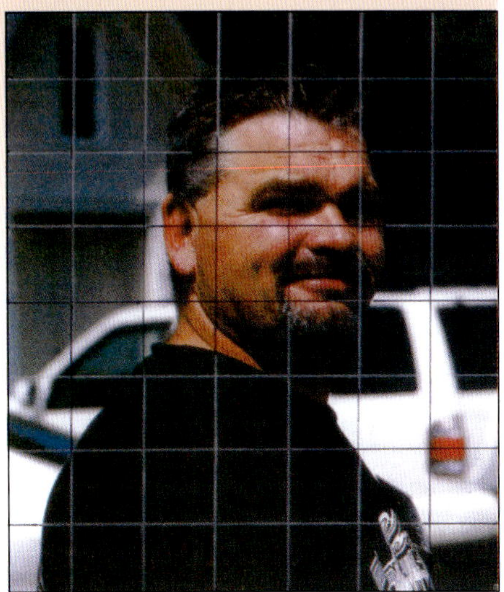

Reference Photo
Use the grid to capture the shape of Mark's face on your canvas paper. Remove the grid lines from your drawing when you are done.

I selected this photo of my friend Mark for the wonderful lighting it provided. The deep shadows created by the outdoor setting give the painting an intensity that fully illustrates Mark's personality. When looking for photo references to use as artwork, I like shots like this. It gives me the "light over dark" (the right side of his face) and the "dark over light" (the left side) theory to work with, giving the painting balance.

Light Complexion Warm
Follow the instructions on page 23 to prepare light, medium and dark versions of this peach color.

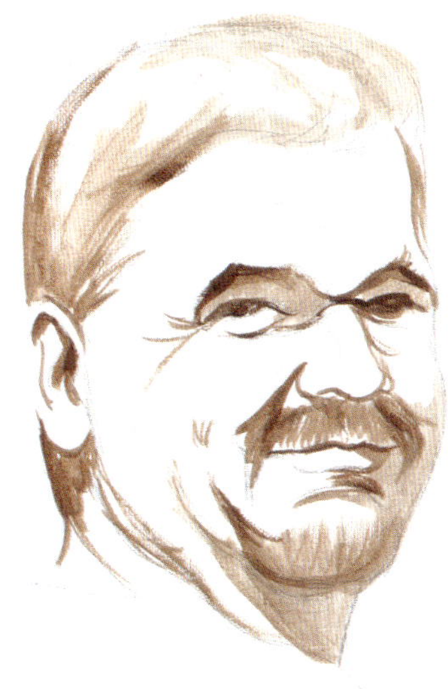

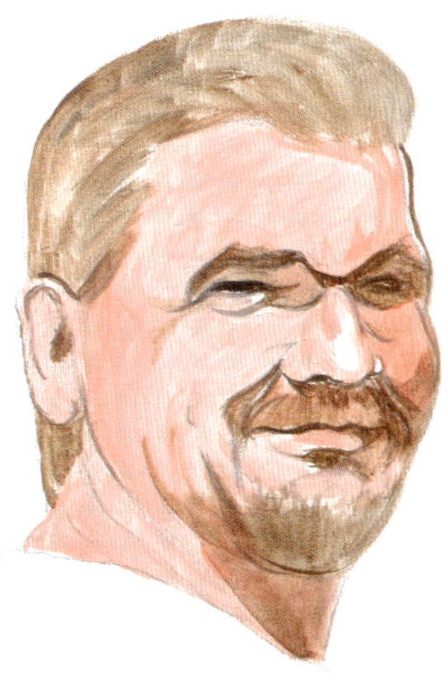

1 OUTLINE AND TONE

Because of the intense lighting and deep shadows of this piece, carefully draw in the details with diluted Burnt Umber and the no. 1 round. This will keep you from losing your line drawing when you begin to paint. Wash in the shadow areas above the eyes, under the nose, along the right side of the face and on the neck. Place some of Burnt Umber inside the ear, behind the ear and in the hair as well to establish the light source.

2 BASIC SHAPES AND HAIR

With a medium version of your skin tone color and a diluted application, wash in the basic shapes of the face, ear and neck with the no. 4 filbert. Add a bit more red to the mix and apply it to the sides of the face and forehead.

With diluted Burnt Umber, continue filling in the hair.

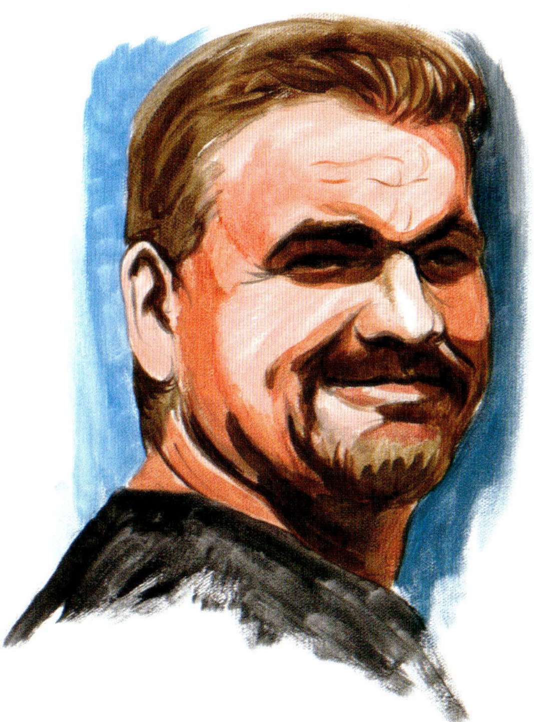

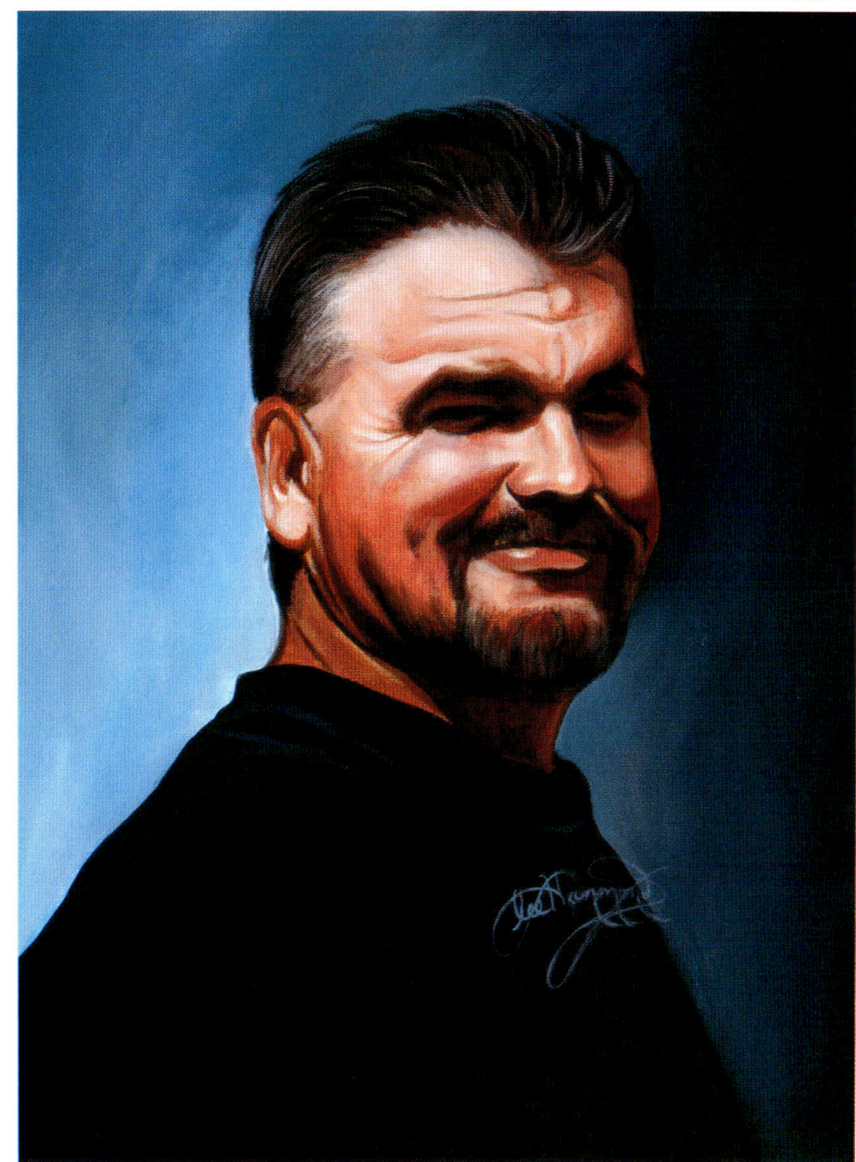

3 THE AWKWARD STAGE

Continue adding tone to the canvas paper with the no. 4 filbert using the light, medium and dark skin tone mixtures. Create the contours of the face keeping the paint very thin. Watch for the five elements of shading and how the shadow areas are creating the roundness and form of the face.

Even though the eyes are heavily shadowed and appear quite dark, it is important to still create the illusion of an iris and pupil. You can envision where the iris is because of the subtle bulge it creates along the lower lid.

With a deeper application of Burnt Umber, strengthen the tones of the hair and facial hair using the no. 2 round. Use strokes that replicate the hair direction.

Wash in some diluted background color with the no. 4 filbert and pure Prussian Blue on the left side and Prussian Blue with a touch of Ivory Black on the right. Use diluted Ivory Black to fill in the shirt.

4 FINISH

Continue refining color and shapes with many layers of thicker applications of the different values of paint you have prepared. Use drybrushing to blend the colors together. Keep the pigments warm in the highlight and halftone areas and cool in the shadows.

Add the reflected light along the bottom edge of the nose, along the bottom edge of the lower lip, and along the crease of his neck. Paint in subtle blue highlights reflected onto the black of the shirt as well.

To finish the hair, use the no. 1 round to apply quick, thin strokes of a combination of Burnt Umber, a touch of pure Titanium White, as well as light blue (Prussian Blue and Titanium White). Apply a little shadow to the skin in the hair line area. To finish, build up and soften the background colors using thicker paint and the no. 4 filbert.

People Together

PIGMENTS
Alizarin Crimson, Burnt Umber, Cadmium Red Medium, Ivory Black, Prussian Blue, Titanium White

BRUSHES
No. 2 round
No. 4 filbert

Nothing is more special than capturing true emotion in your artwork. This piece shows the true love shared between a mother and her newborn child. (In this case, it is my daughter and grandchild.) While the emotions conveyed in the painting are deep and complex, creating it is not.

Light Complexion Cool
Follow the instruction on page 23 to mix light, medium and dark versions of this skin tone.

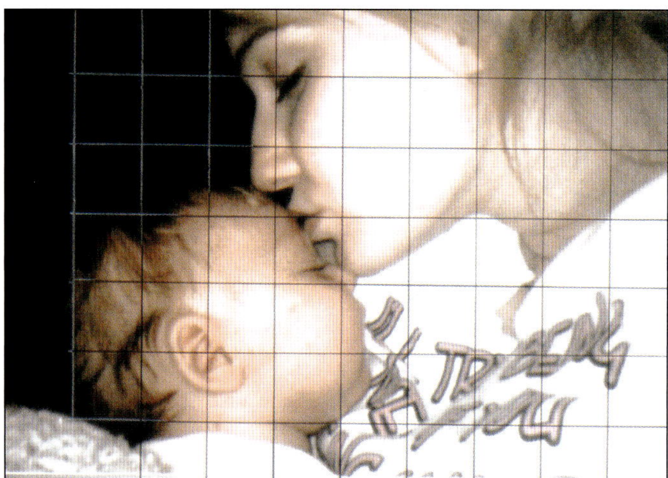

Reference Photo
Use the grid technique to acquire an accurate line drawing on your canvas. Study the photo carefully.

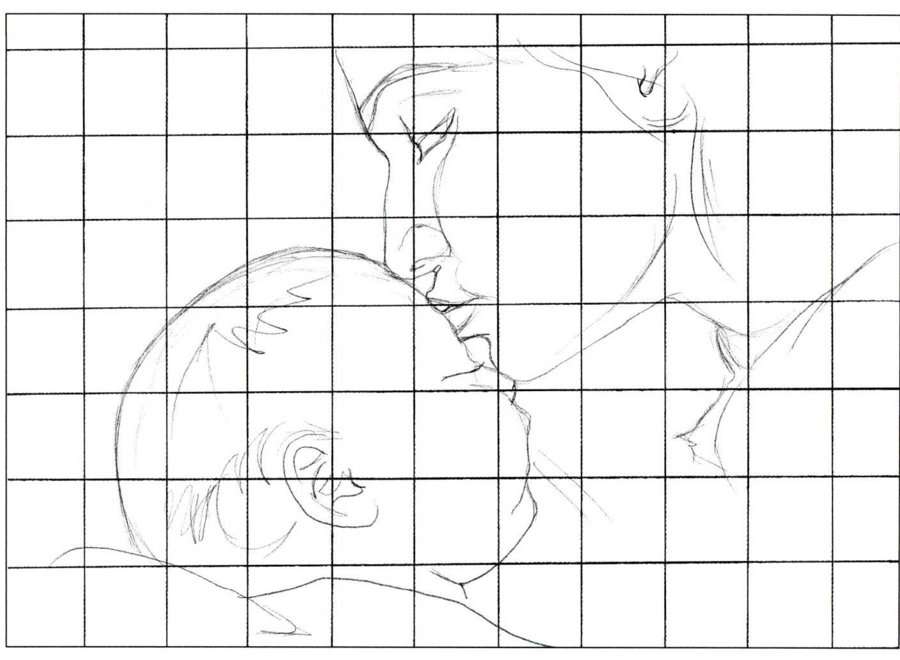

Line Drawing
When you have the shapes accurately drawn, your line drawing should look like this. When you are sure of the accuracy, remove the grid lines with your eraser, leaving the image behind.

1 BEGIN WITH SKIN TONE

With the no. 4 filbert, base in the skin tones of both the mother and baby with the light complexion cool color. Their skin tones are very pink and delicate. Keep the mixture light.

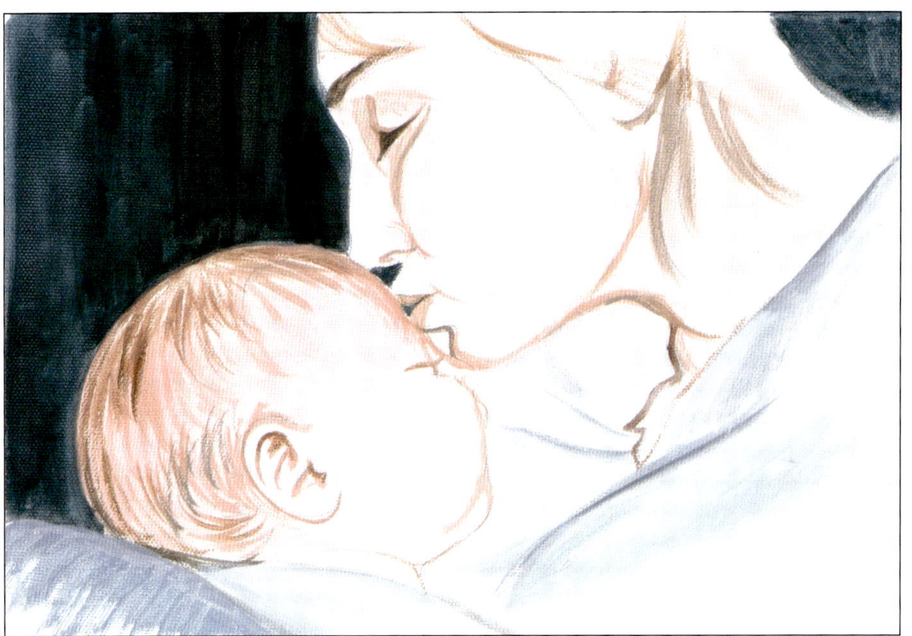

2 THE AWKWARD STAGE

With the no. 2 round, add the dark detail lines of the features using a diluted mixture of Burnt Umber and Alizarin Crimson. Make sure the brushstrokes on the baby's head follow the direction of the hair and the way it grows.

To describe the edges of the head and face, add the darkness of the background using the no. 4 filbert and a diluted mixture of Ivory Black and Prussian Blue. Add Titanium White to that background mixture and use it to block in the clothing undertones. Remember that this is just the undertone and first layer of color. You will add most of the detail in the next step.

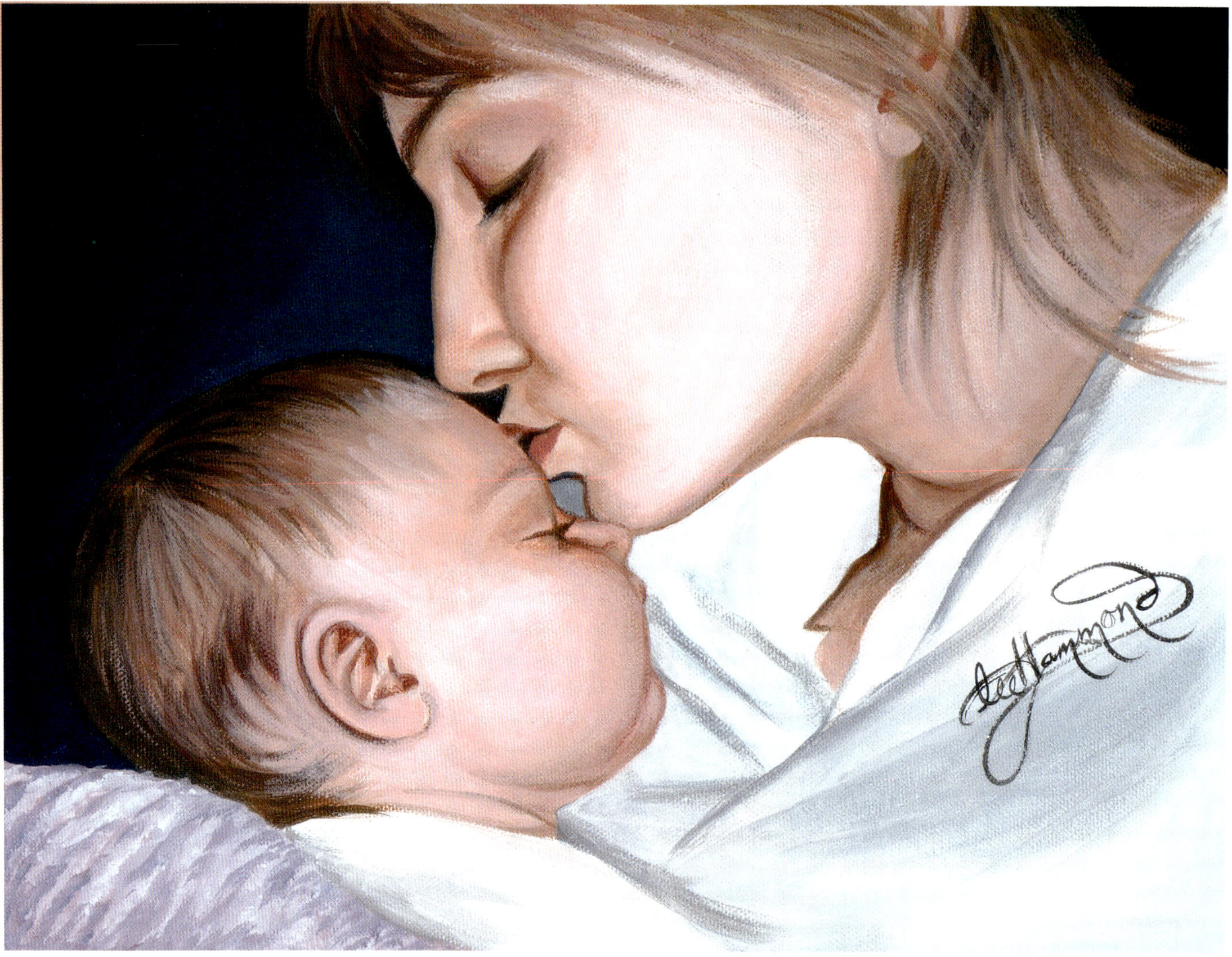

3 FINISH

Use thicker paint applications for the last stages. Prepare two puddles of pigment. One should be the light complexion cool mixture with only Titanium White and Cadmium Red Medium. Leave out the Alizarin Crimson at first to give you a warmer tone. Create another puddle with that mixture, plus small amounts of Burnt Umber and Alizarin Crimson for a nice shadow color.

Fill in the faces with the skin tone mixture until the canvas is completely covered using the no. 4 filbert. Then add the darker shadow colors and gently blend them into the skin tone colors using the no. 2 round. Apply this shadow mixture to the jaw lines, the fronts of the cheeks, the neck and the lips. Apply darker versions of this mixture to the inside details of the baby's ear. Make sure to get the cast shadows behind the edge of the ear. Refer to pages 83–87 for ear practice. Use the techniques from the sphere exercises on pages 31–35 to create the roundness of the faces by carefully transitioning the color from light to dark.

Use the no. 4 filbert to go over the fabric with Titanium White. Add Titanium White to the background mixture (Ivory Black and Prussian Blue) to make the gray color for details. Make the creases and folds with simple brushstrokes.

Add a touch of Alizarin Crimson to that gray fabric mixture to create a lavender for the blanket. Basecoat the blanket with a deep version of this mixture, then add white to the mixture to get a lighter pink. Dab in the paint to create a knitted look. Add some Titanium White on top of that to give it a thick look.

To complete the painting, thicken the background color (Ivory Black and Prussian Blue) and fill it in until the color is smooth and the canvas is completely covered.

People With Backgrounds

PIGMENTS
Alizarin Crimson, Burnt Umber, Cadmium Red Medium, Cadmium Yellow Medium, Ivory Black, Prussian Blue, Titanium White

BRUSHES
Nos. 1 and 2 round
No. 4 filbert

Sometimes a portrait is more than just the image of someone's face. The surroundings and background can play an important part, illustrating what the person is feeling and doing. Incorporating those surroundings into your portraits can add a world of depth to them.

Light Complexion Warm
Since most of this painting is background, you won't need to mix as much of the skin tone color this time. Follow the instructions on page 23 to prepare light, medium and dark versions of this mixture.

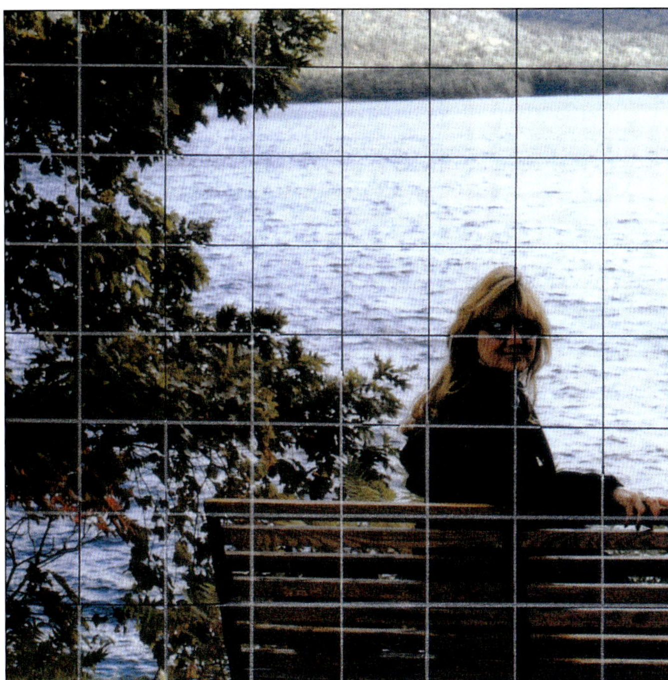

Reference Photo
In this piece, I am clearly enjoying a fall day at the lake shore. The background tells the tale.

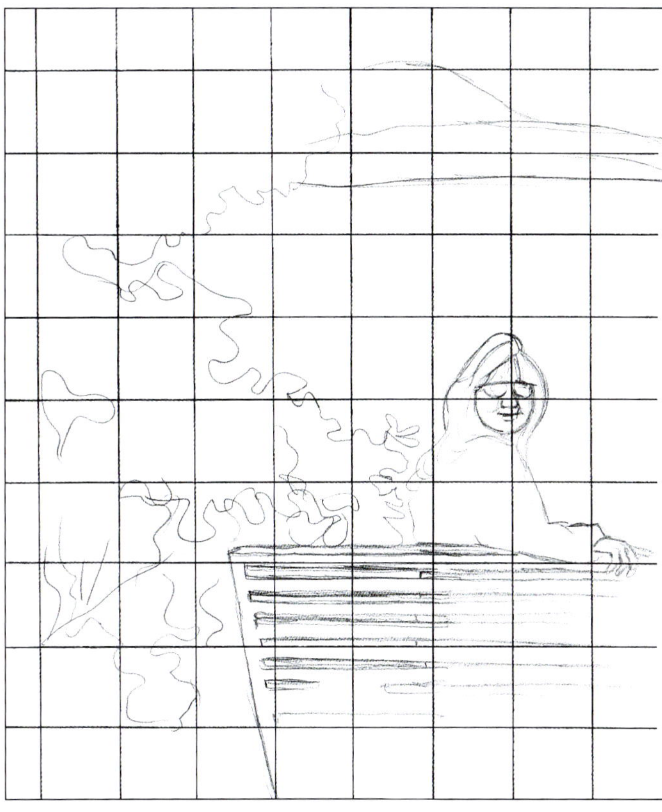

Line Drawing
Use the grid technique to create an accurate line drawing on your canvas paper. Don't worry about a lot of accuracy in the foliage and park bench. You will create it later with paint. For now, just give yourself enough information to serve as a road map. When your shapes look like this one, remove the grid lines with your eraser, leaving the image behind.

1 BACKGROUND

When creating landscape paintings, it is important to start with the background first. In this piece, I started with the extreme background and worked forward. The first application is always diluted and acts as a "color map." Use the no. 4 filbert for this entire step.

Whenever something is in the distance, the colors become weak. The farther back something goes, the more of the atmosphere and sky color it will take on. In this case, the hills take on a pastel color.

Use a Titanium White and Prussian Blue mixture for the sky color in the small area in the upper right corner. Get the violet for the hill right below by adding a touch of Alizarin Crimson to that sky color.

Mix a very light chartreuse color for the large hill with Titanium White, Cadmium Yellow Medium and a tiny touch of Prussian Blue. Use the sky color with a touch of Ivory Black added to create a steel gray color for the hills below. Add more Ivory Black to that mixture for the hill right along the shore line.

Dilute your Prussian Blue and white sky mixture to add the water. Make horizontal brushstrokes. This is the way the water moves and the brushstrokes help create the water surface and illusion of distance.

Make the dark foreground color with Prussian Blue, Titanium White, and Cadmium Yellow Medium. Later, this will become the grass.

2 CONTINUE BLOCKING IN

Continue using the no. 4 filbert to work on the background using thicker applications of paint and being sure to completely cover the canvas. Streak light and dark versions of the large background hill using light and dark versions of the mixture you used in step 1, giving it some texture.

Do the same thing with the water to make it look rippled. You can see how I used the colors of the background to do this. Vary the values from light to dark, following this illustration as a guide. Add some Alizarin Crimson to the upper-right sky mixture to create a lavender. Streak a little of that into both the sky in the upper right and the water.

Complete the blocking-in stage by adding the foreground elements. Prepare a diluted Burnt Umber puddle for the park bench and apply it to the slats of the bench with long continuous strokes using the no. 4 filbert. Use pure Ivory Black and the no. 4 filbert to create the vertical sides and legs and the coat I'm wearing. Switch to the no. 2 round and apply Ivory Black in between the slats to make it look like you are seeing through them.

Use Burnt Umber and the no. 2 round to paint in the hair. Add some Titanium White and Cadmium Yellow Medium to the right side to paint the lighter shades and help develop the light source.

Use the light complexion warm mixture to base in the values for the face and neck.

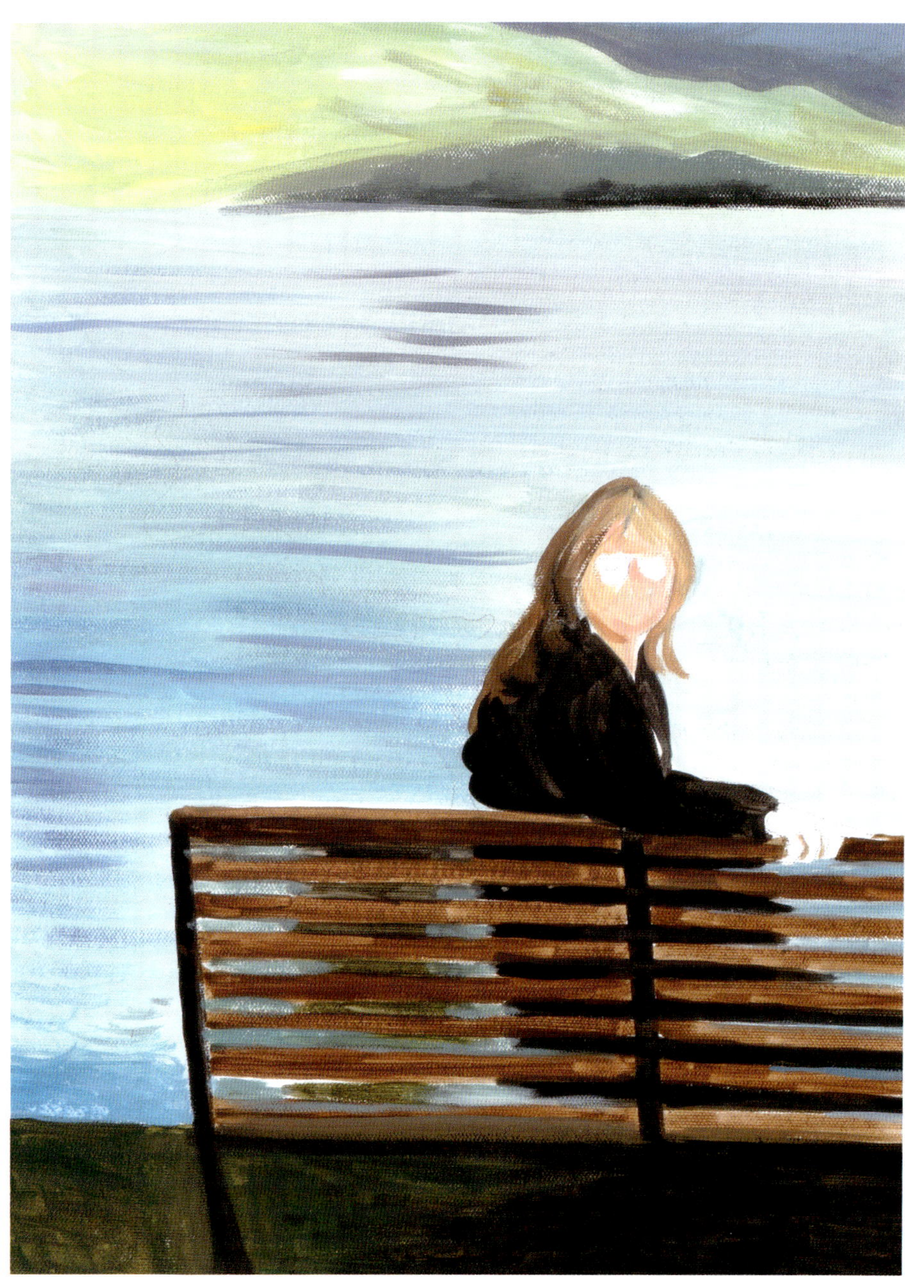

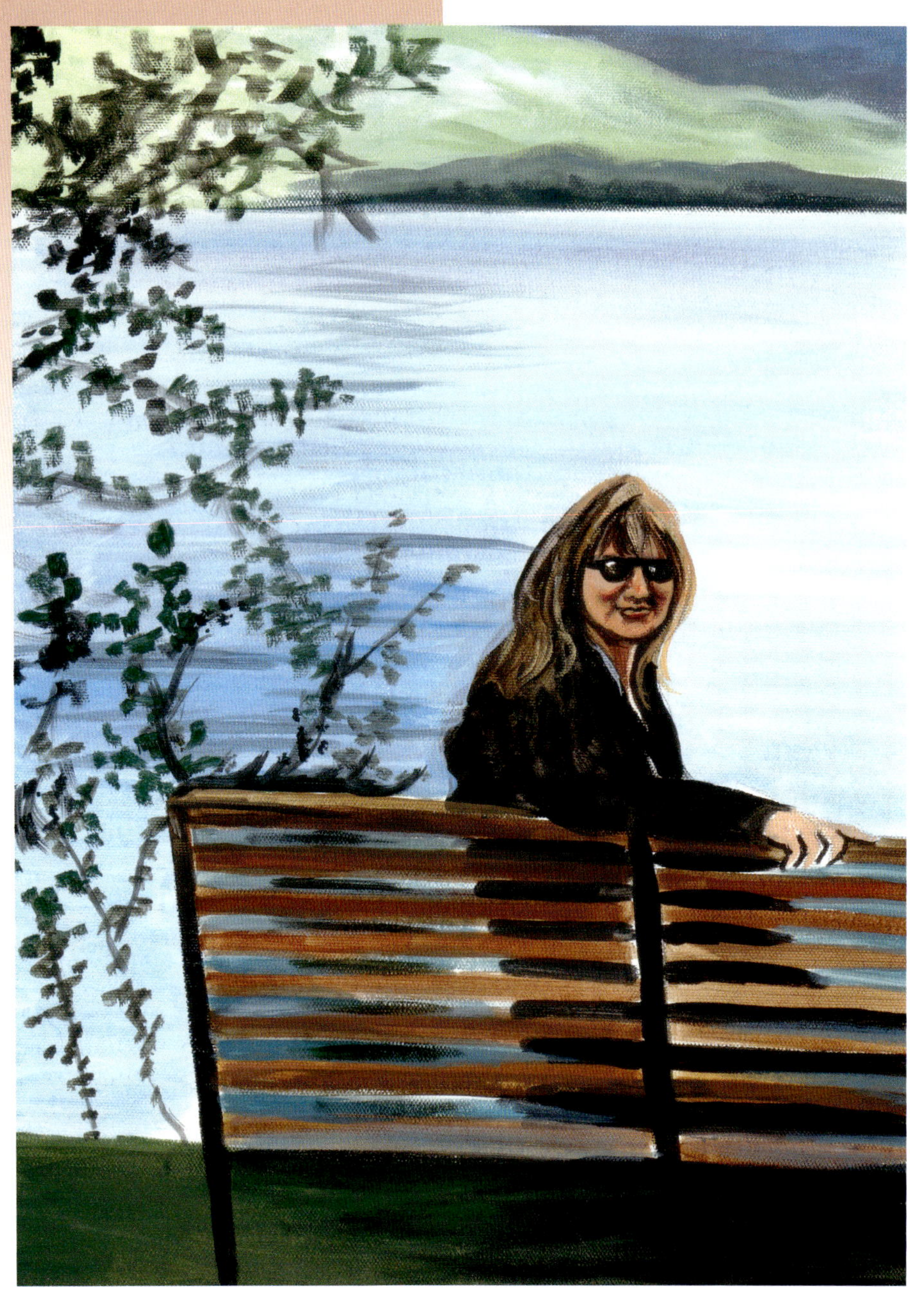

3 THE AWKWARD STAGE

Continue filling in the face using your skin tone mixtures, looking for the patterns of light and dark. The outdoor setting creates extreme contrasts. Make sure to include the dark shadows all around the nose and under the mouth. The shadows curve under the cheeks creating another sphere affect. Use the no. 1 round to apply the tiny details of the likeness. Painting small like this can be frustrating. Apply tiny amounts of paint, so you don't overdo it and make the features larger than they need to be. Go slow! The beauty of acrylic is, if you don't like what you did, you can cover it up right away.

Use the no. 1 round to further develop the hair, adding layers of brown and gold tones created by adding Cadmium Yellow Medium and Titanium White to Burnt Umber. Add a touch of Cadmium Red Medium to this mixture for a redder hue. Use quick strokes, making sure that the strokes curve with the waves and curls of the hair.

Fill in the hand using the skin tone mixture and the no. 2 round. Switch to the no. 1 round again and add some Burnt Umber between the fingers of the hand.

Add the sunglasses with Ivory Black, leaving some small spots of white for the reflection in each lens.

To begin the look of foliage, it is important to have a plan. You need to apply thin lines that represent the stems and branches to give yourself a foundation to build on. Use the no. 1 round with a diluted application of the green mixture that you made for the grassy area of the foreground in step 1.

Look at the photo to see how the branches appear. Follow the same patterns for these lines. This gives the branches direction so you have control over where they end up.

When you have painted the branches, switch to the no. 4 filbert and dab in the leaves using the green mixture. Create darker greens by adding Ivory Black. The leaves will appear as blobs at this point. It will seem very abstract.

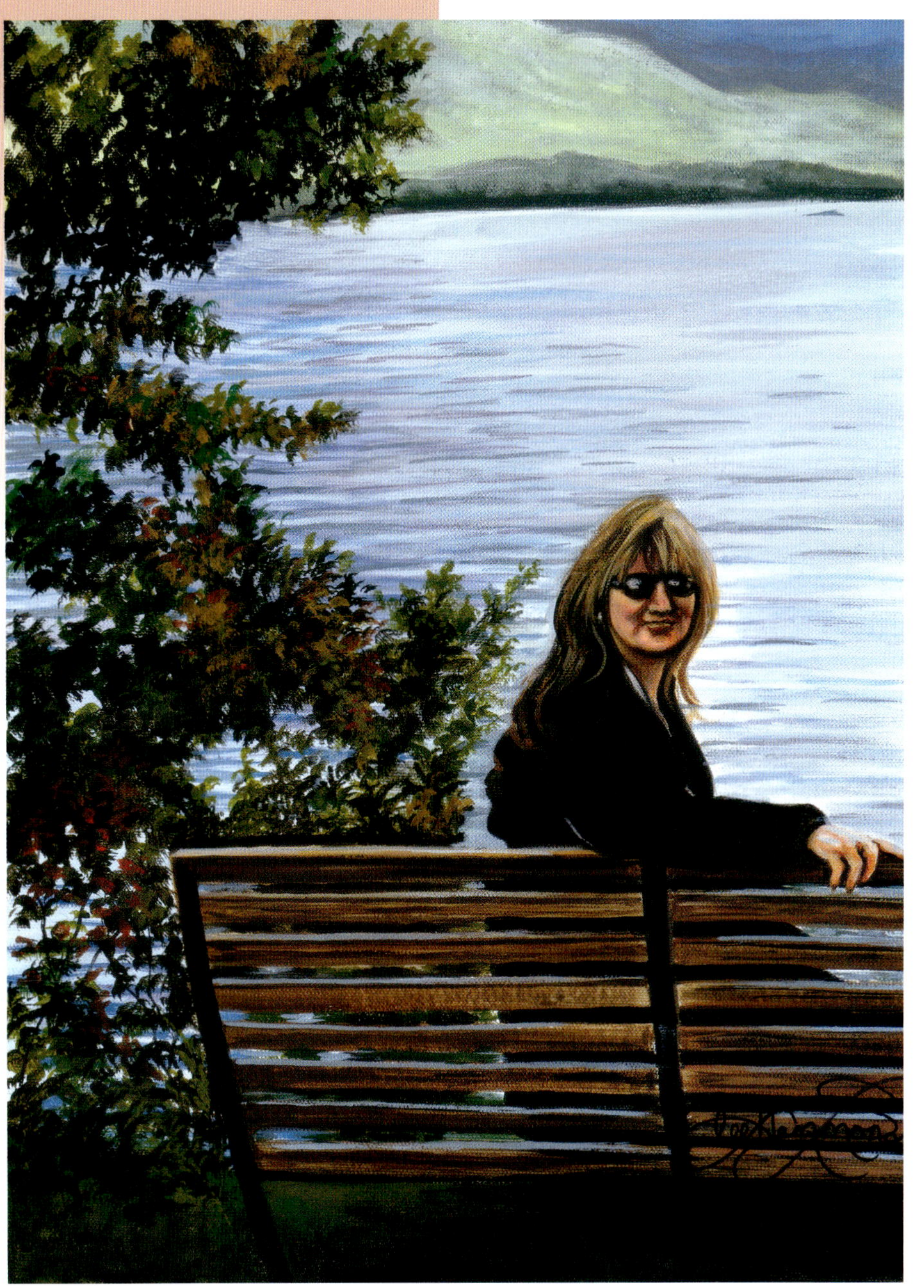

4 FINISH

The final stage of the painting is the fun part. This is where the realism happens. Start with the park bench. Look carefully at the colors reflecting off of the top edges of each slat. Use a light blue mixture of Prussian Blue and Titanium White, and the no. 1 round to streak it to give the look of the sky color reflecting off of the edges. Place this color on top of the hand, too. I always find it so amazing how a small detail can make such a large improvement.

To build up the layers of foliage, add Ivory Black first to show the depth. Mix a variety of greens using Cadmium Yellow Medium with Ivory Black and also Cadmium Yellow Medium with Prussian Blue. Mix these in various values by controlling the amounts of black and blue. The yellow/black mixture creates wonderful olive green tones, while the blue mixture makes more of an emerald. Layer these mixtures on top of your foliage with the dabbing motion. Don't get carried away, though. You want to be able to see through the branches to the background in some areas.

Finally, dab some reds and yellows into the foliage to give the painting an autumn feel. I took artistic license from the original photo. You can add as much fall color as you'd like to create the scene.

Add small highlights of reflected color, such as the reflected blue of the sky on my hand and hair, using the no. 1 round.

Conclusion

If I have learned anything from being an artist, it is that all good things take time. Quitting too soon or taking shortcuts only leads to complacency and mediocrity.

When I look back on artwork I created ten or fifteen years ago, I am not disappointed. I know that I was at a level in my development where I had grown substantially. However, I also see where I could have done better or, more importantly, where I could have continued. Back then, I often "cut to the chase" and presented my subject in a very direct, but isolated way. Now, I want more substance, depth and creativity.

Acrylic painting is a medium that demands your attention, forcing you to take things further. The more I do, the further I want to take it. It is inspiring. It has carried over into my other artwork, and has made me want to deliver more detail in everything I do.

The moral of the story is: If you want to achieve, you must be willing to work at it.

For me, the growth continues and always will. I will never stop learning, experimenting and striving for the best possible outcome with my art. Writing my books helps me do that. You buying and enjoying my books makes it all possible. So, thank you, being your teacher and mentor means "me becoming a better me." For that, I am forever grateful!

Thank you for being a fan, and for sharing this wonderful world of art with me!

Sincerely,

Lee Hammond

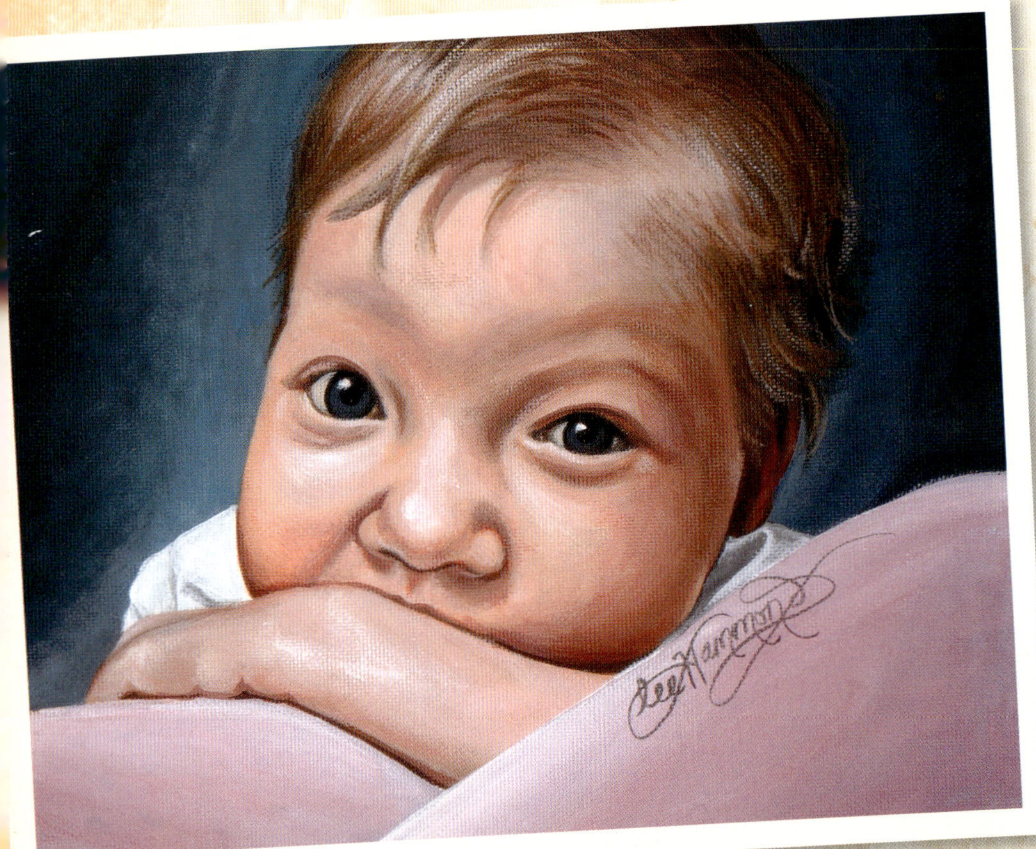

This is an example of creative cropping. I could have easily centered this image on the page, adding more of the blanket and surroundings. But I wanted to focus on the little face of my new granddaughter, Cayla. I didn't necessarily want to capture the image of her blanket for all to see.

To make this painting more meaningful to me, I enlarged her and allowed her shape to go off the page. It places the focus on her and her large eyes, allowing us to connect with her personality.

Whenever you are deciding what to paint, consider different ways of placing your subject on the page. Cropping is a good technique for adding additional interest and focus on your subject matter.

CAYLA LEE

8" x 10" (20cm x 25cm)

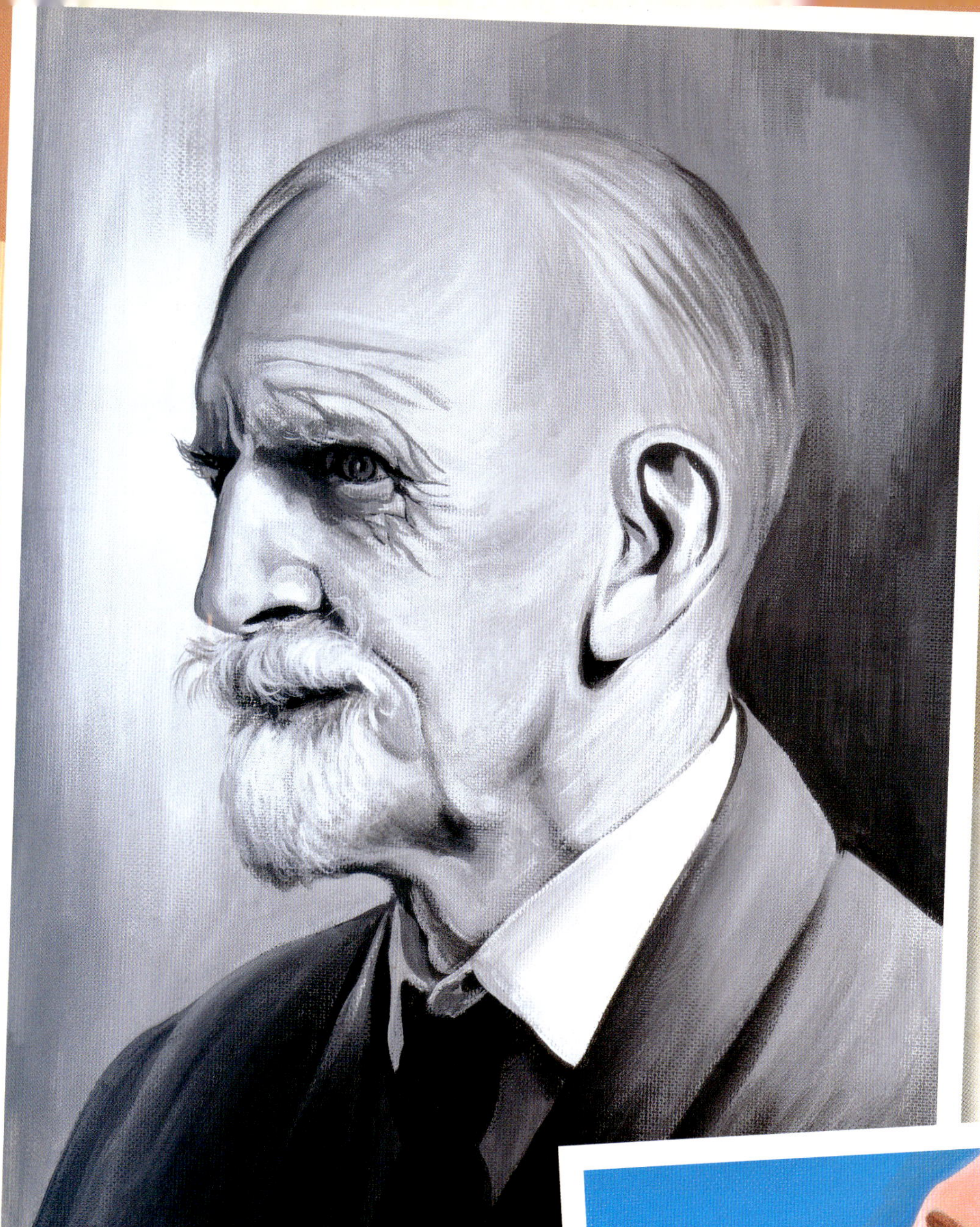

Dark over light and light over dark enhances this portrait. Look at how the shoulder on the right is light against the dark background, and the shoulder on the left is light against the dark background. Remember this in future portraits.

OLD MAN

14" x 11" (36cm x 28cm)

Full-color portraiture can be beautiful, especially when it is as bright and vivid as these skin tones are. This painting uses warm reds and oranges to portray the summer sun. Look closely and see how the reflected light goes along the sides of each finger. This is an example of how the five elements of shading work.

GOLDEN GLOW

10" x 8" (25cm x 20cm)

Index

Master acrylic painting with these other fine North Light Books!

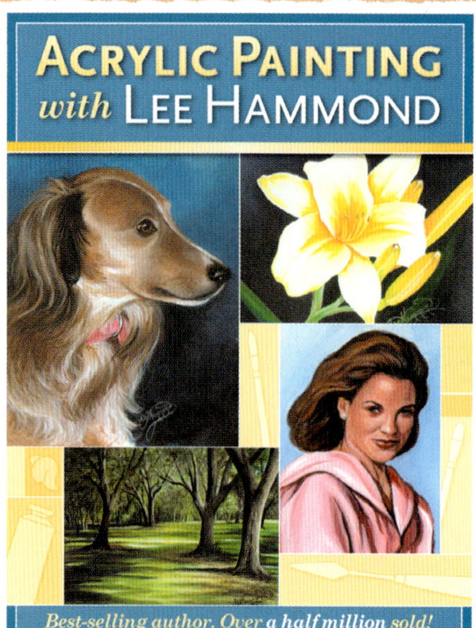

The first of Lee Hammond's acrylic painting books, *Acrylic Painting With Lee Hammond* provides easy instruction for beginners for professional results. Follow Lee's proven methods to experience success painting a variety of realistic, detailed and beautiful subjects in no time.

ISBN-13: 978-1-58180-709-7, ISBN-10: 1-58180-709-0
Paperback, 128 pages, #33375

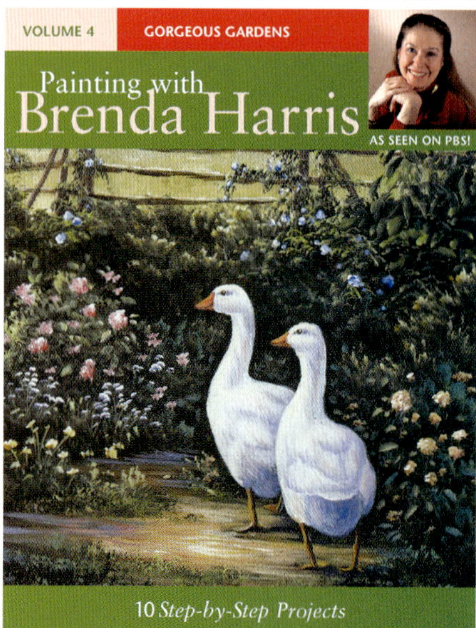

Cultivate stunning garden acrylic paintings in just a few hours with the help of popular PBS television instructor Brenda Harris. Each of the 10 step-by-step projects features easy instructions and even includes a simple drawing template.

ISBN-13: 978-1-58180-791-2, ISBN-10: 1-58180-791-0
Paperback, 112 pages, #33466

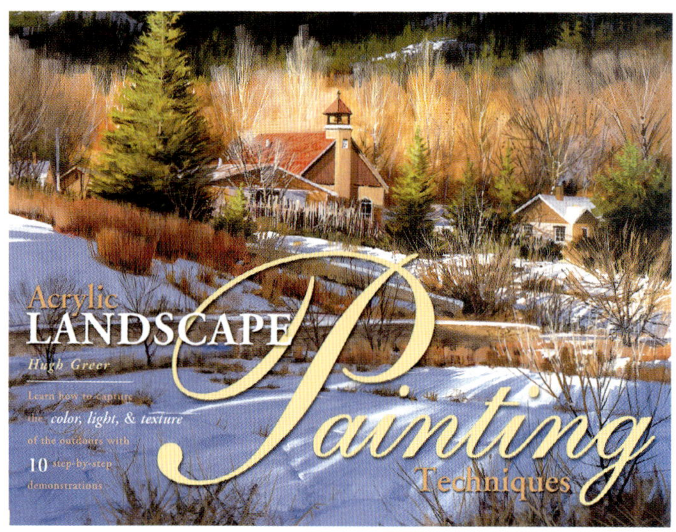

Filled with inspirational artwork and great instruction, *Acrylic Landscape Painting Techniques,* by Hugh Greer makes it easy to learn to paint with acrylics using proven "watercolor" and "oil" techniques with 16 demonstrations.

ISBN-13: 978-1-58180-638-0, ISBN-10: 1-58180-638-8
Paperback, 128 pages, #33217

These books and other fine North Light titles are available at your local fine art retailer, bookstore or from online suppliers.

Or visit us at www.artistsnetwork.com.